POLICING IN THE 21ST CENTURY:

MYTH, REALITIES & CHALLENGES

POLICING IN THE 21ST CENTURY: MYTH, REALITIES & CHALLENGES

K V THOMAS

2012
Kaveri Books
New Delhi - 110 002

First Published in 2012

ISBN: 978-81-7479-125-2

Published by

Kaveri Books

4832/24, Ansari Road

New Delhi-110002 (India)

Tel: 011-23288140, 23245799
Fax: 011 2328 8140
E-mail : kaveribooks@vsnl.com
kaveribooks@gmail.com
Website: www.kaveribooks.com

Typeset in Baskerville BE Font at
Delta Book World, New Delhi - 110 002.

Printed at
Salasar Imaging System, Delhi - 110 052

PRINTED IN INDIA

Preface

The traditional role of police in any democratic society is the effective enforcement of law and order and thereby ensuring the safety and security of law abiding citizens. The globalization and the geo-political developments especially the serious challenges in the global security scenario such as international terrorism have added new dimensions to the present day policing. Nations irrespective of their form of government or economic development are in the radar of this looming threat which now goes beyond the contours of continents. Naturally, this speaks of the need of augmenting the edifice of law enforcement machinery by all nations. India is placed in a unique situation in which the Regional security environment and the terror and radical groups sponsored by hostile neighbors have posed serious challenges to the sovereignty and integrity of the nation. Never in the history of India, has the nation faced such mammoth internal security challenges as in the present decade. It was in this backdrop that this compendium of seventeen essays examine the various aspects of policing from the point of view of their professionalism, public image, accountability to the society, organizational 'deviants', innovations and reforms, role in safeguarding internal security and new challenges from cyber-space and Information Technology (IT).

On analyzing "the past, present and future Role of police in National security, a clear picture emerges that" the critical aspect of National security is closely intertwined with the task of strengthening basic policing at cutting edge level".

Ironically, this task- whether in strengthening grass roots level policing or intelligence set up- has not been properly attended to by the governments or the police leaders, despite a series of national level tragedies like Kargil episode, 26/11, (2009) Mumbai terror attack etc. Keeping apart the inherent organizational and strategic weaknesses of the force, what appears to be the major lacunae of police in successfully undertaking counter-insurgency or counter-terrorist operations was their alienation from the public especially in insurgency affected areas. That is why, Richard Clutterback, who authored many authentic titles on terrorism and insurgency had cautioned the police/ Security agencies that; "the marriage between an uncorrupt police and an alert and co-operative public is the best guard against terrorism". This reminds us the prophetic words of Pandit Jawaharlal Nehru; "the first duty of police is to obtain the good will of the people through their service and integrity. They occupy a position of great responsibility. They can only discharge their duties well if they have the spirit of service to the country and to the people."

Thus, the major theme as how to bring police closer to public/society has been extensively discussed in this book. In-depth analysis has been made on a number of issues such as police image; expectations of the society from police, accountability to Rule of Law, transformation of police into a public service, innovative mechanisms promoting people's respect for police and organizational aberrations such as corruption, human rights violations etc that erode the faith of public on police. While the image of police remains sullied due to a variety of factors, there is dichotomy on the expectations of the public from police and the actual role played by police. So long as this dichotomy exists, the issue of harmonious relations between police and public, which is vital for effective and efficient policing, will remain a myth. Such barriers essentially should be broken for which the police leadership should work out pro active strategies like community policing and internal reorganization and restructuring. The transformation of the force from a vertical to horizontal organization and effective decentralization are pre-requisite for the success of such strategies.

It was in this backdrop, the inter-related organizational mechanisms such as training and development of personnel, privatization and de-militarization of the force and research on police subjects etc were discussed in great detail with a number of constructive suggestions and proposals to rejuvenate and revitalize the force in line with the aspirations of the people and the challenging needs of the country especially in 21st century. The new threats emanating from 'cyber-space' and urban habitat and the means to counter them through wide application of Science and technology particularly the vast vistas of Information Technology (IT) were also lucidly discussed in the pages of this book for the better understanding of police personnel of all ranks as well as laymen. The concluding chapter of the book is on the 'Vision for Police 2020' which basically list out the priorities of the police in the present millennium. No doubt, the vision and the aim of this book is to accelerate the transformation of police as people-friendly as rightly observed by Prime Minister Man Mohan Singh; "Our intention is to create an image of Indian police as professionally competent and technologically advanced force, one that would be an agent of socio-economic change endowed with a spirit of humanism". But we have to go miles before we reach that golden era of Indian police.

Needless to mention that the views and opinions expressed in this book are purely personal based on my research, study and observations. They do not reflect the policy or views of the Central/State governments, Home Department, Police or other Security agencies. Every effort has been made to adopt an unbiased and balanced approach in respect of the issues discussed. I affirm that I have all the moral rights to be identified as the author of this book.

Ernakulam **Adv. K V Thomas**

Contents

1

New Face of Police as Agent of Public Services

As India is marching ahead into the new millennium amidst a mosaic of complexities and challenges arising out of global terrorism, regional security environment, internal security, political, social and economic issues, the natural question that arises in the mind of common man is: what will be the role of security and law enforcement agencies in the present century? Invariably the people might have different answers depending upon their outlook or the overall assessment of the situation. One who is orthodox in his approach and analyses the whole scenario purely from traditional point of view of crime and criminal offences, may foresee the police organization of the future as a well knit professional body of crime fighters who are destined to fight against master criminals or organized gangs for ensuring the security and safety of people. On the other hand, one dominated by liberal and egalitarian views may visualize police organization as the most wide spread government sponsored social service agency destined to perform a plethora of social related tasks (Martin Bard). Another may see police officers in future acting as 'Ombudsman', a representative of the government who responds to the weaker and exploited in the society (A.G. German). Yet another may find them as 'public agents' who are accountable only to the society (Jeffery Riemann). Whatever diverse be the views and perceptions of the people on the future role of police, one need not gaze into a crystal ball to understand the reality that "Police service of today extends beyond the mere routine investigations and disposition of complaints, it has its objective for the welfare of the individual and society" (Daniel Bell). Thus decades ago Pandit Jawaharlal Nehru rightly observed,"It would be remembered that the first duty of the police is to obtain the good will of the people through their service and integrity. They occupy a position of great responsibility. They can only discharge their duties well if they had the spirit of service to the country and the people."

This leads us to certain crucial questions. Whether the police in independent India could attain the good will and co-operation of the masses through service oriented approach? If not, what factors prevented them from achieving such a work culture and image? What are the major causative factors that adversely affect the image and professionalism of the force? What steps should be taken to transform the police into an effective instrument of public service?

The police in free India had continuously operated in highly surcharged, complex and difficult environment. Though they could effectively deal with major law and order challenges and fortify their efforts in safeguarding the democratic institutions, the police-public relations in India remained almost strained, if not hostile. There were strong reasons for the above trend. The police in British India .which was established to serve the interests of the colonial power epitomized aggressive high-handed policing mowing down opposition in ruthless show of terror and strength. The Police Act of 1861 which laid down the foundation of police in independent India inherited this legacy. The vast majority of Indian masses especially the poor and marginalized sections, found the police as an oppressive instrument for sustaining the government in power and thus developed dislike and distrust against them. New dawn of Independence had brought about sweeping changes in Indian polity and system. The nation building exercise which was initiated by great statesmen through a process of proper synthesis and assimilation of different classes, communities, castes, sub-cultures and ethnic groups on a common thread of unity and integrity with a clear socio-economic agenda, instead of bringing the police closer to the people accelerated their (police) alienation. The main reason for this discerning trend was the role played by the police in combating organized violence such as insurgency, secessionism, political extremism, fundamentalist militancy, ethnic conflicts, and caste-communal tensions which had posed serious challenge to the very concept of nationhood. On many occasions police forces have come under severe criticism for their partisan, unprofessional and unethical approach. Side by side, population growth coupled with increase in incidence of crime and the wide spread disparities in respect of the strength of police vis-à-vis their bourgeoning charter of duties and functions aggravated the dilemma of police. Added to this was improper utilization or wasteful deployment of personnel for non-essential duties resulting into an unhealthy trend of overburdened personnel engaging in core areas of policing without doing full justice to their tasks. For example, an all India level survey conducted by National Productivity Council of India revealed that police personnel engaged in law and order duties are working any way between 13-16 hours per day. Such long working hours coupled with lack of proper amenities and infrastructural facilities at work place not only causes stress and strain among personnel but also result into their low morale and motivation. Research studies revealed that increasing instances of corruption, high-handedness, nexus with criminals and anti-social elements, human rights violations, excess against women and other weaker sections by the lower and middle rungs of the police are the manifestation of such aberrations in the organization. When such 'deviant factors' dominate the work culture of the force, the laudable concept of police as a public service organization becomes a myth.

When we discuss various mechanisms for transforming the police into an effective instrument of public service, our first and foremost task should be in the direction of building up constructive co-operation between the police and public. This arises from the general hypothesis that public needs police and police need public co-operation for the effective enforcement of law and order. The practical expression of this concept appeared in the form of various pro-active policing efforts, such as community policing, problem-oriented policing. etc. They have gained much currency and legitimacy predominantly in the West and South-East Asian countries like Japan, Singapore etc. In India also significant attempts have been made in this direction by various State police forces with a view to working out harmonious relations between police and public for effective law enforcement. However most of the efforts by enterprising police managers could not create any sustainable impact on police functioning or making it service oriented, mainly due to absence of institutionalization and systematic support- both organizational and legislative.. Another reason for fading out these schemes was that many of these programs apparently alien were introduced in the Indian soil without re-modulating or remodeling them in our own domestic furnace of socio-economic and political realities. Peter Drucker, in his classic work "*The New Realities*" attempted to highlight this aspect as, "one of the basic challenges the managers in the developing country face is to find and identify those parts of their own tradition-historical and cultural- that can be used as management building blocks. The difference between Japan's economic success and India's relative backwardness is largely explained by the fact that Japanese managers are able to import management concepts in their own cultural soil and make them grow."

The findings of Peter Drucker are true to the core if we assess the grand success of service-oriented policing in Japan better known as 'Kobans'. Basically the police set up in Japan is governed by a management approach (Theory-Z) which provides highly efficient, flexible and cost-effective organization that is characterized by teamwork 'Zolistec', ensuring workers welfare, defined career paths, use of informal control mechanisms and worker inputs in decision making. This approach recognizes that personnel are part of a larger socio-economic matrix of influence including family, religion, economics etc. The management assumes full responsibility for dealing with the whole human being and not a segmental part which is characteristic of any bureaucratic organization. It provides consistency in structure and management processes that allow the National Police force of Japan to be decentralized into a semi-autonomous neighborhood-centered system of fixed posts known as "Kobans" (Police Box) in urban centers and "chuzaisho" (Residential Police Box) in rural areas. This structure positively fosters a high degree of interaction and co-operation between police and neighborhood residents and creates a favorable image of police. They undertake a wide range of tasks such as maintaining peace and safety of citizens through a system of traditional foot-patrolling (which facilitates better.familarity with the residents, houses and area as a whole). Providing consultancy services on crime prevention and security with a view to creating awareness among various sections of society and operating as a nodal centre of "Community Safety & Security" by coordinating different institution, agencies like Family Resident Associations, NGOs, private security agencies, security gadget manufacturers etc.

The National Police Agency of Japan which is role model of policing for the present millennium manifests certain important trends which need a thorough analysis when we think of strategies for transforming Indian police into a more service oriented organization. Firstly, the 'professional model' of policing characterized by mechanization of operations and impersonal law enforcement which is largely reactive and repressive, has limitations to effectively deal with the new challenges against police. Such dilemma in the field of modern policing can be overcome through proactive policing models, which ensure the participation and involvement of community in crime control and order management mechanisms. Secondly, any such proactive model which is properly molded on the basis of socio-economic realities; implemented through sound policing strategies and management principles and sustained and institutionalized by pclice organizations would accelerate the transformation of police into a public service organization. A natural corollary of this exercise is the genesis of participatory process in policing with police and community as key partners, who work together for improvement in quality of life in community.

Innovations and reforms without ground level assessment or proper planning fail to attain the targets or goals and very soon die a natural death through oblivion. This is more relevant in a country like India, a land of sub-continental proportions with regional, religious, cultural, linguistic and ethnic differences and diversities which have created a mosaic of law and order problems unique for each region and State. For example urban India, especially our mega cities like Mumbai, Delhi, Calcutta, Bangalore, Hyderabad, Noida, Ghaziabad etc which are in the grip of a 'third wave rhythm' (Alvin Toffler) characterized by new values and way of life, can be categorized as the major centers of organized crimes such as economic and cyber offences, drug-menace, trafficking in persons 'supari-killings,' kidnapping for ransom etc. On the other hand such offences may be unheard of in many parts of rural India where caste conflicts and killings, atrocities against women, dalits and other weaker sections, social exploitation etc dominate the crime scenario. At the same time, vast areas of the country cutting across urban-rural differences are in the grip of militant and radical groups whose depredations and dastardly acts have posed serious challenge to police and other security agencies. Thus instead of importing and implementing any uniform policing model or strategy to deal with such complex and diverse nature of offences in our pluralist society, the endeavor of police leadership should be to work out different strategies (in relation to different type of offences/crimes) or to formulate common strategy to combat those offences of same nature or interlinking dimensions. To cite an example, it is now proved beyond doubt that conventional policing with ill-trained personnel bereft of sophisticated weapons or not familiar with Guerilla/jungle warfare is not a match to effectively face the serious challenge posed by Left Wing Extremists (LWE). groups operating in different parts of the country. Same is the case with the growing trends of different shades of terrorism which transcend beyond geographical boundaries having sophisticated net work and vast financial resources.

Two aspects are important in this regard. First one is proper pilot or project studies in different locations especially in areas where society has been highly fragmented due to violence and crimes so that practical difficulties involved can be fully understood before a concept or strategy is institutionalized. The best technique available is 'Crime analysis" or "Crime Mapping" which "identifies trends and patterns within crime data in an attempt to solve crime or prevent their repeat occurrence" (Melissa Miller Reuland). It also equips police management with data on economic, geographic and law enforcement aspects for launching long term projects. The significant success attained by "Grey-hounds." in combating CPI (Maoists) in Andhra Pradesh and the causalities suffered by Chhattisgarh Police and Central Paramilitary Forces in their anti-Maoist operations in Chhattisgarh are typical examples as how important are the proper project studies/ assessment of situation in the formulation of right strategies by police before dealing with major challenges in the law and order front. The 'Grey-hounds' a highly professionalized and motivated special police force to exclusively deal with LWE menace, over a period of time had rightly assessed the socio-economic-demographic features vis-à-vis the activities and depredations of Radical ultras in their citadels as prelude to their systematic operations against LWE groups. This was their major secret of success in anti-Maoist operations in Andhra Pradesh. On the contrary, Chhattisgarh police and Central forces had had heavy causalities in their sporadic anti-Maoist operations in 2009 and 2010, without proper assessment, planning or preparations.

The second aspect is redefining the role and functions of the police in accordance with changes and challenges in the society. We should come out of the traditional approach that prevention and detection of crimes are the only areas of concern of police. With the advent of modernity, technological advancement, urbanization, economic reforms and liberalization and growth of market economy, the demands upon policing have undergone major change. The police in the present century have to play a major role in a plethora of tasks and functions which are closely intertwined with the concept of welfare State and well being of the masses. They are concerned with the feeling of fear of crime, rights and privileges of all sections of people especially weaker sections, physically handicapped, women and children, distress situations like earthquake, cyclone havoc, flood damage, famine, rail accidents, collapse of buildings, maintenance of order in general and during huge congregations in particular, which are more of service oriented objectives than core policing tasks. The crucial question now is how to equip and transform the police organization to perform such functions?

The efforts to transform police into an effective instrument of public service by redefining their role and functions and adopting proactive mechanisms would meet with success only when such moves are accompanied by internal re-organization and re-structuring of the force. As we move from 'professional model of policing' to strategic 'problem solving' model a more decentralized structure is needed to achieve the policing goals/ tasks. Herman Goldstein was perfectly right when he observed, "if police department is to be truly professionalized, the authority and responsibility should be de-centralized. The brass should surrender some of the prerogatives and must empower those down the lines to define the challenges of the work and the means of achieving them."

The process of de-centralization would accelerate the transformation of the force from a vertical to horizontal one with more and more personnel imbibing common traits such as flexibility, fluidity, tact and initiative as against the present characteristics of regimentation, command and control mechanisms which are unique features of any vertical organization. Such a transformation in the structure and complexion of the organization is essential for the police to play a pro active service oriented role in the society. The personnel with the changed attitude and traits under proper guidance and supervision of their senior officers can successfully involve the community or the people of their area of operations in crime prevention and peace keeping, social defense and a number of emergency tasks such as disaster management, conflict management etc. The formation of such police-public committees and their expansion with the inclusion of apolitical organizations, reputed NGOs/ community organizations and their institutionalization under proper legislations or organizational procedures would facilitate police to play a more service/ welfare oriented role in the society.

The concept of de-centralization should trickle down to the work culture and utilization of resources and amenities for wide range of policing tasks. For example, vertical organizations like police design policies and strategies at hierarchical level and then implement them through rules and procedures promulgated downward; professionally de-centralized organizational set up entrust such mechanisms to those closer to the ground(example cutting edge level personnel) who are in the best position to design solutions and evaluate them because they have more information about the immediate situation and direct access to the effects of their techniques. For example, a beat constable who remains posted for a pretty long period in a communally sensitive area with warring groups on the issue of taking out religious procession etc would have been better idea about the likely trouble- spots or the lumens elements responsible for communal tension or conflicts, than a newly appointed Superintendent of Police. One cardinal principle of the strategic management of public service organizations is that their professionalism improves by reducing the distance between task conception, task execution and concrete results. The Police management system and human resources development techniques that are basically the functions at senior management level need thorough overhauling and re-orientation. The officers should encourage a work culture at each level and allow them to use their initiative and potential to the optimum advantage of the organization. For example, more than 85 per cent of our police force comprises constabulary and about three-fourth of total expenditure in police budget in the States incurred on constabulary related expenditure. And yet this important rank in the police force that interacts with the general public is treated as a mere mechanical cog in the police machinery and not expected to exercise his discretion or initiative. Such aberrations in the proper utilization of manpower should be rectified.

Similarly proper procurement, utilization and distribution of material and technical resources are important tasks for quality improvement of the force. Unless the personnel are equipped with sophisticated weapons, electronic gadgets, communication and audio-visual aids, they are unable to meet the challenges of new generation of criminals or the underworld mafia who have no dearth of such devices. No doubt, the State governments or police organizations spend substantial funds for large scale procurement of such equipment or devices as part of modernization of Police. But irony is that they seldom initiate any imaginative or innovative measures for their utilization. For example, computers had been introduced in a big way by many State police forces as early as in 1975, but neither there was any serious effort on their proper use or application in important areas of policing such as crime analysis/mapping, nor any systematic move to impart proper computer-literacy to the personnel at cutting edge level. On the other hand, the bitter truth was that while bulk of such equipments were used as decorative pieces in the spacious rooms of senior echelons of the force, the majority of middle level personnel who had acquired some proficiency in computers were shamelessly deputed to impart training to the better haves of senior officers or their school-going wards. And the computerization in police initially remained only in papers and was confined to routine activities such as preparation of pay bills or establishment matters.

Similarly the police departments in many States have procured large number of vehicles to give more mobility to the personnel especially those engaged in patrolling or surveillance duties. But any objective survey on the utilization of these vehicles would reveal that sizeable percentage of them is not used for actual policing tasks. There is no moral or ethical concern for the majority of senior and middle level supervisory officers to depute such vehicles with 'Police' name plates and beacon lights to regularly carry their wards to educational institutions or their wives to beauty parlors or ladies' clubs. More real irony was that some senior echelons of the force insist that at least a couple of brand new vehicles should be permanently parked in their residences to satisfy the sagacious ego of their life partners. A random survey in 2006 on the number of senior police officers in Madhya Pradesh having their own personal vehicles/drivers and sparingly use such vehicles for personal purposes, disclosed that their number was less than 5 per cent of the total strength of senior officers of and above the rank of Superintendent of Police. The situation is not different in other States as well. The above fact clearly indicates as how huge and extensive is the misuse of departmental vehicles in the Police organization which keep a conscious silence on such matters and adopt all dubious and illegal means to silence those who try to expose such illegalities. Of late, substantial funds have been spent for improving infrastructure facilities notably office and residential buildings. But hundreds of police stations which are the most frequent and perhaps the nearly all crucial domain of police-public co-operation function in dilapidated rented buildings without basic amenities or facilities. The personnel who manage such police stations take away stationery items like pens, re-fills, white paper, carbon-sheets, torch light batteries etc from the shops that fall in the close proximity of police stations for their regular office work. The more unfortunate among them have to drain out their own pockets or force somebody else in the street to meet the expenditure for the transportation of unclaimed dead bodies and their funeral. Their living conditions are equally dismal. The barracks of the beat constables or the living in accommodation of the constabulary in many States are centuries-old structures with leaking roof, cracked walls and broken doors and windows, devoid of basic amenities like drinking water, toilets or sanitation facilities. The other side of the spectrum is entirely different. The quantum of funds utilized to re-construct/renovate and furnish/re-furnish the office spaces for senior police leaders with all ultra modern facilities and gadgets is astronomical. Demolition and re-construction of Office accommodation are very common in police organization as majority of senior echelons are blind believers of 'vastu' or Sooth-Sayers/astrologers. Every new incumbent in a senior post goes for alteration/modification of the office space in line with such beliefs; for which huge departmental funds are wasted without any impunity. Such disturbing realities and images in the force create strong "mental blocks" among the right thinking personnel and act as major impediments in inculcating service, welfare oriented traits among the personnel.

The ultimate effectiveness of any police department depends upon the quality of the personnel. Based on this hypothesis, James H. Auten has developed a new approach to management for productivity in the public service organizations especially the law enforcement agencies. Auten's theory otherwise known as 'P' management underlines that in law enforcement agencies it is the people whether they function as administrators, managers, supervisors, detectives or patrol officers determine as how much productive their organization is or functions. It also highlights that organizations will become more productive when human resources who are motivated by properly created goals and objectives realize their growth potential. On a closer analysis we find that the basic principles of the above management concept are intricately interwoven into three main features of human resources development viz. recruitment, training and leadership qualities which are vital for any professional organization like police.

The police in the new century needs new breed of personnel with a healthy blend of 'knowledge' and 'cerebral skills' and have the right aptitude and capability to successfully undertake a variety of complex and arduous tasks. Ironically, the present recruitment procedures appear to be grossly inadequate to recruit such personnel to the force. One main lacunae is that the age of recruitment is going higher and higher in all ranks which reflects badly on the policing. For example, the age limit of 18/20 years, which was fixed by the Police Commission of 1860 for the competitive examination for the recruitment of personnel to Indian Police (IP) cadre of the British India, has now gone up to 30 years for candidates seeking entry to IPS through All India Civil Services Examination. The situation is worse in respect of the age prescribed for direct entry to the ranks of Deputy Superintendent of Police (DSP) and Sub Inspectors which varies from 30 to 38 years in various States. In the case of constable which represents vast majority of police service, there exists no uniform pattern in respect of age limit or educational qualifications. The irony is that most of the personnel are inducted into the force at the age of 30-35 years when skill generation or attitudinal modification efforts will not succeed in giving 30-50 per cent positive results. Rather the results may be negative in the form of apathy, rigidity and mental blocks which continue with the personnel through out their career. Such human resources seldom show any interest or sincerity in undertaking service/welfare oriented tasks in the organization. These realities have prompted the government and policy makers to initiate various administrative reforms to implement "catch them young concept" in the All India Services to give new orientation and dynamism to administration and governance. Needless to mention that proposals like the introduction of an Entrance Examination for All India/Central Services to Class XII students on the pattern of NDA, IITs, Medical Entrance Examination etc and the selected candidates undergoing a two part five year course at a National Academy before allotting them All India Services on the basis of merit and choice should be vigorously pursued. Simultaneously, the job avenues for Professionals/specialists to Central services including Police should be kept open through direct entry of Officers from the disciplines of Engineering, Law, Forensic Science, Economics, Statistics, Forest Management, Management, and Public Administration by conducting All India level competition. A two-tier system of such recruitment with specific syllabus and examination pattern would definitely help to improve the quality and professionalism of our All India Services and allied cadres including police. The State governments should also launch administrative reforms and enact proper legislations for the recruitment of young and talented candidates to other ranks particularly constabulary. The age limit for the recruitment of constables should be fixed as 18 years with the minimum educational qualification as 10+2.

Another factor interconnected with the recruitment is "man-power planning" which is now almost absent in the organization. Too few men for too many jobs and too many men for too few jobs are not healthy for the balanced development of any organization. Very often ad-hoc methods and extraneous influences dominate the very concept of manpower recruitment policy in police. In many States, it has become a common practice of recruiting large number of constables or middle ranks like Sub Inspectors whenever there is a change of government in power. Mere political populism demands such decisions. Such en-masse' recruitment leads to wastage of manpower which a country like India cannot afford. Such ill-conceived and lop-sided recruitment policies defeat 'Career-planning' which is yet to take concrete shape on professional lines. The Career planning inter-alia includes the promotional aspects and better placement of those taken in the department. Unfortunately, in many States the promotional prospects of personnel at cutting edge level especially constabulary, Sub-Inspectors, Inspectors and DSPs are far from satisfactory. Stagnation is too stifling in the case of constabulary. The Dharma Vera Commission highlighted their plight when it says; "a large number of constables retire as constables without even one rank promotion in their entire career. No system can remain healthy if such a large number of personnel vegetate and waste out after working for nearly 30 years in the same rank at which they entered in the system." No amount of sermons or motivational techniques can change the attitude of these personnel to the betterment of the organization, unless corrective measures are taken to improve their career prospects especially those who are keen and committed to come up in the ladder of the force. Suitable organizational measures such as linking promotions with performance and suitability (instead of seniority alone) which have been introduced in defense forces like Air force for the promotion of the lower ranks (Airmen, Sergeant etc) on the basis of their Annual Confidential Reports (ACR) and the grade/score in the prescribed Departmental tests/ examinations may be explored to ensure the timely promotion of professionally competent personnel at the cutting edge level of police.

Once we have the right manpower, the next important aspect is training. In fact training is considered to be the best investment in any professional organization. Unfortunately, training takes a back seat in the whole scheme of policing. Except a few premier Police Training Institutions like National Police Academy (NPA), Hyderabad, majority of the Police Training establishments in the States are ill-equipped in terms of infrastructure and resources and also handicapped due to poor level of human resources. More over, militaristic orientation of training programs through greater emphasis on outdoor curriculum and physical exercises coupled with old, out worn and obsolete training modules and methodologies largely based on traditional law enforcement mechanisms failed to develop humane or welfare-oriented attitude among the majority of the personnel. Designing such Training curricula with modules covering traditional areas of policing which occupied only a small percentage of personnel's on duty time and not in accordance with the expanding role of police and their wide spectrum of duties and functions defeated the main objective of training namely, equipping personnel to perform various tasks and functions associated with their present and future role. This dichotomy in the concept and actual practice of police training has prompted National Police Commission (NPC) to observe; "if the police men are trained only in how to deal with crimes and criminals and not how to deal with the rest of the population, it is not their fault that they failed to come up to the expectations of the general public". Thus in order to bring desired attitudinal change among the personnel especially for developing traits and qualities essential to undertake service-oriented missions, special emphasis has to be put in giving a new orientation to police training. The Annual Conference of Directors' General and Inspectors' General of police held in September 2000, had identified this aspect and it adopted a 'Vision Statement' (Training Vision-2010) which recommended a three point strategy viz. attitudinal change leading to shift from enforcement mode to service mode; enhancement of capabilities of personnel and creation of Mother Trainers in order to achieve the above goals.

However, much has yet to be done to improve the quality of police training with a humane touch. For that purpose training mechanism capable of developing general spirit of service and professionalism among personnel for dealing with service-related tasks like conflict resolution, juvenile delinquency, gender justice, disaster management, neighborhood conflicts, enforcement of social legislations meant for the protection of the rights and privileges of weaker sections etc. should be worked out after conducting proper empirical studies and public surveys. New modules on above policing tasks and inter- related themes like theory of policing and its application to police-community relations etc should be incorporated in the training curricula. Practical schemes such as deputing police probationers to those communities and areas which need a more service oriented policing, may be designed to help the new generation of police leaders/ personnel to shed their inhibitions to interact with various cross-sections of the society. These exercises should be properly evaluated in order to identify the right personnel with right attitude and approach for assigning them service related tasks.

The proper development of human and material resources-both within and outside the organization- is one of the key functions of police leaders. In this regard, the police leadership comprises two components namely, the internal leadership governing his leadership behavior with his subordinates in the force and the external leadership which means leadership role in the community. For reforms and changes like the transformation of police into public service, proper synthesis or integration of these two elements is essential. While the internal leadership through a strategic management style that implies high concern for human resources and performance motivate personnel to exhibit true spirit of service in a wide spectrum of duties and functions, the external leadership develop support and resources and proper liaison within the community to undertake service oriented proactive policing tasks. Thus, the more pro-active a police leadership, the more speedy will be the transition of police into an effective instrument of public service.

The police in the present millennium should come out of their assumed role as traditional law enforcement agency and shed their work style largely influenced by cops-and-robbers syndrome. Their ever-bourgeoning role and functions go beyond the contours of battle against crime and criminals and now touch upon almost all important fields of human activity. The most challenging task confronting the police in the present century is how to equip the organization to successfully deal with such a wide spectrum of complex and diverse activities which on many instances are not directly related to the core-areas of policing. Internal re-organization and re-structuring based on new strategies and innovative mechanisms play a significant role in meeting such tasks and re-orienting the style and functioning of police. But police need the help, input and support of every member of the community in improving their professionalism and providing the public with better and more affordable service. Such a comprehensive partnership between the police and community built on the firm foundation of "social accountability" and mutual trust will influence their role and functions on pro-active lines and enable them to attain the image of a public service organization.

2

Image Crisis of Indian Police:
Causes and Remedies

The image of professional organizations like police depends mostly on their performance and the impressions and perceptions of their major stake-holders. The more popular the image of an organization, the greater will be their acceptance in the society. The Police whether under British Raj or in independent India could not exhibit an exemplary performance in the core areas of policing; nor rise up to the expectations of common people. Men in 'Khaki' were viewed with fear, suspicion and sometimes with animosity. All sections of people had had some fair idea about the omissions and commissions of police, as police or crime related stories spread like wild fire especially in rural areas. From time immemorial, village grandmas through their bed-time tales or folklores to naughty babies immortalized them as cruel and fearful characters. Now, the virtual media through cinema, Serials and exclusive Police or 'crime stories' bring them to our drawing rooms as symbols of brutality, cruelty and terror. They bring live stories of 'khaki-clad men' brutally beating and battering a hapless helpless woman for a petty theft or tying a youth behind a motor-bike and pulling him all through the street in the presence of dismal crowd. In all such 'stories', they intrinsically interweave facts, fiction, myth and reality and their subjective impressions in such a way to create permanent adverse imprints against Police.

Over the years the nuts and bolts of the Police structure in the country have been loosened; its morals and confidence had been destroyed making it unreliable and undependable. Thus the image of police remains poor and sullied among the overwhelming majority of Indian masses. The Second Police Commission (1902-03) appointed by the British government observed; "there can be no doubts that the Police forces through out the country is in a most unsatisfactory condition, the abuses are common every where, that this involves injury to the people and discredit to the government and that radical reforms are urgently necessary" Ironically not much had been done to change the dismal image of the police. Thus the First Police Commission of free India (1977-81) commented; "Functioning under the constraints and handicaps of an outmoded system, the Police performance has fallen short of public expectations. The present culture of the Police system appears as a continuation of what obtained under the British regime when the Police functioned ruthlessly as an agent for sustaining the government in power". The above image of Police had strongly reflected in the pungent words of Justice A.N. Mulla of the Lucknow Bench of the Allahabad High Court as; 'There is not a single lawless group in the whole country whose record of crime is anywhere near the record of that single organized unit which is known as the Indian Police.'

A number of empirical studies on the public image of Indian Police had clearly reflected the image crisis of Police. For example, the study conducted by the Banaras Hindu University (1972) and Indian Institute of Public Opinion, New Delhi (1978) brought out a highly unattractive and eclipsed image of the Police in the minds of the people. Similarly the impressions of the future generation particularly adolescent students on Police were revealed in another such recent study undertaken by U.N.B. Rao, IPS among over 2000 students from different mega/metropolitan cities of India. The overwhelming majority of respondents expressed negative impressions on the style of functioning of Police; Police mechanisms including non-registration of complaints/ cases; their unsympathetic approach towards common people and the over all image of the Police. One of the main conclusions of these studies was that Police are ill-equipped, power-drunk, corrupt, immoral without any professional ethics. Some real time statistics on policing speak this cardinal truth. As per Transparency International 2005 survey, around 62% percent of citizens have first hand experience of paying bribe to Police totaling to the tune of Rs.3900 crore per year; 22389 departmental proceedings are pending against police personnel as on Jan 01, 2005 and about 5.2 lakh exhibits are pending examination in States and Regional Forensic Science Laboratories. The National Human Rights Commission's (NHRC) Annual Reports for the last four years (2007-2010) showed that the complaints against police ranged from 50000 to 75000 with a steady increase of custodial deaths. The studies and statistics bring out certain major factors that adversely affect the public image of Police. These factors which influence the perception of the general public on police can be broadly classified into historical, organizational, personnel/functional and extraneous and include:

(a) Historical legacy/image of Police as an oppressive instrument meant for safeguarding the colonial interests of the British and subsequently the rich, the privileged and the powerful sections of the society.

(b) The Police Act of 1861 and the adversarial nature of the Police with archaic and outdated organizational procedures and practices which lack professionalism.

(c) Regimentation and paramilitary orientation which alienate the Police from the public.

(d) Lack of strategic planning, collapse of command-control mechanisms with weak, uninspiring, self-centered police leaders playing fiddle to the tunes of political masters to safeguard their cozy posts.

(e) Political interference which appears more prominent in rural areas and manifests itself in the misuse or abuse of police power and disregard to law by the Police.

(f) Police demeanor and "behavioral aberrations" such as corruption, use of Third Degree methods, custodial deaths, atrocities and excesses against women, dalits and other marginalized sections.

(g) use of authority, power and discretion indiscriminately for vested and partisan interests,

(h) biased or unethical Police behavior during investigation of sensational cases, maintenance of law and order and caste-communal conflicts.

(i) increase in incidence of crime, delay in investigation of cases/ arrest of criminals and acquittal in large number of cases.

(j) role of electronic media in sensationalizing 'Police Stories' detrimental to the image of Police.

A closer analysis of the above factors reveals that the adverse impact being created by these issues on the overall functioning of the Police, its performance and image could be overcome through radical reforms and internal re-organization of the force. Over the last three decades such efforts have been going on at various levels. For example, National Police Commission (NPC) made a number of recommendations such as adoption of Model Police Act (drafted by it) and formation of State Security Commission in order to accelerate the process of structural and organizational changes in Police in line with the radical changes in the society and expectations of the masses. Similar worthwhile recommendations and proposals were made by other Committees headed by eminent administrators, legal luminaries and Police leaders such as Justice V.S. Malimath, K Padmnabhaiah, Soli Sorabji, Julius Reibero etc advocating radical reorganization of the force and thereby checking adverse factors like political interference with Police which is the greatest evil.

For example, setting up State Security Commission/ Police Boards and Police Establishment Committees etc with specified functions such as selection of Police officers for appointment to the post of Director General of Police, transfer/ postings and promotions of middle and senior supervisory cadres and review and evaluation of the organizational performance of the Police with special emphasis on efficiency, standard performance and behavior etc would help to buttress the image of Police.

However, two aspects are crucial in this regard. The first one is the question of implementation of Reforms which is still uncertain due to the organized moves by political masters to out beat the meaningful Police Reforms. The Draft Model Police Act of NPC is yet to be implemented by many States. The only matter of consolation is that the Apex Court has already seized the gravity of the issue and passed necessary directions to the Political Executive to vigorously pursue the Police Reforms in view of the fast changing socio-economic-political and security scenario in the country. The second aspect is the genuine apprehensions in the minds of general public as how the proposed Reforms, even if implemented will help to refurbish the present image of the Police, their competence and professionalism, unless there is radical transition in the attitude and approach of Police leaders who govern the Police. Such apprehensions are not unfounded if we make an introspection on the exact role played by Police in a number of recent sensational cases like Best Bakery, Jessica Lal, Priyadarshini Mattoo, Nitish Katara, Nithari, Aarushi etc. Some genuine questions and doubts stir up our minds: whether the rampant political interference or pressure was the sole causative factor for such lapses which created wide spread criticism against Police? Can the Police be totally exonerated themselves for their failures in the proper investigation of these cases? How many Police leaders attempted to resist the apparently illegal orders/directions from Political masers or higher-ups? What happened to their solemn pledge to protect the lives and properties of citizens without any bias or prejudice? Perhaps the angry, revengeful and hapless souls of Shorabuddin Sheikh, Kausabi, Jessica Lal, Priyadrarshini, Aarushi and thousands of others who had attained martyrdom in the altar of law enforcing agencies may be staring at us without getting any answers to these crucial questions which still haunt the Police organization in the country.

Basically, such questions are reflective of the complicity in the existing system particularly the relations between the Political Executive and Civil Service, which no longer have the image of 'steel frame' due to complex reasons. But purely from policing perspective, such unfortunate happenings or incidents are the outcome of "Professional Model of Policing" characterized by mechanization of operations and impersonal law enforcement which is largely reactive and repressive. This need to be changed and instead pro-active policing models which ensure participation and involvement of community in crime control mechanisms should be developed. Any such pro-active policing model on the basis of socio-economic realities, implemented through sound Police strategies and management principles would accelerate the transformation of the force as people- friendly with improved professionalism and performance. A Draft Model Police Act for Kerala police, recently brought out by Peoples' Union for Civil Liberties (PUCL) has envisaged such pro-active policing model institutionalized with rules and regulations at State Police hierarchy level and decentralized at police station limits having Community Liaison Groups comprising respectable local residents and Beat Officers undertaking regular beat and patrolling of cluster of villages. The Model Act also stipulates the formation of Citizens' Policing Committees for each locality or group of localities or colonies including slums for effective pro-active policing in urban areas. The pro-active policing mechanisms both at urban and rural areas shall focus on crime and social disorder through the delivery of police service that include traditional law enforcement as well as prevention, problem-solving, community involvement and partnership.

Re-defining the role and functions of the Police is imperative for the success of pro-active policing mechanisms or the efforts to transform the Police people-friendly. The police should come out of the conventional age-old approach that prevention and detection of crime are the only areas of concern of Police. With the advent of modernity, technological/scientific advancement, globalization/ liberalization and economic reforms and the growth of Market economy and free trade, the demands upon policing have undergone major changes. The Police in the present century have to undertake a mosaic of tasks and functions which are closely connected with the concept of welfare State and well being of citizens. The Police personnel of the present millennium have to deal with the very element of fear of crime among citizens, rights and privileges of all sections of the people especially weaker sections, physically handicapped and emergency situations like earthquake, cyclones, floods, rail accidents, collapse of buildings, bridges etc. The Draft Model Police Act of NPC and similar model Acts drafted by Non-Governmental Organizations (NGOs)/Civil liberties-human Rights groups have come up with a number of recommendations/proposals focusing on the social /public service role of the Police in order to make them more humane and acceptable to various cross sections of the society. The "Social responsibilities of the Police" as envisaged by them include a plethora of issues such as proper assistance to the members of public, particularly senior citizens, women, children, the poor and indigent and the physically and mentally challenged persons who are found in helpless condition on the streets and other public places or other-wise need help and protection, victims of crime and road accidents etc. These proposals are salutary considering the growing trends of consumerism and materialism that are making steady inroads into the society and the new generation relegating traditional values, human bonds and relations to the background.

The above issues of expanding horizons of Police-charter of duties especially social functions are basically intertwined with the attitude of Police leaders and extent of internal reforms in the Police. We should not forget the truth that there are still a strong school of Police leaders who are deeply committed to the concept that Police organization is nothing but a regimented team of 'crime fighters' who have nothing to do with public/social service or such other functions in the society. It is an established fact that the nature and quality of policing mainly depend on leadership. The Police unlike other public organizations have certain cognitive features namely, power/authority and discretion. They enjoy wide range of powers while discharging core functions of Police such as maintenance of law and order and prevention and detection of crime. In fact Police personnel have absolute powers and authority on such Policing functions as rightly observed by Lord MR Denning, "I hold it to be the duty of the Commissioner of Police as it is of every Chief Constable to enforce the law of the land. No Minister of the Crown can tell him that he must or must not keep observation on this place or not; he must or must not prosecute this man or that one. Nor can any Police authority tell him so. The responsibility of law enforcement lies on him; he is answerable to law and law alone". Once the Police leaders uncompromisingly uphold the true spirit of the rule of law, the Political Executive/masters would not overstep their jurisdiction and illegally encroach into the domain of Police. On the other hand when the Police leaders hobnob with the political masters and are too willing to oblige them in pursuance of their vested interests, the latter dictate terms with them to do illegalities. The higher echelons of the Police in majority of the States are over enthusiastic to implement the agenda of the governments in power, in contravention of the rules or regulations or the established procedures and practices. No structural mechanisms like State Security Commission or Police Complaint Authority can end such trends unless there is a real change of heart or approach at senior hierarchy.

Similarly, Police discretion is yet another feature that can be used or misused by the personnel and evoke controversies adversely affecting Police image. Very often the personnel at cutting edge level while enforcing the complex laws and regulations confront the dilemma, "To be or not to be" i.e. should they strictly enforce all laws or ignore some violations? This 'Hamletian' dilemma could be resolved through proper application of the "power of discretion" for which the timely guidance and directions by Police leaders to the personnel on the ground are necessary. The personnel are bound to exercise the power of discretion strictly in accordance with the procedures that lay down processes and formalities. But those intoxicated by tremendous powers or dominated by selfish motives out rightly misuse them at the cost of the general image of the Police. In fact the major 'deviants' at cutting edge level negate the very concept of good policing and evoke considerable public furor and erode the credibility of the force. Politicization and communalization of such issues by the vested interests aggravates the dilemma of police.

Another major 'deviant factor' that brings down the public image and credibility of the Police is the increasing nexus among Police-Politicians and criminals/ goons. A more dangerous and disturbing trend is the entry of criminal- turned terrorists into this unholy nexus having transnational linkages and sophisticated net working for money-laundering, fake currency transaction, drug-peddling and trafficking in manpower. Our major metros have witnessed the existence of such gangs and their organized operations. At times such 'syndicates' collude with communal and fundamentalist elements and create a reign of terror through serial bomb-blasts, communal riots or gang wars which shatter normal life of common people. Our major cities in the recent past have witnessed such bizarre incidents, which to a great extent; have shaken the faith of people over law enforcement agencies. A more distressing aspect is the booking of innocent persons in such incidents, apparently due to the failure of Police in identifying and apprehending the real groups behind such dastardly crimes. Unless the Police leadership strongly deal with such incidents and restore the faith of common masses, their efforts in effecting lasting make over on Police image would not be fructified. Ironically, on many occasions the approach of Police leadership on such matters is not healthy or conducive as rightly observed by Aravind Varma, Senior IPS Officer now teaching Criminology in Indiana University, USA, "the Sauvé police leadership rather than the ill-mannered Constables could be responsible for the Police-politician-criminal nexus". Another inter-related factor of this unholy nexus is the organized efforts of political and police leadership to shield the delinquent police personnel on the pretext of safeguarding the morale and image of the organization. Even attempts have been made to scuttle the directions of Judiciary or bodies like National/State Human Rights Commissions in this process. Very often they put forth seemingly convincing reasons. Thus Lord Delvin had rightly commented, 'it is the general habit of police not to admit the slightest departure from correctness.' This approach instead of protecting the morale and image of the organization cause more embarrassment to the organization when the vigilant media or detractors of the force come out with highly exaggerative and speculative stories on such nexus; misdeeds and omissions of the Police. In fact the present 'culture of secrecy' or 'no comment policy' on one hand and 'big mouth' approach of egregious police officers have been exploited by the media for 'police-bashing'.

No doubt, the media play a crucial role in building up or tarnishing the image of Police. The 'police stories' especially in respect of sensational or sensitive investigations are pet themes of the print as well as electronic media, attracting large clientele. The more the readership or rating of any such 'story' or program in the print or electronic media, the greater will be its impact over the people. Ironically, various surveys and studies on the approach of media towards Police revealed that around 75% of reporting/telecast by the media on Police project a negative image, which in the long run will erode the credibility of Police and their acceptance in the society. There is no surprise on such trends, as even the most popular

'British Bobby' had worst ever image and suffered humiliation from British Press in the wake of Second World war. The Bobby could refurbish its image after the implementation of the recommendations of a Royal Commission in 1962. While endorsing the great influence of the British Press and British Broadcasting Corporation (BBC), the Commission recommended that the media/press should maintain highest standard in reporting the Police news and features so that the people should have confidence on the Police. Incidentally, in our country the National Police Commission (NPC) had examined the whole gamut of Police-media relations and made a number of recommendations to work out better co-ordination and synergy between Police and media. The Commission also felt that the Police should demolish their culture of secrecy and should remain more open and accountable to the media so that the tendency of the latter to come out with highly speculative and sensational 'police stories' much against the interests of the organization can be checkmated. For that purpose the District Police Superintendents of Police were empowered to directly brief the media, while the Police stations were allowed to furnish routine statistics such as number of cases registered, arrests made etc. Despite such efforts, a happy and harmonious Police-media relationship has not grown up as manifest by 'trial by media' in a number of sensational murder cases such as Jessica Lal, Aarushi, Shivani etc. Thus, in the current scenario, the endeavor of Police leadership is to establish" mutual code of honor' between the Police and media by appreciating the role and responsibilities of the both so that their interest and of the public that are ultimately served by the both would be well protected.

The process of broadening the spectrum of .duties and functions of Police and implementing the structural changes in the force depend on a myriad of factors. First and foremost is the proper development of human resources, as ultimate effectiveness of any Police department depends upon the quality of the personnel. Gone are days when all the able-bodied youth were found to be the best bet for Police force. Such manpower with brute physical force was essential for the force which then played the typical role of an oppressive instrument with its basic function of 'crime-fighting'. In the modern welfare State, the Police need to shed this image and should try to become a friend of the citizens through their service-oriented approach. For that purpose the force requires educated, well-balanced and humane personnel devoid of any rabid communal, caste or political leanings or proclivities. A challenging task before the Police leadership is the recruitment of such personnel; imparting proper training to ignite their knowledge and skills for developing right attitude and approach and application of right strategic management mechanisms for motivation, leadership and ensuring better performance. Ironically, the existing recruitment procedures especially for Constabulary and middle level officers are grossly inadequate to recruit such personnel. The higher age fixed for recruitment, lack of uniformity among States in the recruitment process, corruption, malpractices and political interference and lack of career policy and planning at Police leadership level .are some of the major lacunae adversely affecting the present recruitment system of Constabulary and middle ranks of Police. Irony is that despite much rhetoric on Police reforms, neither the Political Executive nor the Police leadership has made any serious thought to introduce radical changes in the present recruitment system in Police especially the Constabulary. The heart of the matter is that the Political masters irrespective of their ideologies and policies are inclined to have a Police force with their sympathizers, where as the Police leadership playing second fiddle to such elements is keen to have more pliable and weak personnel blindly obeying their dictates and directions. In the ultimate analysis in such a scenario with overwhelming majority of weak, uninspiring personnel prone to corruption and malpractices, the Police organization and the general public suffer at the cost of the vest- interested political masters and a set of self-centered and over-ambitious Police leaders.

Along with radical changes in the recruitment policy, proper training of personnel assumes considerable importance in the process of remodeling the police. Though Training is considered to be the best investment in any professional organization like Police, much could not be done yet to streamline the training program as in the case of countries like USA, UK and Holland where such programs are intended to adapt the personnel to changing needs of the society. For example, Pennsylvania Police in the US added incident simulator as part of the training aimed at attaining competencies matching core tasks. These programs cover a wide spectrum of the newly emerging challenges to the police at ground level, which facilitate the personnel at cutting edge level to professionally handle such real time situations. Though we can claim for argument's sake that such incident simulated programs are included in the training module of Training institutions like NPA, the reality is that overwhelming majority of personnel have not been imparted such training. On the contrary, majority of our Police Training establishments in the States are ill-equipped in terms of infrastructure and resources; devoid of well-qualified and competent Faculty members and are bereft of training modules and methodologies capable of developing skills and talents to perform various tasks and functions or desired attitudinal change to inculcate traits and qualities to properly interact with people in the course of their policing tasks. In the present scenario, the major task of Police training institutions in the country is to bring out a new breed of police personnel with high level of professionalism, right attitude and approach helpful to improve the image and acceptance of the organization in the society.

No doubt, the training alone will not complete the transition or transformation of the personnel in line with the declared aims and goals of the organization. Much should be done by the Police leadership to encourage a work culture that should empower Police personnel at each level and allow them to use the initiative and potential to the optimum advantage of the organization. For that purpose the personnel inducted into the organization through sound recruitment strategies and properly trained and empowered to meet law and order challenges should be entrusted with important tasks and goals which would inculcate in them a feeling of involvement and importance within the organization. Such a transformation of the personnel especially at cutting edge level will help to eliminate their present perception and impression that they are mere 'mechanical cog' in the highly impersonal Police Machinery and are free to do anything legal or illegal on the strength and color of the uniform. Only a force with such transformed personnel can overcome the present image crisis of the Police and fulfill the mission of Indian Police as rightly highlighted by Prime Minister Man Mohan Singh, 'our intention is to create an image of the Indian Police as professionally competent and technologically advanced force, one that would be an agent of socio-economic change endowed with a spirit of humanism'.

3

How to Make Police Professionally Competent to Face National Security Challenges ?

Police is the most vital instrument of the State in the context of National Security. The security scenario of the country had undergone critical changes during the last three decades. Transnational threats such as global terrorism with its seminal links to smuggling of arms, explosives and drugs, money laundering and information-war fare and internal problems like terrorism. Left Wing Extremism (LWE), insurgency and different shades of caste-communal and ethnic violence and conflicts that are jeopardizing the unity, integrity and sovereignty, are the major challenges to the internal security of the country. Added to this are the organized efforts of a hostile neighbor and non-State players to disintegrate and destabilize the nation through 'Low Intensity Conflicts' (LIC) or 'proxy wars'. The manifestation of these threats appear in different forms such as terrorist/extremist attack, serial bomb blasts, mass killings, communal and ethnic violence etc which shatter peace and tranquility in the society.

The crucial question is whether the Police organization with the present infrastructure, resources, manpower and professional skills can effectively deal with a plethora of internal security challenges. The answer is 'no'. Many factors contribute to this reality. First is certain basic statistics in respect of inadequate presence of police in the vast areas of our country. While the strength of the total Police force in the country showed a marginal increase during the period

2009-2010, the index for police per 1000 of population showed a marginal decline during the same period. Similarly, the Police for per 100 sq. km. which stood at 133 (2009) manifested their inadequate presence in vast areas of the country. A typical Police Station with one or two Sub Inspectors/ Assistant Sub Inspectors and ten Constabulary has to meet the law and order requirements of over two lakh-population spread around an area of 200 sq. kms. in rural areas. In many States especially those infested by LWE or insurgency, such vast areas remain inaccessible to police personnel due to unique geographical features like forests, rivers, ravines and mountains. The aberrations in the proper utilization of man power and resources worsen the situation. For example, major percentage of constabulary which constitutes more than 85% of the total force, are not deployed for any 'core-policing tasks', but are treated as obedient mechanical functionaries mostly acting in compliance of specific orders from their superiors and not doing anything positive on their own initiative or judgment. This leads to a unique situation in which the Police organization is being operated, supervised and led by around 15% of the total force; which cannot do full justice to the department or the major stake-holders in respect of core policing tasks like maintenance of order and prevention and detection crime.

Similarly, overwhelming majority of personnel at cutting edge level is bereft of adequate professional skills or expertise to effectively deal with the new challenges in the National Security front. Their understanding on different shades of terrorism, molded in highly puritanical fundamentalist or revivalist concepts and the ideological or tactical/ operational framework of Left Wing Extremist groups is abysmally low. Same is the case with other threats like insurgency, Low Intensity Conflicts, cross-border terrorism and intricacies of 'covert warfare' by hostile intelligence/security agencies. Their knowledge is peripheral in respect of the vast technological advancement made in the fields of 'cyber space' and the wide spread of cyber-related offences like appropriation of cyber cash/credit card manipulations, cyber obscenity, corporate espionage, 'hacking'/manipulation of cyber data etc.

The irony is that the 'knowledge explosion' and 'information revolution' that have made 'big bangs' in different spheres and made substantial contributions in changing the profile of organizations are yet to create any major ripples in the Police which is still wedded to conventional practices and procedures adversely affecting its competence and professionalism. This was despite the organized efforts by the Central and State governments to modernize the force to cope up with the new challenges in the internal security scenario. The Centre's ambitious "Modernization Program of Police (MPP), commenced in 2000-01 with an annual allotment of Rs. 1000 crore was basically intended to improve the fitness, strike capability and mobility of the forces including secured Police Station buildings and modern communication and office equipments. No doubt, State Police forces have spent substantial funds for the purchase of vehicles, modern gadgets, communication equipments and weapons and construction of buildings especially office complexes. However these infrastructural developments have not contributed much in strengthening the basic policing due to gross misuse or under utilization of the newly procured logistics and resources. The impact analysis of Police Modernization programs in many States revealed that the main aim of the scheme namely, enhancement in the 'capability' of the force through the better application of the technological up gradation by the personnel could not be achieved. It further highlighted that this lacunae was mainly due to the difficulty in choosing the appropriate technology and delay in procurement, much less making the personnel adept in handling them. At cutting edge level 'capability' factor remained low, thereby incapacitating the personnel to cope up with the new threats. The tragedy is that the State Police forces are vying with each other to get maximum funds from the Centre under MPP, but are less objective or realistic in the proper utilization of these funds for the greater professional advantage/competence of the force. The main bottleneck is that there is no proper monitoring mechanism on the utility of these funds; nor effective accountability on the proper application of the resources/logistics so procured with these funds.

The strengthening of basic policing at cutting edge level especially in areas infested by extremism, insurgency, militancy and other organized crimes was one of the major recommendations of the four Task Forces constituted by the Government of India in March 2000 to evaluate various aspects of National Security, after the 'Kargil episode'. The Task Force on Internal security headed by N.N. Vohra; the former Union Home Secretary, specifically observed that almost all the States have defaulted in their crucial obligation to progressively expand and maintain fully trained and equipped Police forces in adequate strength to meet the rising challenges in the maintenance of internal security. The Group of Ministers (GoM) that had studied the recommendations of the Task Forces came out with a number of proposals to augment the internal security management with the active involvement of police at cutting edge level. One of the significant proposals of the Group was on the revamping of the State Intelligence/ Special Branch units which have well knit organizational set up and grass roots level presence. Their major finding was that the induction of more professionally competent personnel into these units and their proper training, orientation and motivation with better resources and specific charter of duties would facilitate the police to get ground level intelligence inputs enabling the civil police to effectively deal with serious internal security threats. The Centre had initiated certain pioneering efforts in this direction. An apex level body namely Multi Agency Centre (MAC) and its State counterparts, State Multi Agency Centers (SMAC) with representatives of major Security and Intelligence agencies were formed. This was aimed at the proper collation, analysis and sharing of inputs having Internal security implications with concerned agencies for timely action and neutralization of threats. Similarly, another body namely Joint Task Force Intelligence (JTFI) with their counterparts in the States have been constituted for better liaison and co-ordination between State Special Branches and Central agencies with more focused efforts to counter major Internal security threats such as terrorism, extremism and militancy. More ambitious programs like imparting training to State Intelligence personnel on such threats by opening Regional Training Establishments manned by Faculty of Central agencies were also launched. The Conference of DGPs/IGPs in 2007 endorsed the need of strengthening State Intelligence/Special Branches which according to them can operate as effective instruments in identifying the groups or organizations posing threat to internal security.

However, a closer analysis of various new mechanisms initiated by the Centre/States for reinforcing the police at cutting edge level to meet the internal security threats, indicates that they could not achieve much in commensurate with the vast resources and funds utilized by them. Basically, the newly constituted bodies whether at the Centre or in the States lacked transparency and accountability and on many occasions functioned on bureaucratic lines without showing the spirit of co-operation and co-ordination among all the stake -holders. In some instances, these bodies were headed by incompetent leaders devoid of conceptual or practical knowledge and whose apparently perverted actions invited criticism. Thirdly, while there was infrastructure and technology up-gradation, no corresponding improvement was made in respect of the professionalism and competence of the manpower associated with such Centers. More over induction of hand-picked superannuated personnel on contract basis without proper assessment of their competence or professional experience had had adverse impact on the overall performance of such bodies. This was more relevant in the case of many octogenarian Faculty members of Regional Training centers who teach decades old concepts and practices on information gathering, to the Special Branch personnel much to their disadvantage of collection of ground level real time tactical intelligence. On the contrary, the success stories of elite forces like 'Grey hounds' in Andhra Pradesh reveal that properly selected, trained and motivated police personnel commanded by Police leaders with proven competence, experience and integrity are the best bet to effectively combat major internal security threats.

There is no dispute on the need of strengthening State Intelligence Machinery especially the State Special Branches which should act as the eyes and ears of the police in camouflage to closely monitor the developments in each and every police station limits, having a bearing on internal security. This aspect was prominently highlighted by Prime Minister Man Mohan Singh during the Chief Minster's Conference on Internal Security (New Delhi/February 01, 2011) as, "best actionable and prompt intelligence on internal security often comes from police Stations". But re-vamping State intelligence/ Special Branch units seem to be a Herculean task in the present scheme of things when these special units with mediocre or frustrated lot function as the appendages of State governments in power or a set of senior Ministers or leaders of the ruling party. More over, a wide plethora of routine tasks and duties assigned to these personnel occupy bulk of their time and energy, depriving them to undertake any core-policing tasks connected with National security. .So long as this scenario exists; the basic policing especially in relation to internal security suffers. Thus the need of the hour is that the Political Executive and the Police leaders should come out with a clear-cut action plan to re-structure and re-vamp these units so that they can play a constructive role in policing. The success of special units or civil police in combating organized crime depends on the extent of public support and co-operation that they enjoy at grass-roots level. This is more relevant in the case of Police organisation's fight against extremists, militants or insurgents who build up their bases and broaden their net work with the help of local population, either due to ideological sympathies or under intimidation/threat by these groups. Thus Richard Clutterback rightly commented; 'The marriage between an uncorrupt Police and an alert and co-operative public is the healthiest guard against terrorism.' The Police personnel at cutting edge level who maintain good rapport with the local or indigenous population through effective enforcement of law and order and service-oriented approach are front line warriors of the force to deal with such threats. The institutional mechanisms like the Village Defense Parties (VDP), Community Interface cells, and Police Complaint Board etc at District/Police Station level with the representatives of Police and public help to augment Police-public relations.

In fact, the Police Stations where the common man comes into contact with Police have pivotal role in strengthening basic policing and Police-public relations. Their importance of police stations in grass-roots level policing has been significantly increased with the growing trends of terrorism, extremism and other organized crimes in different parts of the country. In this backdrop, the statement made by the Prime Minister Man Mohan Singh during DGPs/IGPs Conference in October 2005 that there is need to strengthen civil police at the cutting edge of Police station level at which the basic policing functions are discharged assumes considerable significance. Such impressions on the police set up are not unfounded considering the track record and image of police. Non-registration of FIRs of the poor and under privileged and lackadaisical investigation of cases are the common complaints against police stations. A typical example was Nithari case (Noida) of murder of poor children, in which the local police station initially refused to register FIRs lodged by the parents of missing children, from the poorest strata of the society. The 'Nithari episode' was a clear pointer to the malfunctioning of police stations and the break down of police at each level particularly at the cutting edge. Many factors like corruption, extraneous influences notably political intervention, approach and attitude of personnel and lack of proper supervision by senior personnel lead to such unhealthy scenario. Much should be done to streamline the functioning of police stations both in respect of their administrative procedures and manpower requirements. Clear norms and procedures should be laid down and meticulously followed in respect of registration of FIRs, follow up investigation of cases and timely submission of charge-sheet etc. For example, every SHO should be made duty bound to register FIR immediately on every complaint. Every police station should be provided with computers for registration of complaints and the Email address of SHO should be published. There should be an option for the aggrieved person to send the complaint by Email to the officer concerned with a copy to the higher authorities whose Email should also be widely published. Every complainant should be given a receipt for the complaint lodged with the intimation to higher authorities. The procedure for registering complaints should be widely published in vernacular press and electronic media so as to enable the aggrieved persons to correctly approach police with their petitions. It should be made mandatory that all police officers should give an action taken report of all cases within ten days of the receipt of the complaint, to the senior officer. All police officers should desist from prompting or pressurizing the complainant to withdraw his or her case. If such actions are reported, the higher authorities should take stern action against the erred police personnel. Meanwhile, the Police leaders should explore suitable strategies from the corporate world and utilize vast advancements from the cyber world to simplify the procedures and process. In fact, the modernization funds should be utilized for strengthening the basic policing at police station level instead of lavishly spending them for purchasing fleet of modern vehicles or constructing huge complexes with ultra-modern facilities.

While we discuss other strategies for strengthening basic policing at cutting edge level, some of the proposals by Padmanabhaiah Committee on Police reforms are worth pursuing. One important proposal is the selection of Sub

Inspector cadres after plus + level education and their 3 years training before regular induction into the force. One added advantage of such a recruitment mechanism is that the SIs so inducted who are well molded in proper police ethos during their formative years and well-versed with law, criminology, Forensic Science etc by virtue of their three year curriculum, will be professionally competent to deal with major threats connected with internal security. The Committee also suggested the replacement of certain percentage of posts of Constables with Sub Inspectors till teeth to tail ratio of 1: 4 is achieved against the present ratio ranging from 1:7 to 1:15. Another inter-related proposal is that the minimum functional rank in Police stations should be fixed as Sub Inspectors. Such restructuring and re-organization of civil police will help the organization to have sufficient number of professionally competent personnel including experienced Investigation Officers (IOs) who will undertake speedy and timely completion of investigations. The availability of sufficient number of professionally competent personnel at cutting edge level will not only ensure better enforcement of law and order but also the effective control of emerging threats to internal security.

Just like the structural/organizational changes in civil police set up, revamping of Armed Battalions and Armed Forces is also needed to equip the police to meet the challenges in internal security field. In many States structural changes are in the offing to narrow down the differences between these units and local police. The relevance of armed police Battalions with right manpower and better logistics has increased in the backdrop of mounting activities and depredations of terrorists, extremists and insurgents in different parts of the country. Properly trained, motivated and engaged personnel of these units can operate as the front line forces to handle sporadic and adventurous acts such as hostage-taking, hi-jacking etc, perpetrated by these groups. If the Police has to remain the pivot of internal security management in the country, their dependence on Central

Paramilitary Forces (CPMF) and Defense Forces to tackle internal security related issues has to be reduced. An ill-equipped Police force has the limitations to effectively deal with serious internal security challenges that we are now confronting through out the length and breadth of the nation. Thus, instead of ad-hoc arrangements and cosmetic changes in the Police, what is required is all round radical structural, organizational and personnel changes that will facilitate the force to meet the major threats in the internal security scenario. After all, the concept that defense forces and Central Paramilitary Forces which are basically recruited, trained and deployed to fight against our enemies across the borders, should not be engaged for long in aid of civil authorities to combat internal security related threats, is gaining general acceptance in the country. Very often the prolonged deployment of such forces alien to a particular region or State opens a Pandora's Box of sensitive issues like high-handedness or excesses, violation of Civil/human rights of civil population and turf battles between Central and State forces adversely affecting joint operations etc. For many years, the North East had witnessed such issues, whereas, we are still in the midst such serious issues in the Kashmir valley.

While preparing the police to effectively meet the challenges in the internal security front, one main task of the police leadership is to make the personnel at cutting edge level more tech-savvy. They should be imparted better knowledge, training and practical skills on the wide range of modern weapons, explosives and communication equipments easily available to terrorists and extremists. Attitudinal change is also vital in professionalizing the personnel on the above lines. The general approach of majority of personnel at cutting edge level is that special units or areas are the exclusive domain of a handful of experts, whereas they would remain happy and contented with conventional style of policing without paying much heed as what is happening around them. The proliferation of organized crimes impinging on national security is so wide spread that a few experts cannot effectively deal with them. The genesis of 'cyber-crimes' and their escalation to almost all major spheres of human activity have compounded the situation. The law and order and internal security scenario in the country have now become so complex and complicated that each and every personnel of the law enforcement machinery should be equipped with professional knowledge and expertise to successfully deal with the situation. Thus, the former Union Minister Shivraj Patil, while addressing the7th International Conference on Cyber Crime in Delhi in September 2007, rightly observed; "these new offences (cyber crimes) are serious enough to capture the priority attention of law makers and all members of law enforcement agencies".

The task of professionalizing personnel at cutting edge level is a serious challenge before the police leadership. Basically majority of the personnel at the middle or the fag end of their stressful career in police organization is averse to changes or innovative mechanisms within the force. Thus, the leadership has to learn a lot from the corporate world as how human resources with diverse qualities could be developed to the optimum advantage of the organization. The successful managers encourage workers and employees to come out with independent suggestions that will help in cutting cost and improving efficiency. It is a commonly endorsed 'corporate philosophy' that those at the bottom of the corporate hierarchy are well versed with individual duty and tasks better than their superiors and are therefore to give most useful proposals to the advantage of the organization. This concept of' 'cognitive repairs' in professional organizations which was succinctly propounded by Professor Joshua Klayman and Richard Larrick underscores the significance of 'bottom up' repairs such as employee-derived slogans, procedures and proposals more beneficial than 'top-down' repairs that are designed and implemented by mangers or outside experts. This management concept appears to be of much relevant in police organization. The personnel at cutting edge level are the best judges to objectively bring out various flaws in basic policing and suggest corrective measures to overcome them. For example a beat constable who sincerely performs his duties in a particular beat for a reasonable period is the best judge to make practical suggestions to improve patrolling mechanisms or basic policing tasks in that area in tune with the new challenges in the law and order front. Same is the case with an intelligent traffic constable who can make any number of constructive proposals to resolve traffic jams or congestions in his functional area. However, majority of personnel at cutting edge level seldom come out with any such proposals due to vertical character of the organization coupled with regimentation and tightening controls. Such lacunae in the force should be rectified by police leaders by making the organization more open and flexible without eroding discipline and decorum.

Thus, formulation of sound human resources development/management strategies assumes considerable significance in improving the professionalism of the force especially of the personnel at cutting edge level. In majority of the State police forces, the induction of a large number of personnel with better educational qualifications and high career aspirations has changed the complexion of these forces. An arduous task before the police leaders is to keep up the morale of these personnel and develop them as true professionals to improve the quality of basic policing. For that purpose, the leadership should work out a number of pro-active strategies like comprehensive growth and co-ordination studies, rationalization of promotion policies, better service conditions, financial and non-financial incentives and above all creation of a feeling of involvement and importance for the cutting edge, in the organization.. The endeavor of police leadership should be to empower the personnel at each level, allow them to exhibit their intelligence, initiative and innovation and exploit their intrinsic potential for the larger interests of the organization.

In the new millennium when major threats to National security are looming from various corners, half-hearted approach on populist lines by the Police leadership or Political Executive in the area of law and order enforcement will neither help to strengthen basic policing nor prepare the force to effectively deal with the threats to national security. What is seriously required in the present context is real changes in the structure/organizational set up, complexion of .human resources, leadership qualities, tasks and priorities and style of functioning of the force The police leadership should work out well defined strategies and mechanisms to accelerate the process of changes that will help to refurbish the image of the police.

4

Police Community Relations:
A Role Model for the New Millennium

Police do not function in vacuum. The premise that the public need police service and the police need public co-operation is the essence of the ideal concept of policing in any democratic society. The quality of policing can be greatly improved by developing harmonious and constructive police-community relations. The National Commission on Criminal Justice Standards and Goals, USA in their report observed, in the absence of citizen's assistance, neither more manpower or improved technology, nor additional money will enable law enforcement to shoulder the momentous burden of combating crime. Co-operation between the police and community is the first say in crime control.

The traditional concept of community participation in policing tasks has now attained new dimensions with modern jargons like 'community-policing'- an area which has provided new horizons to policing and aims at both prevention and detection of crime by increasing the involvement of society/community in policing tasks. Nationally and internationally, several strides have been made in this field. For example, the concept has become an integral part of US Law enforcement system and different shades of CP schemes have been in practice in all the metropolitan areas in the US. The 'Neighborhood Scheme', 'Guardian Angels', "The Portland Burglary Preventive Program", "Crime

Stoppers" etc are some of the most popular and successful programs there. Similarly Japan has become a model State in the implementation of such schemes like "Kobans" ensuring direct interaction between citizens and police especially in crime prevention tasks. South Africa, Netherlands, Brazil, Mongolia, Philippines, Malaysia, Singapore, China, Papa New Guinea, Maldives etc are other countries that are currently going in community policing in a big way.

In India, a number of innovative techniques/schemes were adopted by different States to elicit public participation and co-operation in policing. The Neighborhood Watch Committee (New Delhi), Mohalla Committee (Maharastra), Friends of Police (Tamil Nadu), Gram Rakshak Dal (Gujarat), Sallahkar Samitis/ Community Interface cells (Punjab), Village Defense Committees (West Bengal, Madhya Pradesh, Assam), Nagarik Samitis (Rajasthan), Alert citizens (Mumbai) Citizens Police (UP), Maithri (Andhra Pradesh) Jana Maithri (Kerala) etc were some of the popular schemes. The expertise and financial support of International organizations such as United Nations Development Program (UNDP), Overseas Development Agency (ODA), UK, Common Wealth Human Rights Initiative (CHRI) etc have been utilized to study the intricate aspects of this concept viz- a- viz training and reforms in order to successfully launch the pro-active policing schemes in India. The National Conference of Directors General of Police in early 2000 had established a study group to assess the implementation of community policing schemes. Despite these efforts, community participation as an organized and planned policy of crime prevention is yet to be developed in our policing efforts. Thus the pertinent question is where we went wrong?

Basically, any effort to introduce a scheme or program alien to the country without re-molding or re-modulating it in the domestic furnace of socio-economic and political realities would not meet with any major success. This had happened in respect of many of our CP programs and projects. No doubt, our police managers undertook foreign jaunts and vigorously took up CP schemes which were modeled on the pattern of community policing in western countries notably USA and UK where the police force at all levels is a highly professional and refined body. There, the people with the exception of those in 'ghettos' are basically law abiding, whereas we, the people generally have not got much respect for law and most of them would not mind committing minor offences, if sure of not being caught. Three centuries of British rule and various forms of struggle during the freedom movement especially the civil disobedience coupled with the post independent phenomenon of violent struggles and conflicts by various sections of the society in pursuance of their demands built up such a 'mass-psyche' among large majority of Indian masses. Added to this is the poor and sullied image of police in India. The historical legacy and image of police as an oppressive instrument during the British Raj and as a biased partisan force perpetrating the interests of' the rich, powerful and privileged' in free India have created adverse 'imprints' on police in the minds of overwhelming majority of Indians and acted as major stumbling blocks in harmonizing police-public relations. The outdated organizational structure and legislations like Indian Police Act of 1861 failed to reform the police in line with the democratic aspirations of the people. Given the image of police in the country, many law-abiding citizens especially of rural areas are less enthusiastic to actively associate with police in community policing schemes. On the contrary, any politicization of community policing mechanisms through the active participation of political activists opens a Pandora's Box of controversies adversely affecting the credibility and accountability of CP. Moreover, many of these schemes which are initiated at the instance of a few police managers are seldom sustained or followed up by their successors. Thus many of these programs had gone into oblivion when their innovators were transferred out or took up more challenging assignments. Now, a serious introspection is essential to get a clear picture as how these programs can be streamlined and coordinated with the active involvement of the civil society?

Detailed case studies of three successful CP schemes in the States of Karnataka, West Bengal and Punjab have brought out certain important factors which are applicable to CP programs elsewhere. The first one was the experiment in Hubli, the second biggest town in Karnataka with an appropriate population of eight lakhs, of which around 30% are Muslims. Apart from communal divide between Hindus and Muslims, belonging to weavers community, "Idgah Maidan issue" (on the issue of hoisting National Flag on a piece of land belonging to Hubli Municipal Corporation, which has been used by Muslims for long for offering Namaz etc) had further vitiated the communal and law and order scenario especially after the attempt of fire-brand BJP leader Uma Bharathi to forcibly hoist Tricolor there. Two incidents of police firing in 1994 & 95 resulting in the death of six persons had further alienated the public from the police. Added to this were calculated moves by local political leaders to tarnish the image of police through their campaign and agitations highlighting that a large number of police personnel working in the twin cities of Hubli-Dharward for decades had developed vested interest and adopted biased approach in law enforcement.

It was in this background that the Commissioner launched the new experiment. Three- pronged strategy was adopted. Firstly, the public mood and temper on police have been objectively assessed with the help of a well-drafted questionnaire which was published in local news papers for getting feed back/response from the people. On the basis of the response/views, a list of tasks to be done on priority to regain the public support and confidence was prepared. Secondly, bold and effective personnel and organizational mechanisms were initiated to reform the force and refurbish its image. A number of steps like transfer of police personnel who remained posted in the area for long and developed vested interest, reshuffling of Constabulary, launching of welfare schemes for the serving personnel/their family, better interaction with personnel at various levels, sanctioning of financial and non-financial incentives to those personnel who performed good work, training/in-service courses for various ranks etc have been initiated in order to reform the force from within. Thirdly, a well planned strategy had been worked out for building bridges with the public, besides sorting out issues of public concern such as regulation of traffic, eve-teasing, molestation etc. Specific projects namely 'Police in the service of the people' and 'Police with children' etc had been launched for properly projecting the humane face of the police and creating awareness among children on the challenges and perils of the force. For implementing the above three- pronged strategy at ground level, the assistance of vocal groups such as Advocates Association, Medical Association, Chambers of Commerce etc as also the electronic and print media (which play decisive role in mobilizing public opinion in any society), has been ensured. An impact study of the scheme revealed that there was 25-30% reduction in crime; substantial improvement in the condition of slum/ colony dwellers and noticeable change on the approach of children and women towards police.

In West Bengal, a successful CP scheme was launched in Asansol in Burdwan District which was also unique in many respects. Asansol, once a major commercial and industrial centre had become a hot bed of illegal activities owing to the closure of many industries and resultant unemployment. Rail par area of the city was the epicenter of various anti-social activities such as wagon-breaking, unlawful iron-racketeering, arms-peddling, etc. The area was a conglomerate of lower class and underclass suburbia bereft of important anchors like industry, schools, hospitals etc and was a breeding ground of different kinds of common law and order problems such as communal disharmony, mafia-violence, industrial unrest, dacoity, theft and violence.

The Asansol experiment of community policing which was undertaken during 1994-98 by the then Additional

Superintendent of Police /Superintendent of Police was unique in many respects and was an attempt to develop co-operative and consensual relations between the Police administration and civil society in larger canvas of welfare and service oriented schemes. The establishment of a Children's park at an abandoned area, (the hub of illegal liquor and gambling), vocational training center for under-privileged women, Library cum Medical Polyclinic, with other facilities like Bank, post office and computer center and an ecological park on the outskirts of the city and rehabilitation of around 800 sex workers by providing them alternate source of income etc were the major projects undertaken by the police administration as part of its community policing endeavors. Another noteworthy feature was the initiative shown by the Police to form an NGO namely "Disha Janakalyan Kendra" for undertaking welfare schemes among the marginalized sections. The Police leadership was also successful in getting the support of international organizations such as Red Cross, CARE etc in consolidating the programs. Equally significant was their success in raising Victims Benevolent Fund- the proceeds of which were given to the victims of rape, child-abuse, industrial mishaps etc. One major finding of Asansol experiment was that improvement in the infrastructure and basic amenities in backward areas occupied by marginalized sections and creation of awareness among them on various law and order issues have positive impact in the crime scenario of such areas.

The Patiala experiment in Punjab was of a different nature. The objective of the scheme which was undertaken by District Police, Patiala in1999 was to improve the behavior of the police with the public so that the police-community relations could be strengthened. Accordingly it was decided that all police personnel during their interaction with the public would address all male members as "Shrimanji" or "Sir" and all ladies as "Bhenji" or "Mataji" or "Madam" depending upon their age. A similar change of attitude of police personnel during interaction with the public in police stations or other public places was insisted upon under this scheme. The scheme was implemented in three different phases namely;

(a) briefing of all Gazetted police personnel and Inspectors, SHOs, I/Cs of units,

(b) one month trial period and;

(c) formal public announcement to this effect. The result of this experiment was very positive and the public greatly appreciated the general behavior of the police personnel. It had also helped to improve the overall image of the force. However, its impact was short-lived.

The above case studies which were successful stories in Community policing could identify certain positive traits, conducive for strengthening police-community relations. These factors include:

(a) Proper assessment of the mood and temper of the public on the image and functioning of the police before launching the scheme;

(b) Effective organizational/personnel strategies including reforms within the force in order to refurbish its image and improve the community support. Lord Denning had rightly commented that between the police and the public, the former had duty to change first. In the case of police, such positive changes could be effected without much resistance in view of the vertical character of the organization and paramilitary orientation;

(c) Shift in the role of police from traditional law enforcer to an advisor, facilitator and supporter of new community based police initiative in the fields of development, welfare, social-service etc;

(d) Institutionalization of various reform measures and schemes in order to ensure their sustainability;

(e) Apolitical approach by police leaders during the implementation of innovative techniques/procedures meant to augment police-community relations;

(f) Proper initiative, drive, imagination and commitment of police managers to undertake community policing techniques without any vested interest like undue personal publicity or image building efforts;

(g) Involvement of NGOs, Community liaison groups like Resident Associations, Neighborhood Watches, Student-youth organizations in specific community policing initiatives targeting marginalized and under-privileged sections like women, children, dalits etc and;

(h) Effective use of vocal groups, print and electronic media in the dissemination of themes which help to bridge the gap between the police and civil society.

Any scheme or mechanism for strengthening Police-community relations should have clear cut objectives or mission. The broad contours in this regard should include:

(a) Bridging the gap between the police and the public so as to work closely in a creative way to prevent crime, physical and social disorders etc;

(b) Change of attitude of police and the public. For that purpose the police should develop a work culture upholding that policing is a service to the community, where as the public should properly understand the constraints and difficulties of the police in their mosaic of duties and responsibilities;

(c) Identification of breeding grounds of crime and initiating corrective steps with the help of community;

(d) Improving the quality of policing by increasing public co-operation through generation of free flow of information from the community to the police; and

(e) To wean away people from falling into criminal way of life and promote activities to make them useful members of society.

Based on the above broad objectives and parameters, specific tasks or issues which need the immediate attention of the police and community from law and order or crime prevention in a particular area (preferably the jurisdiction of a Police Station) should be identified and proper strategy should be worked out to effectively deal with them. Sound institutional mechanism should be developed in order to attain the objective/tasks. Under this program, local units comprising 200/300 households should be formed in each village or locality. The Station House Officer (SHO) of the police station should function as Convener between the people of that village/locality and the police station. The Convener should make all efforts to personally know every person of the area to which he is assigned and need to be familiarized with the geographical, social, economic and cultural background of the area. He should identify suitable members and nominate them to local level Police-public committees, which should constitute sub-groups for assisting the police for specific tasks such as maintenance of social order, crime prevention, welfare schemes for the under-privileged, road safety, women issues etc. The Convener should maintain high standard of personal conduct and integrity; rise above considerations of caste, community, creed and politics and adopt impartial and unbiased approach in all matters. Besides he needs to develop skills in professional matters, communication and public relations for effective functioning. For coordinating and supervising the activities of Police-public committees, suitable police personnel should be designated in each police district. Their suggestions and views may be sought by the local units whenever they take up major programs or schemes that require more manpower and resources. Similarly proper schedule should be worked out for the effective functioning of these committees. As far as possible, the committee should convene fortnightly meetings, presided over by the SHO of the Police Station concerned and attended by the Convener and members of the committee, besides the members of the sub-groups. The Committee should deliberate mainly on the general action relating to the objectives/tasks as also the action plan to achieve specific results. The decisions in the committee should be through general consensus. It should encourage suggestions/complaints from the general public in respect of its functioning as also the maintenance of law and order and related issues for which complaint box should be installed. The police should promptly attend to the genuine complaints and efforts should be made to resolve the difficulties/grievances of the general public pertaining to law and order.

The concept of co-operative and consensual relations between the police and civil society has been gaining ground in all democratic societies which uphold the rule of law. In all such societies, means and methods of securing public support for policing tasks have caught the attention of police administration and Political Executive. We now hear a lot about community policing or pro-active policing and a wide spectrum of innovative schemes and techniques to bridge the gap between the police and the public, almost on the same lines of such schemes in the West. However, their rhetoric is more than the actual practice or success at ground level. The irony is that while majority of the police leaders in the forefront of such schemes have their own career or image oriented agenda, the political masters mainly utilize these programs to project that all is well in the law and order front with harmonious police-public relations. Such dubious designs never help us to achieve tangible results through CP schemes. What we require now is a thorough introspection of such matters and earnest and sincere efforts to implement the schemes at grassroots level through sound institutional mechanisms and by ensuring real and constructive support of the civil society.

5

Indian Police in the New Millennium

India has stepped into the new millennium with a mosaic of challenges in the areas of law enforcement and internal security. Inevitably, these issues in the field of law enforcement compel us to revisit our understanding on the future policing tasks. No authentic futurological studies have been conducted in India on this sensitive subject and the literature available at present mainly consist stray thoughts or subjective impressions of police professionals or social scientists who take keen interest on internal security or policing. Thus, based on past trends in India and elsewhere and the contemporary scenario, the challenges and tasks are to be identified and right action plan has to be formulated in order to equip the police to effectively meet the requirements of the present century. The reality is that ad-hoc arrangements or cosmetic populist measures no longer will help the police to meet the looming threats posing serious challenge to the integrity of the nation.

Unlike in the 20th century, policing tasks in the present century will be greatly influenced by international security scenario, regional geo-political developments and the global economic trends. Though the possibility of global or nuclear war has receded following the emergence of a uni-polar world with USA as the only super power, the threat to world peace continues to exist from unconventional forms of struggles and violence such as international terrorism, Low Intensity Conflicts (LIC) or 'proxy wars' and 'ethnic cleansing'. Take for instance the growth of Islamic fundamentalism or terrorism. Though Samuel Huntington predicted confrontation between Islam and the West because of the conflicting interests, the world did not attach much credibility to his findings till the fag end of the last century when the Islamic terrorists started striking their targets, particularly of USA in Mexico, Saudi Arabia, Egypt, Algeria, Sudan, Afghanistan, Kenya and Tanzania with much precision and sophistication outwitting the intelligence and security agencies in the West, USA and other European countries had awaken from their slumber and felt the pressure of global terrorism. But, the whole world was pulsated by Al Qaeda's dare-devil attack of World Trade Centre and other US establishments in September 2001. Thus global terrorism and the counter-operations had transcended beyond geo-political barriers, with more and more countries in Asia, Europe, Africa and America facing the threat of terrorist violence. In fact, Osama Bin Laden, the most inspiring force of Islamic terrorism, was not merely an international fugitive, but the architect of Sunni-sponsored Islamic terrorism whose tentacles have spread to many countries through a net work of Pan-Islamic Militant outfits, foreign trained mercenaries and fighting groups like 'Fidayeen'. The active presence of such organizations like Harkat ul-Ansar (Harkat-ul-Mujahideen), Jaish-e-Mohammed, HUJI, and foreign trained mercenaries from Afghanistan, Sudan, Algeria and Egypt, in Kashmir continue to pose a real threat to our internal security. The Mumbai terror attack in November 2009 and series of explosions and blasts in different parts of the country indicate the presence of the "sleeper cells" of such groups in the hinterland of our country.

India's entry into the nuclear club, her initial reservations to sign Nuclear Non-Proliferation Treaty (NPT) and Comprehensive Test Ban Treaty (CTBT) as dictated by the West, shift in foreign policy relations and the change in the regional security environment had created new challenges to internal security. Though there is a clear shift in the approach of Obama administration towards India after the signing of Civilian Nuclear Treaty, the 'Wikie leaks' clearly indicated that US would continue their 'cloak and dagger operations' in various countries including India to safeguard her strategic and economic interests. The Police, intelligence and security agencies in India should have to upgrade their professionalism through technological advancement to defeat the clandestine operations of US and other Western intelligence agencies in India. At regional level, the relations with China are not yet cordial especially in the backdrop of unsettled border dispute and her moves to emerge as 'big brother' in Asian subcontinent by dabbling in the affairs of neighboring countries like Pakistan, Bangladesh, Nepal etc. Her rapid economic advancement and frantic efforts to capture foreign markets to sell out products will intensify competition and conflicts with neighbors like India. Pakistan is not only antagonistic but also hostile and vigorously pursues 'proxy-war' against India as part of her long term strategy of 'encirclement and balkanization' of India by abetting and assisting the forces that are inimical to us-both within and outside the country. The emergence of non-State players with their strong roots in parts of Pakistan and anti-Indian feelings has made the scenario more complex and precarious as such groups pose permanent threat to country' s security. The 'Mumbai terror attack' had exposed their strong linkages with ISI and other agencies/groups in Pakistan and demonstrated as how dangerous are these groups/operatives. Bangladesh, Myanmar, Nepal and Bhutan with their fluid and fragile political set up have become the sanctuaries of major insurgent and militant groups operating against India. The emergence of Nepali Maoist groups into power in Nepal has added new dimensions to the CPI (Maoist) threat especially in parts of Uttar Pradesh and Bihar. Though the ethnic strife in Sri Lanka is almost over with the elimination of LTTE and their supremo Prabhakaran, the fringe elements in various Tamil militant groups continue to pose some problems in Southern India.

The growing Islamic fundamentalism and militancy in Maldives is yet another challenge to internal security as there are sizeable floating Male population in Southern States like Kerala and Karnataka. All these factors naturally increase the possibility of 'proxy-wars', espionage, sabotage and subversion adversely affecting National security. Added to this is the mass migration of people-legally and illegally- across the international borders. The steady influx of migrants from Bangladesh, Nepal and Bhutan to India as a result of internal conflicts, ethnic strife, natural calamities/famines and economic factors, which has already changed the demographic pattern and created socio-economic problems in the North East will be continued as one of the most volatile and complex issues of the present century, with increasing incidents of ethnic conflicts/violence and serious law and order problems in the affected areas.

The emerging global economic trends will create an array of problems in the areas of security and public order which need the intervention of a professionalized police. Gone are the days when the industrialized West has dominated the world economy. In the present century, the newly emerging economic giants of Asia would hold the key to the global economy indicating the shifting nature of world economy. The People's Republic of China has already established strong foothold in the world economy posing a serious challenge to the western world including USA which is now reeling under recession and unemployment. India is also marching ahead with significant industrial and infrastructural growth. These developments would accelerate the process of 'globalization' and 'economic liberalization' which may lead to heightened industrial and popular protests, urban unrest, the fragmentation of traditional class-based life style and steady increase in economic offences mainly due to slow trickle down effect of economic reforms and the widening gulf between the haves and haven't... The mass protest and resistance against the entry of Multinationals and big corporate groups in West Bengal, Orissa, Chaattisgarh etc were clear manifestations of these trends. The depletion of job opportunities due to automation, increasing unemployment, exodus of people from rural to urban areas in search of job and above all denial of social justice to the marginalized sections are likely to evoke serious issues in our socio-economic fabric of society. These are bound to affect the management and administrative style of various institutions including police which has to play a crucial role to maintain public order and ensure economic advancement with social harmony.

The internal security scenario is unlikely to show any signs of drastic improvement during the early decades of the present century. There won't be any immediate let off to Left Wing Extremism (LWE) which is now the most serious challenge to internal security especially in view of their killings, violence and other depredations in many parts of the country. So long as the economic disparities, lop-sided development, deprivation of basic necessities for marginalized and weaker sections and class conflicts continue, the radical extremists would maintain their pockets of influence mainly in backward-tribal areas of West Bengal, Bihar, Jharkhand, Chattisgarh, Maharashtra, Orissa and Andhra Pradesh. The insurgency and turbulence in Kashmir valley which had grown up into a full-fledged 'proxy-war' may continue as negotiated settlement to the vexed issue is far off sight in view of the conflicting line of approach of the major stake-holders. Though Sikh extremism is ceased to be a major threat, efforts to keep alive 'Khalistan' slogans in Punjab by section of expatriate Sikh intellectuals in USA, Canada and UK through their extensive net working and financial clout along with the fringe elements of Khalistan Commando Force (KCF), Babbar Khalsa and other extremist outfits indicate that Sikh extremism is not fully eliminated. The North East continues to be a seething cauldron of violence and militancy with the active presence of a number of insurgent and ethnic groups and militant movements which are engaged in mafia type executions and killings, kidnapping, ethnic cleansing, extortion and destruction of arterial roads, bridges, oil-pipe lines and rail lines. The prospects of peace talks with major insurgent groups like United Liberation Front of Assam (ULFA) or Nationalist Socialist Council of Nagaland (NSCN/Khaplang-Issac Swu faction) and working out a negotiated settlement with them are not bright in view of their recalcitrance and rigidity of demands. Though many senior ULFA leaders like Aravind Rajkhowa (Chairman), Pradeep Gogoi etc have now come out of jail, neither they are willing to sit across the table for negotiations nor to shun their slogan of' sovereignty of Assam'. More over, Paresh Barua, the Supreme Commander in-Chief is still elusive in Bangladesh and not favorably inclined to any negotiation with Government of India/Assam government. Similarly, decades-long peace talk stage-managed by a set of retired bureaucrats with one faction of NSCN failed to take off properly or to bring permanent peace in Nagaland and other Naga occupied areas in the North East. The irony is that neither the official negotiators nor the leaders of insurgent group are serious to end the exercise which goes on for years within the country and outside spending huge amounts from national exchequer. A more serious and distressing trend is the emergence of religion based extremism and militancy in almost all States. The large scale explosions engineered by such groups at religious/pilgrimage centers, trains and other public places resulting into the death of hundreds of civilian population was a matter of serious concern for police and other security agencies. Unfortunately, the tacit support extended to such groups by certain mainstream political parties and their front bodies make it difficult for the police and other agencies to conduct free and fair investigations into these dastardly crimes. On the other hand, the concept that the government should fully utilize police to deal with internal security challenges and dispense with the practice of constant deployment of Armed forces in aid of civil administration, which has the inherent danger of the erosion of constitutional authority and demoralization of the forces, is gaining ground. Further, majority of these movements are closely intertwined with local issues or problems which can be dealt with by police. Thus, the role of police in the internal security management will become more relevant and significant in the future.

The internal problems having direct bearing on law and order will be aggravated. One such major issue will be the demographic changes. Though population explosion could be marginally controlled, there was rapid increase in urban population which was 25.9 million (10.84% of the total population) in 1901 had increased to 217.6 million (25.72% of the total population) in 1991 and 285 million (27.8%) in 2001 The estimated urban population, according to certain projections, will be around 535 million (38.2%) in 2010, 590 million (40%) in 2020 and will cross 50% of total population by 2050. This will lead to certain major geographic and demographic shifts with crucial impact on policing. The first and foremost is the continued exodus of rural people to urban areas in search of jobs and better living conditions resulting in the formation of more and more urban agglomerations and sprawling slums within and suburbs of the mega cities. Naturally, the number of cities and urban centers will be increased. The increased urbanization, adding to haven't and rootless in urban areas by millions with consequent stress on civic services/amenities, housing etc will create new law and order problems. Many of these areas particularly slums and colonies will turn into breeding grounds of a wide spectrum of crimes such as gang wars, mafia strikes, organized and syndicate crimes, drug-trafficking, prostitution, sale of spurious liquor etc.

Keeping with the trends in the past, the crime in general will increase. For example, the violent crimes and property crimes showed a steady increase since independence with an annual growth rate ranging from 2 to 3.5 for all crimes. Another trend which is really a matter of concern is the increase in crimes against women. Statistics tell us that a woman is raped in every 40 minutes; a dowry death in every one and half hour; while a woman is molested in every 30 minutes and also an act of criminal offence against women is committed in every seven minutes. The crime against women is unlikely to show any decline in this century in view of dominating male chauvinism inherited and practiced by the orthodox sections of the society; degeneration of traditional values and the general trend of commoditization of women and the spread of consumer culture. Thus, gender sensitization will be one of the priority items in the future agenda of police. Similarly, the technology-oriented sophisticated crimes like white collar, computer-manipulated, drug-related, Bank/ Insurance/Telecom/Credit card frauds, money-laundering and rigging up of share prices will increase as a result of economic liberalization and the circulation of large quantum of black money in Indian economy. Another issue of serious ramifications is the increasing instances of corruption which have engulfed almost all institutions in the country and the helplessness of democratically elected governments to effectively deal with this menace. In order to combat such crimes, police has to keep abreast of the modus -operandi followed by various crime syndicates. For that purpose, it is necessary to maintain close watch on banking institutions, insurance companies and major players in international trade and establish effective liaison with other agencies like Customs, Enforcement Directorate, Income Tax, Revenue Intelligence, Narcotics Control Bureau etc.

The order maintenance tasks of police are likely to increase in 21st century. Social tensions will increase due to political awareness among the weaker and down-trodden sections who will demand greater role in the scheme of things. The formation of caste-oriented political parties and their vituperative propaganda and campaigns on militant lines have intensified caste-communal conflicts in many States. Centripetal tendencies manifested through demands for autonomy, violence by ideologically committed groups, exclusivist expressions and regional and parochial sentiments are likely to remain unabated. Disputes on sharing of river waters, construction of hydroelectric projects, fixation of inter-state boundaries, and creation of new States etc will become more focused and intensive due to politicization. Similarly, caste, communal and ethnic identities instead of getting resolved during the process of national integration are likely to get consolidated into divisive political boundaries. The unhealthy trends like 'criminalization of politics', 'politicization and communalization' of criminals, increasing role of money and muscle power in the elections and the nexus between shady politicians and the under-world are likely to strain our polity with steady increase in political crimes and violence.

The emerging scenario in the country indicates that police in 21st century will be confronted with multi-faceted challenges of which the most definitive one will be the 'knowledge explosion'. The information revolution that has already conquered new horizons of knowledge and the application of Science &Technology will soon revolutionize the functioning of almost all institutions. The police cannot remain aloof from this great transformation which is knocking at our doors. Unfortunately the professional knowledge or skills acquired by the personnel at the fag end of the last century have become redundant. Percepts are changing continuously. In many threat- areas like terrorism, militancy, secessionism, religious fundamentalism and Left Wing Extremism, the present level of knowledge of majority of police personnel is nominal. Unless the police improve their understanding of the ideology, methodology, techniques, inter-linkages, sources of economics, arms-holding etc of these groups/movements, police efforts to neutralize them will not attain any major success. Thus, if the police have to keep up with the times, they have to update their knowledge and skills on a continuous basis. This is all the more important in the case of the application of Science and technology in the policing. The training inputs in the field need a drastic review and efforts should be initiated to introduce the latest technical and scientific innovations in the Training institutions so that the new generation of police personnel should develop scientific temper and culture with professional touch in their policing tasks. For example, new branches of Forensic Science such as "Forensic linguistics' (test analysis to determine the authorship of disputed documents),' Forensic cheilocopy" (the print of the lip of human being which is never identical with another is developed like Finger-print) 'Forensic Deontology' (test analysis of the bite-marks on the skin of a victim) DNA Profiling etc are yet to be introduced in the majority of our Police Training Institutions. Similarly, application of 'cyber-technology' or computer-based finger-printing etc could not make much headway in many State police forces. The approach of some sections of police leaders that such areas are part of the scientific and academic pursuit which the police at cutting edge level are not much interested will work against professionalism in the force. Such a line of thinking should be shelved and more serious efforts to be made to impart proper knowledge and expertise to all sections of personnel which will enable the force to meet the new challenges in law and order front.

These new threats mainly emanate from terror groups or organized crime syndicates. For example, a wide range of explosives, explosive devices, remote control mechanisms and ingenious concealment techniques of such devices have been used by militants and insurgents who obtain their expertise in these fields from international terror groups, foreign intelligence agencies or foreign mercenaries. Similarly, there is steady inflow of sophisticated weapons and small arms to these groups from external arms markets with a net-work of arms dealers and agents. Very often nexus exists between arms dealers and operatives of organized crimes/ movements such as smugglers, drug-mafia, communal syndicates or fundamentalist outfits. The Mumbai blasts of 1993 and Purulia arms dropping are examples. The proliferation of explosives and weapons and the spread of organized and syndicate crimes are so vast that a handful of experts cannot effectively deal with the situation.

The advancement of science and technology and significant strides that are anticipated in these fields during the next few decades will pose major challenges to police. These threats have become more serious in view of the country's nuclear power status and ongoing efforts to develop advanced missile system. Reliable inputs indicate that terror and mercenary groups are engaged in serious efforts to lay their hands on nuclear materials or the chemical or biological weapons. Al-Qaeda's leaders like Chemical Ali remind us how this dreaded terror group meticulously workout their terror-plans to create havoc and terror! The police knowledge on 'cyber-crimes' or' ecological crimes' such as illegal disposal of and trafficking in hazardous wastes or illicit implantation of genetically engineered organisms into the environment is rudimentary. In order to meet the new eventualities, the professional standards of the department need a thorough review and the personnel should be sensitized on the wider dimensions of the threat of misuse of nuclear or chemical weapons.

The concept of human rights is getting more acceptances in India due to the ratification of many International Covenants and Protocols on human rights by the Government and the formation of National Human Rights Commission (NHRC) in1993. Naturally, the police need to be more sensitive to human rights issues. With the decentralization of structural mechanisms to check the violation of these rights by constituting State level Commissions and Human Rights Courts, the police would be under great pressure to uphold these rights. More over, the Judiciary also steps in when there are major issues of human rights violations such as "encounter-killings' by police. This will further aggravate police-dilemma. A pertinent question is as how the police will effectively function in a democratic set up without transgressing the civil/ human rights of the masses especially when there is steady increase in organized crime such as terrorism, militancy and political extremism? Perhaps the answer lies in the true professionalism of the force by changing their 'sub-culture' and upholding the rule of law of the country.

The change in police 'sub-culture' is imperative to improve police public relations-another sensitive area of policing in any democracy. Due to historical and other reasons, the police -public relations in the country were never cordial. Though efforts have been made to harmonize these relations, much success could not be achieved yet. As the police has now entered into the new millennium, the uneasy relations that exist between police and public should give way to healthy interaction which may facilitate the former to operate effectively in our plural society. This can be achieved by doing two things. One is the transparency in police functioning and the other is proper response to those who approach the police with grievances and complaints. The accent should be on improving the working of police stations especially in rural and backward areas.

In any action plan for police in 21st century, the first priority should be to professionalize the police. Now, the Indian police service, in many respects is 'generalist' as ad-hoc and need-based arrangements dominate their functioning. Neither the present selection procedure nor training curriculum helps them to become true professionals to deal with law and order issues. The cult of 'generalism' is hopelessly out-dated in a knowledge-driven world. True professionals and specialists now dominate such a world in which our police organization stand exposed. The crucial question is as how to professionalize Indian police or how to improve its professionalism? The basic requirement, according to a police specialist, James Watson, is; "a starting point, definition of its (organization) role and set of standards for fulfilling it, so that the members of the organization can better measure the quality of service provided by them" On both these accounts our police is lacking. There is much ambiguity on the core functions of the police and the means for achieving them. Re-defining of police functions accompanied by the re-structuring of police organization with corresponding changes in the procedural and penal laws should be taken up on priority basis. Though some of the recommendations of National Police Commission (1977-81) had become slightly outdated, major proposals such as enactment of a new Police Act to replace the Indian Police Act of 1861 should be speedily implemented, while another Commission should be set up to go into police Reforms in the light of 21st century challenges and problems confronting the police. Similarly, a thorough review may be undertaken on the provisions of Cr Pc, IPC and Indian Evidence Act in order to enable the police to undertake speedy investigations by strictly adhering to the rules and procedures.

The concept that all areas of law and order-the prevention and detection of crime and the enforcement of various social legislations etc are the exclusive domain of police needs to be changed. Serious thinking in respect of 'privatization' and 'civilianization' of certain functions of the department should be initiated by the Political Executive and Police leadership. The core issue would be how much of the present policing functions and responsibility would be shared with properly equipped and competent private or semi autonomous agencies without jeopardizing the interests of the citizens. Basically, this tasks vest with the Political Executive. However the police leaders and internal security experts who are well versed with country's security scenario should be involved in the formulation of policy matters on such sensitive issues. Certain factors should definitely be taken into account. One is the multiplicity of agencies or forces doing almost same nature of duties causing the waste of money from the national exchequer. On many occasions the formation of such bodies is not out of security requirements or considerations, but to satisfy the ego or career ambitions of a few at the hierarchical level of police or other security agencies. For example, for many years, in the aviation security area, there were agencies like 'Bureau of Civil Aviation Security'. Airport Security (of State Police), the security wings of Air India/Indian Airlines, Private Airliners, National Airport authority etc which were earmarked almost the same nature of security duties in the area of civil aviation security. Ironically, despite such a plethora of agencies, major offences in civil aviation front including the infamous hi-jacking episodes occurred under the nose of these agencies. With the induction of Central Industrial Security Force (CISF) in the major airports in the country, for security duties, there is drastic improvement in the overall aviation security. Similarly with the increasing demand of individual-oriented security, there is mushroom growth of agencies at the Centre and States, causing major drain of manpower and resources. It is high time that the governments should rationalize the functioning of such agencies or privatize them. For that purpose the government in consultation with the National Security Council (NSC) should make a thorough and objective review of various police, paramilitary, intelligence and security organizations vis a vis their role, functions, manpower and cost factor and prune those agencies which have become redundant by virtue of the changing security and law and order scenario in the country. Truly speaking, no serious exercise in this direction has been done during the last few decades as a result of which these organizations have expanded in manpower, logistics and resources incurring astronomical expenditure, but totally failed to cope up with the situation in the internal security front. This has happened mainly because of the failure of Political Executive to make their own assessment/studies on the professionalism, accountability and transparency of these agencies, but blindly implemented the proposals. Recommendations made by the serving or retired personnel of these agencies who exhibited their fraternity and camaraderie rather than the larger National interests. And whenever, the Political Executives made any moves in the direction of pruning some of these bodies, there were organized efforts of bureaucrats and 'so-called' security/ intelligence experts to browbeat them as happened in the case of former Prime Minister Morarjee Desai who drastically cut down the manpower and budget allocation of Research & Analysis Wing (RAW) in the wake of large scale allegations of irregularities in the selection/appointment of personnel of this external intelligence organization. Perhaps, Desai was the only prime Minister who took brave political decisions to streamline the functioning of Security/Intelligence agencies in the country, whereas all other Prime Ministers of the past and present remained silent spectators on the follies and failures of these agencies which were largely due to their lack of accountability and organizational 'deviants'.

Another equally important aspect is re-structuring or privatization of agencies or organizations which should be linked with productivity (performance), cost effectiveness (value for money concept) and proper management of manpower in order to achieve better performance in core areas. Unfortunately, the present trend in many security/law enforcement agencies is go for routine re-structuring for re-structuring sake without properly assessing or considering the requirements. In some States, DGP posts are created in dozens to accommodate those senior officers closer to the ruling set-up. The situation is not different in many sensitive Central agencies where the organizational pyramid at the top becomes lop-sided with too many Heads, whereas the bottom becomes fragile and weak with stagnated and frustrated "line" personnel. Such re-structuring seldom help to improve the competence or performance of the organization.

The strategic management system in policing needs re-orientation in view of the rapid socio-economic changes and widely disparate law and order problems in different parts of the country. In many places, minor offences like consuming of liquor in open places, or gambling in private clubs etc are no longer looked down upon by society. The crucial question is whether the police should adopt a puritan line and overstrain their machinery for strictly enforcing laws in such case? In fact, there are many areas in which the primary concern of the police should be the order maintenance, more than the strict enforcement of law. Then, many laws should be 'under-enforced'. The proper identification of such issues and application of right strategies to deal with them will constitute one of the major tasks of police during the present century. This requires that the police should develop proper faculties of assessment and analysis of emerging situations in the changing socio-economic milieu.

The concept of 'Policy, Planning and Research' which is vital in the case of any professional organization, is yet to be developed on scientific and practical lines in the police. It is high time that such organizational strategies should be given structured form for which persons having right insight, professional aptitude, and grass-roots level experience on real policing problems should be inducted into police. This body should be entrusted with important tasks like futurological studies on new trends in crimes, their likely socio-economic impact, identification of crime-prone areas and sections, existing policing mechanisms to combat crimes, image of police, human resources related issues in police, training modules/impact of training mechanisms at ground level of policing, infrastructure, logistics and facilities to effectively deal with the new saga of crimes etc. The conclusions and findings so arrived at by such empirical studies should constitute the basic data for the formulation of policies and, strategies on policing by Political executive/police leadership, instead of the present practice of introducing reforms or changes in the force on the basis of the subjective impressions or perversions of a set of police leaders to meet political expediency. In the backdrop of a mosaic of law and order issues in the country, strategies such as setting up of Special Task Forces to deal with problems having inter-linking dimensions or spread beyond the contours of one State should be actively considered. For example, such a force for the North East specialized on the demographic and ethnic features and law and order issues in the region can definitely plan and execute sound operational strategies to deal with the highly complex and complicated law and order scenario in the North East where the slogan of 'sovereignty' and 'xenophobia' of all outsiders by ULFA; 'ethnic cleansing' by Bodos and the vagaries of NSCN permeate beyond the State boundaries with highly clandestine inter-linkages and net-working. Similar task forces can be constituted to deal with Left Wing Extremism (LWE); different shades of terrorism etc whose internal and external linkages go beyond the contours of geographical boundaries, having extensive net-working with organizations and movements within the country and outside. In fact, the formation of bodies likes National Investigation Agency (NIA) with personnel, drawn from different Central agencies and State Police forces are of limited use to undertake major challenges to the internal security. These agencies devoid of proper structural mechanisms/organizational set up at ground level or professionally competent personnel and inheriting the legacy of their parent organizations, have limitations to undertake independent, impartial and efficient investigations or other tasks. They depend more on their Central or State counter-parts and parrot their findings in important cases of internal security jeopardizing the very concept of 'due process of law 'or natural justice. Meanwhile at the higher plane, there is need for setting up an institution like National Crime Authority of Australia in which officers of drug enforcement, police and customs headed by a Judge monitor the response to organized crime and suggest mechanisms to effectively combat them.

Another major agenda in the action-plan for the police in 21st century is the qualitative improvement in the professional traits of personnel and their proper handling by the leadership. The induction of large number of educated personnel with high career ambitions into the lower echelons of police is likely to alter the very character of the force very soon. These factors coupled with other unique problems in the force such as distinct culture, service conditions, stress and strain in policing, alienation from the public etc are likely to spill over and precipitate as major human resources development problems, if not properly dealt with. In order to cope with the situation, the police leadership should develop better human resources development concepts, which are minimal in the police now. Gone are the days when platoons of constables deployed in the Poultry, Diary or Agricultural Farms of senior echelons of the force 'on duty', silently worked for months in order to get regularization in the Special Armed Battalion! The existing practice of half a dozen constables working as orderlies in the office, household or plantations and doing everything at the beck and call of senior officers and their better-haves should be dispensed with. Formulation sound policy-guidelines and organizational initiative to improve service conditions of personnel by treating lower echelons as employees of the State and not 'personal servants'; comprehensive growth and co-ordination studies to ensure career progression of various ranks; building up high morale through proper motivation and mental well-being of the professional, rationalization of transfer/ promotion policies and above all bridging the gap between the lower and higher echelons of the force are some of the key areas in which the police managers need to pay more attention in the present century. The endeavor of the police management should be to empower policemen at each level and allow them to use their initiative and drive and exploit their intrinsic potential. An effective de-centralization should percolate down to the lower levels as rightly highlighted by James Q Wilson; "If the police department is to be truly professionalized, the authority and responsibility should be de-centralized. The brass should surrender some of the prerogatives and must empower those further down the lines to define the challenges of their work and the means of addressing them". Such trends of decentralization should pave the way for the drastic revision in the existing norms of discipline and command and control mechanisms in the force. Instead of regimentation and tightening controls, the emphasis should be on flexibility, fluidity, fraternity, tact and understanding from the part of police leaders so that the new breed of police personnel with better education, knowledge, class-consciousness and competence would operate as the best assets of the organization. Many States have initiated measures on the above lines. For example, Kerala has recently in February 2011, taken initiative to change the regimentation and paramilitary orientation of the force for which the Civil and Armed wings of the police were rechristened as Kerala Civil

Police with the introduction of the rank of Civil police officers against the centuries old existing ranks of Constable and Head Constable. However, mere re-christening of the force or rank-structure will not help the assimilation of the force unless the police leaders adopt a more humane and flexible approach towards the lower functionaries.

Such well-founded policy and planning in the organization coupled with the wide application of science and technology in the investigation of cases will enable the force to overcome many challenges emanating from human rights field. Justice (Retd) V.S. Malimath, a former Member of the National Human Rights Commission (NHRC) aptly highlighted this aspect as; "Criminal justice can be made more effective by relying on scientific evidence. It will reduce police over-dependence on witnesses which in turn will bring down the allegations of human rights violations against them. The "third degree method" is the only vital weapon with the police and if that is taken away from them, a suitable alternative should be shown them or they may find themselves in helpless condition". The alternative, no doubt, is the modernization of the force with the wide application of science and technology in policing. The extent of human rights issues which the police and other security agencies confront during day to day policing or in dealing with organized crimes like terrorism or insurgency can be brought down if they switch over to modern technical operations by fully exploiting the wide spectrum of applications in cyber space and modern technology. The wide ranging invisible capabilities in the field of electronics/cyber space (like satellite surveillance, bugging, digital monitoring etc) and other tools of trade such as Acoustics, and sensitive sensory devices should be made use of for generation of intelligence which on proper collation and analysis will be potential weapon in undertaking successful counter-terrorist/insurgency operations, without causing causalities to the civil population of affected areas.. But it is also equally important that the police personnel should be sensitized on human rights especially the International

Covenants, Declarations and Protocols such as "UN Code of Conduct for Law Enforcement Officers" which make the personnel obligatory to respect and protect human dignity and uphold human rights of all persons while enforcing law and order.

Thus, at the end of the first decade of the new millennium, one can visualize a mosaic of challenges to the police, which unlike in 20th century, are interlinked to global security and economic trends, regional security environment, internal security and socio-economic changes. The complexities that are likely to develop in the political, social and economic fields during the present century will definitely aggravate these challenges. The general notion that police can mange these challenges just as what they had done in the past should be dispensed with as the present century which is expected to be entirely different from earlier civilizations and societies will open a myriad of problems-moral and ethical, new values and systems-which may be unique and unprecedented. The 'knowledge explosion' and 'information revolution' may virtually hi-jack the world to new horizons where the crime and criminals will appear much beyond our imagination and anticipation. We need not go to any sooth-sawyer to confirm such trends. We have witnessed the early indications of such trends at the fag end of the last century when global terrorism had reached at the centre stage of the world polity with their dreaded dare-devil acts of destruction and violence. None had ever imagined or anticipated the dare-devil act of terrorists striking the Twin towers of World Trade Centre by using high-powered aircraft. Perhaps, the present century may be destined to witness more such dastardly acts of destruction and genocide even by using miniature nuclear devices or biological weapons that the terrorists would lay hands sooner or later. It may not be prudent to think that such serious threats to entire humanity whether emanating from within the country or outside can be successfully contained through the present style conventional intelligence collection, security system or routine policing or need based arrangements and adjustments that we are accustomed to. As rightly commented by Nicholas Machiavelli, the civil servant of the 16th century," one who adepts the way he acts, according to the quality of time succeeds", the success of the police organization in combating the challenges of this century depends much on its adaptability to the emerging situations. Changes are inevitable in the role, functions and priorities of the organization; in the professional knowledge, skills and attitude of the personnel; their management and utilization and above all in the attitude of the force towards the society and people. For that, what is required is formulation of right policies, strategies and planning with special emphasis to professionalize the organization and take it closer to the people. Much initiative, imagination, drive, vision and understanding should come from police leadership and administration in preparing such a blue print for Indian Police in the present millennium.

6

Need for Demilitarization and Civilianization of Police

The police in India have to face diverse and complex issues and unforeseen challenges due to a variety of factors such as regional geo-political developments, socio-economic issues etc. These policing problems reflect on the whole gamut of police work like prevention and detection of crime, maintenance of public peace and order, collection of criminal intelligence, crowd-control, handling of riots and civil disturbances and combating organized crime, violent movements, insurgent and subversive activities, different shades of militancy and terrorism and other threats to internal security. Besides, the process of social evolution and interplay of societal forces have made the law and order scenario highly complex and complicated. Hardly any of these challenges or threats existed on the horizon of our country when the Police Act of 1861 was drawn up or the police set up was established in the British India. Thus, a pertinent question arises as whether the police force in the country still governed by an archaic act of almost two centuries old, can effectively tackle the new era of offences, crimes and criminals? The answer definitely is 'No'. In fact, the police to a great extent, are ill-equipped and handicapped in combating organized crimes such as terrorism, insurgency or new forms of cyber and economic crimes. The theme of reforms and structural changes in police and new concepts like privatization and demilitarization of police assume considerable significance in this backdrop.

When we talk about privatization and demilitarization in police, we should be clear as what exactly is the character of Indian police? A brief account of the police system as developed during the British rule and its transition in Independent India would provide us a specific answer to the above question. Historically, the evolution of the organizational structure of the police during the 19th century was conditioned by the political needs of the colonial State. The English East India Company which became the de-facto ruler of vast territories of India, desired a police system for the whole of colonial India on the pattern of the police set up in Sind Province, established by Sir Charles Napier in 1843. It was modeled on the pattern of colonial Irish Constabulary; commanded by the British Army officers who closely supervised, controlled and disciplined the force. Thus in1856, the Court of Directors of the East India Company through a directive to the Governor General highlighted; "the police of each District should be taken out of the hands of the Magistrate and should be equipped, clothed and disciplined so as to render it efficient and serviceable without giving it an absolutely military organization". When the British government appointed the First Police Commission for India in1860, one of the policy directives to the Commission was that;" though the duties of the police should be entirely civil, not military, the organization and discipline of the force should be similar to that of a military body". While issuing such directive, the British government was also influenced by the success of the new Metropolitan London Police which was set up in Great Britain under an Army officer, Col. Charles Rowan in 1829. The police system which was set up by the British in India subsequent to the report of the Commission in 1860, by the enactment of Act V of 106 (The Police Act of 1861) was civil as far as its duties were concerned, but militaristic in its orientation. The Second Police Commission further standardized and reformed the structure on a national basis within the ambit of the 1861 Act. During 1902-1947, the main growth area in the police organization was the Central

Intelligence Machinery and Central Paramilitary forces which were grossly misused by the British to perpetrate the colonial interests of the British regime through ruthless repressive measures against the freedom fighters.

The basic structure and character of the police namely centralized functioning and paramilitary orientation remained in tact even after independence. The recruitment norms and procedures with more weight-age to physical traits rather than the educational or intellectual faculties of candidates, pattern of training and above all the built-in element of regimentation and discipline in the force clearly reflected the above image. Further, the force exhibited characteristics akin to that of an alien army while dealing with peoples struggles in different parts of the country. Although steps were taken on and off, mostly ad-hoc basis to increase the strength and capabilities of the force, there have been few basic reforms to improve the organization and administration of the police in way which would have enhanced its image and transformed its functioning in line with the democratic aspirations of different sections of people in free India. Thus the First Police Commission of free India (1977-81) headed by late Dharma Vera had observed; "functioning under the constraints and handicaps of an outmoded system, the police performance was fallen short of public expectations. The present culture of police system appears a continuation of what obtained under the British regime when they functioned ruthlessly as an agent for sustaining the government in power."

The colonial and militaristic image of the police is the major factor which alienates the force from the public. For common people, the 'khaki' has become the symbol of fear. The 'khaki-clad' police men are traditional characters of cruelty, brutality, corruption, sexual escapades and other vices in Cinema and electronic media. The out-dated organizational structure and legislations like Indian Police Act of 1861 failed to reform the police to the expectations of all sections of people. Given the present character and image of the police in the country, overwhelming majority of people especially in rural and backward areas have reservations to extend assistance to police in the areas of crime prevention or detection or innovative proactive policing mechanisms. The lack of public support and co-operation adversely affects the professional competence and overall efficiency of the force in the area of law enforcement.

Thus shedding the present character and image of the police especially its militaristic orientation and style of functioning would help to bring police closer to the people and community. The professional and organizational advantages of any such transformation are manifold. Basically, the quality of policing will be improved by developing harmonious and constructive police-community relations. There are many areas of policing in which public assistance and co-operation would augment police efforts to effectively maintain law and order or to combat organized crime. Take for instance the danger of insurgency or extremism that has engulfed many States and strategic areas. As the maintenance of law and order basically falls under the jurisdiction of States, the police forces are bound to deal with such challenges. Time and again, it has been proved that the success or failure of any counter-insurgency or counter-extremist operation by police or other security agencies depends much on the extent of public support or co-operation that they enjoy at ground level. For example, the professionally competent Special Task force in Andhra could achieve significant success in their protracted operations against Left Wing Extremist (LWE) elements only after making inroads into the indigenous population of the affected areas. Similarly, the much trumpeted joint operation (Bajarang) by Police, Army and Central Paramilitary forces against the cadres of United Liberation Front of Assam (ULFA) in 1990-91 failed to achieve any tangible results mainly because of the lack of support and co-operation of local population. The situation had changed, to some extent during the second stage of the operation (Rhino) when sections of the civil population affected by the excesses of ULFA cadres had started co-operating with the forces on the ground. The situation in Kashmir valley is yet another example as how the public hostility and opposition adversely affect even the well organized counter-insurgency operations. A police force which operates on militaristic lines and gets alienated from the civil society through their excesses and harsh methods can seldom win over the confidence and co-operation of the civil population. Once the State Police fail to restore normalcy in the affected areas, they would naturally be relegated to the background and the Army and paramilitary forces step in to deal with the situation. Such a police force with beleaguered image but forced to assist the other agencies on ground level operations get further alienated from the masses. The frequent deployment of Army or other Armed forces in aid of civil authorities to deal with law and order issues seriously erodes the authority of the constitution and opens a Pandora's box of legal and moral issues; that is why the Parliamentary Committee on Defense on a number of occasions had recommended that Army should not be deployed for counter insurgency operations. In conventional areas of law enforcement, better police-public relations would help to improve the quality of policing. This was universally accepted and pro-active or community policing mechanisms with the active involvement of police and public have been accepted in various formats all over the world including India. However, the paramilitary orientation of the force is the main irritant in successfully working out community policing programs with public participation.

The police management system and human resources development techniques need re-orientation for the demilitarization process in police. The new breed of police personnel with better drive and initiative need to be treated with more tact and understanding than the old generation of personnel whose subservience to authority to a great extent, had contributed to the regimentation and militaristic orientation in the force. This change in the character of the police inevitably demands drastic revision in the existing norms of discipline and command and control mechanisms. Instead of regimentation and tightening controls which are unique features of any vertical organization, the emphasis now is on flexibility and understanding which are the characteristics of any horizontal organization. The need of the hour is the transition of the force from vertical to horizontal format especially in view of the changing complexion of the force and its diverse tasks. One crucial question is how this change could be effected without eroding dignity, decorum and discipline. To begin with, the recruitment and selection system need a thorough revamping in which the focus should be to induct personnel with good education, character and conduct and humane qualities. The back door entry of personnel with dubious background at the instance of political masters or other extraneous forces should be dispensed with.

Another equally important task is re-orientation of training programs at all levels. Unfortunately, police training in the country is patterned on the training to Armed Forces personnel in Military Training establishments with more emphasis to out-door curriculum and physical exercises. The Gore Committee which was set up by the Government of India in 1971 to review the whole gamut of police training in the country identified this lacunae and rightly recommended that the focus of the training from drill and regimentation should be shifted to the development of proper attitude. However even after four decades, the training pattern for police remained almost unchanged except in the case of some Central police training institutions. In majority of the States, the focus of training is not only in the case of regimentation but also to develop total subservience to the hierarchy so as to reinforce the vertical character of the organization, It is not an exaggeration that trainee- constabulary especially of Special Armed Battalions in many States have been engaged for Manuel works in Agricultural or Poultry Farms owned by senior Commandants etc on the plea to shape them well for serious policing duties! The Conference of the Directors General and Inspectors General of Police which was held in

September 2000 had taken a serious note of the lapses in Police training and observed; "there was no change in the basic colonial philosophy of policing. The present training curricula discouraged individual discretion and decision making and replaced individual identity with group identity. It dehumanizes recruits and instilled unquestioning loyalty to superiors. It was not linked to the job the recruits were to perform, besides over-emphasizing outdoor activity". The conference adopted 'Training Vision-2010' with three point strategy which included:

(a) attitudinal change leading to shift from enforcement mode to service mode;

(b) enhancement of capabilities of personnel; and

(c) creation of mother trainers to improve quality of training.

However just like the rhetoric and hype in every DGPs conference, 'Training Vision-2010' met with a natural death in majority of the States except the fact that substantial funds were absorbed by the police hierarchy for erecting huge complexes and procuring equipments in the name of improving policing Training facilities. The irony was that neither the mother trainers were created nor there was any qualitative improvement in respect of the Faculty of Training institutions or the Training modules meant for the enhancement of the professional capabilities of the personnel. Training is one among the many mechanisms for improving performance or the attitudinal transformation of the personnel and thus in turn the overall character of the organization. A heavy responsibility rests on the police leaders to build up congenial organizational climate. In the present context, there is greater need to develop attitude of service among the personnel. Such attitudinal change especially decent and polite behavior, the fair, honest and impartial discharge of duties would enable the personnel to earn the goodwill, respect and co-operation of the public.

Demilitarization process in police should be accompanied by radical changes in the role and functions of the police. A paradigm shift in the role of police from' traditional law-enforcer' to 'facilitator' or 'advisor' in the fields of security, development, social welfare etc has already come up in many countries where the concept of privatization in policing has made significant strides. In Great Britain, private security sector which had expanded rapidly during the 1970s had been recognized by the government as a legitimate provider to criminal justice system. There, the police service itself had been subjected to 'privatization mentality' with increased emphasis being placed on the measurement of effectiveness, efficiency and performance. In Canada, there is overt recognition that private sector has significant role in policing. Similarly, privatization and 'civilianization' have become the basic features of US law enforcement system. New schemes like 'para-police'- a concept modeled on the lines 'para-medical' or 'para-legal' have been introduced in many metropolitan areas with great success. They are trained semi-professionals who perform important but routine, preliminary or peripheral police tasks usually connected with service to citizens. The 'para-cops' who are usually females are not responsible for investigating crimes or apprehending or arresting those suspected of crimes. The concept of private sector has also started attracting the police in our country. In States like Kerala ' Student-cops' almost on the lines of 'para-cops' have come into existence in important cities with routine tasks like traffic regulation, assistance to the aged and poor etc. Besides, Home Guards in large numbers have been engaged on contract basis for traffic regulation in big cities.

There are many factors which emphasise privatization of certain policing tasks. Firstly, during the last few decades police role has expanded considerably because of social dynamics and inter-related factors like population growth, rapid urbanization, industrial growth and increase in the number of social offences. The situation was further compounded with the organized crimes such as militancy, extremism, terrorism and insurgency. The expanding role of police coupled with their social obligations made the force vulnerable in effectively dealing with basic law and order duties ensuring the safety and security of all citizens. There was no qualitative or quantitative improvement in respect of police organization to cope up with these changes. A study conducted by the National Police Academy, Hyderabad revealed that on an average an investigating officer was able to devote only 37% of his time for investigation works, while the rest of the time was spent for other duties like VIP protection, petition enquiries, administrative works etc. These factors adversely affect the professionalism and competence of the force as well as the scope of successful investigation and prosecution of cases leading to conviction. The delay in investigation of sensational cases/arrest of the suspects/accused erodes the public image of the police. Secondly, the economic liberalization and corresponding developments have brought about radical changes in the functional profile of professional organizations which are greatly influenced by 'privatization culture' through the process of 'outsourcing' of a number of tasks so as to enable the organizations to concentrate in their core-functions. The police cannot remain an exception to this global trend.

Certain well-defined parameters should be adopted by police while going for privatization. The core areas of policing which essentially constitute statutory functions should be properly identified and should remain in the exclusive domain of police. Any ambiguities in this regard should be set right at the leadership level. Similarly tasks/functions outside the core areas that can be assigned to private or semi-autonomous bodies should also be properly identified considering the quantum of works that police have to perform in a particular State or area. As far as possible, privatization should be linked to 'productivity', 'cost-effectiveness' (Value for money concept) and 'quality of service'. An effective structural mechanism should be worked out to ensure transparency and to monitor the performance of the private agency, assigned with specific policing tasks. Privatization of policing tasks with unbridled powers and discretion to police leaders will definitely breed corruption and malpractices which will bring discredit to the organization.

A core issue connected with privatization is as how much of the present policing tasks and responsibilities should be handed over to the private sector. Basically, this task vests with the Political executive or the government. However, a beginning can be made by transferring some of the functions that can be effectively performed by the private sector. For example, a large force is now tied up with VIP security duties. In many States, 'security cover' to many 'so called VIPs' has become a status symbol. 'There is much scope for reducing the number of protected persons as well as police personnel assigned to each protected person. The Home department in various States should take initiative to review the list of' protected persons and prune the list realistically. The States should also explore the scope of privatizing this sector with the provision that the individual who needs protective cover to pay the cost. Similarly, many of the guard and escort duties now undertaken by the police can be conveniently entrusted to private agencies as private security sector has already occupied substantial space in various security tasks. In view of the rapid technological advancement and introduction of wide range of modern devices and gadgets like Close Circuit Television (CCTV), Simulators, Alarm system etc, in the area of personal and perimeter protection schemes, the reputed private security agencies can be assigned with such security duties. Besides the traditional beat and patrolling duties of police have attained new dimensions in view of the emergence of a large number of high-rise buildings and chain of multi-storied residential apartments in urban and semi-urban areas There are other tasks and functions of police which can also be assigned to well -established private agencies. For example, the verification works for fresh appointments or for issuance of passports which absorb substantial time of police personnel can be outsourced. Same is the case with traffic control and regulation. But the irony is that police leadership is not keen to divest such duties and functions which are fertile grounds for personnel to make quick money through corrupt practices. Such attitude and approach should be shelved by police leaders who should act as 'prime-movers' to catalyze the process of privatization to more and more areas of policing.

One noticeable trend is that the privatization culture has spread to more and more sections of people especially in urban areas where enforcement agencies cannot cope up with various challenges in the law and order front. For example, the services of private security agencies have been extensively used for watch and ward duties in residential areas, Hospitals, Hospitality establishments, Super-markets, small and medium industrial establishments etc. Residents, for example are increasingly willing to pay for security patrols or beats to protect their communities. Of late, community groups such as Residents Association, Tenants bodies, Chambers of Association etc take initiative for organizing such security duties. Besides security related tasks, these bodies also assist police in various pro-active policing schemes making policing tasks easier. Another advantage is that with the help of such bodies, the law enforcing agencies can better evaluate the services provided by private security agencies in particular areas and adopt corrective steps to improve their functioning.

Privatization may basically improve choice, quality of service and customer control in certain respects. But there are inherent dangers as well. On questions of legitimacy and delivery of justice, there is no sacrosanct for private agencies especially those floated by vested interests. When a number of constitutionally sacrosanct institutions are under cloud for their dubious and unethical role even on issues of natural justice, there is no wonder that some of the private agencies may plunge into undesirable activities. For example, in the recent past, a number of private security and detective agencies have been floated by retired defense, Police and Intelligence personnel who try to use or influence their serving counterparts in these departments. Instances have come across that some of these agencies using coercive and black-mailing tactics with the help of serving personnel to speedily settle issues or cases. Many of the private security agencies are purely guided by pecuniary and commercial interests and compromise with the actual requirements of the clients. However such lacunae or drawbacks should not be used as a ploy to close the doors of police or other security agencies for the private sector. After all police or other agencies are also not totally free from such deviations and lacunae, albeit, their public image is worse than that of many private establishments. Proper legislations plugging the possible loopholes in the Private Security agencies with effective structural mechanisms should be enacted to make them more responsible and accountable so that they can work in tandem with law enforcement agencies and the community at large. It is salutary to note that the government has already enacted such a legislation to streamline the functioning of Private Security agencies. But the pertinent issue is the implementation of the Act by taking stringent action against those private security agencies which operate purely on business lines and jeopardize the security of citizens and ultimately the larger national interests.

As the society evolves, the police would be confronted with new challenges and issues that would definitely influence the policing concepts. Thus changes are inevitable in the complexion, character, role, functions and modus-operandi of the force in order to effectively deal with the new situation. When professional organizations are becoming more flexible and open in order to fully exploit the talent and expertise of human resources, police cannot remain immune to such approach. Demilitarization essentially is the need of the hour in police, to fully utilize the capabilities of the personnel and to establish cordial relations with the people/ community. Same is the case with privatization of certain policing tasks which will facilitate the force to concentrate more in core areas of policing ensuring better performance and professionalism. Whatever lacunae or bottlenecks are there in the process of demilitarization or privatization such as dilution of discipline and regimentation in the force or lack of legitimacy of activities, the effort of police leadership and Political Executive should be to overcome such issues. After all no institution or system is cent percent sacrosanct or perfect in the existing socio-economic-political milieu of the country.

7

Cyber Crime:
Prevention and Investigation

The genesis of cyber space which is characterized by the convergence of communication technologies, Computer and broadcast media is the most significant development at the fag end of the 20th century. The revolutionary advancement made in the cyber space during the first decade of the new millennium and the 'looming space' and Information Technology (IT) which are ever expanding with 'Third-wave rhythm (Alvin Toffler) have influenced almost all areas of human activity. The new wave of cyber-crimes is an offshoot of these changes taking place in cyber-space. Basically, while the developments in the cyber-space is a matter of jubilation for the entire humanity, the misuse of these facilities have become a matter of serious concern for the law enforcement and Security agencies world over. Thus, it is pertinent to examine the conceptual, legal/jurisprudential intricacies of cyber-crime in order to enhance their understanding of the problem thereby enabling the enforcement personnel to effectively deal with them. Equally important is the task of the sensitization of the people on the various nuances of the problem in order to work out proactive strategies/mechanisms to prevent or minimize the occurrence of cyber-crimes, with community participation.

The cyber-criminal activity transcends beyond the realms of space, place and time and encompasses a virtual environment in which values are generally attributed to ideas rather than conventional physical property. These characteristics of the cyber-space challenge many of the conventional jurisprudential assumptions based on two-dimensional models namely physical presence and space. It is a well established principle of international law that control over physical space and people is an attribute of sovereignty and Statehood. But cyberspace is a borderless environment and its electronic frontiers transcend beyond geographical boundaries of nations through, Internet, E-mail and other communication channels. Nation-States have limitations to exercise their jurisdiction in cyber-space over persons who may not be within its territory or events or transactions which have no meaningful nexus with the States. This has evoked crucial debates on the question whether cyber-space should be subjected to any sort of regulation? Incidentally, the issue got mixed up with constitutional provisions like Freedom of Expression in USA who plays a decisive role in cyber space with its products like Internet and IT giants like Microsoft. The Supreme Court of USA struck down the Communications Decency Act 1996 in Reno *vs* ACLU on the ground that the Act which was enacted to prevent access by minors to the indecent material in the Internet was unconstitutional as it negated the freedom of expression guaranteed by the US Constitution. This caused a set back for the proponents favoring some form of control over cyber space. Subsequently many countries like UK imposed censorship on Internet and interpreted that there could be healthy regulations in Internet without imposing censorship over cyberspace.

But what is more significant for law enforcement agencies is the proper identification of actors in cyber-space. Since Internet makes it possible for individuals to camouflage their original identity or personality and assume different identity in cyber-space, identification of real persons behind the virtual or digital personality is essential for the effective control of the cyber space. Unless the real person behind the virtual personality is known to law enforcing authorities, fixing criminal or civil liability will not be possible in cyber space. Many countries like USA have tried to address the problems ensuring individuals to reveal their true identities while applying for user ID in the web. This is based on the commonly accepted jurisprudential concept that pseudonym just like anonymity is generally dishonorable and lacks accountability. Domain names are now assigned by the Internet Corporation for Assigned Names & Numbers (ICANN) on behalf of the National Science Foundation of the US. But such regulatory mechanisms cannot contain wide range of cyber crimes especially those committed by hackers and trespassers who adopt ingenious methods to break into the net.

Global definition of cyber-crime is yet to be attained in view of the steady expansion of cyber-space. In simple terms, it is the criminal activity largely using computers/internet. These include anything from down-loading illegal music files to stealing millions of dollars from online banking accounts and intellectual non-monetary offenses such as creating and distributing viruses on the computers or pushing confidential business information on the Internet. The most frequent and prominent form of cyber crime is 'identity theft' in which criminals use the Internet to steal personal information from others. Two of the common ways this is done is through 'phishing' and 'pharming'. Both of these methods lure the users to fake websites(appear to be legitimate) where they are asked to enter personal information such as login information, user name, password, phone number, address, credit card number, Bank account details etc.

However the most comprehensive attempt to define cyber-crime was undertaken by the United Nations whose Manual for the Prevention & Control of Computer related Crime (1995) gave the functional definition of cyber crime by interpreting that 'such crime exists because 'the computer has created a host of potentially new misuses and abuses that may or should be criminal as well'. The European Committee on the Crime Prevention of the Council of Europe also avoided formal definition of cyber crime; it highlighted the functional characteristics of target activities The Committee left the individual countries to adopt functional classification to their particular legal systems and historical traditions. Some Researchers like Young (1995) and Wasik (1999) have focused upon the individuals and have tried to identify the offenders like hackers, players, updated white collar criminals ,pornographers, perverts, traditionalists, computer-spies, computer terrorists etc Another school of researchers have concentrated upon behavior and classified six group of offenders namely:

(a) theft, embezzlement and fraud of intangible property;

(b) sabotage and vandalism;

(c) automatic destruction of data;

(d) appropriation of data;

(e) theft of computer service; and

(f) alteration and modification of data.

With the rapid strides made by Internet in the cyber space, the above classification has become obsolete. The National Computer Crime Squad of the Federal Bureau of Investigation in USA had given a broad-based classification of cyber-crime namely:

(a) intrusion into the Public Switched Network;

(b) major computer Network intrusion;

(c) Network integrity violations;

(d) Privacy violations;

(e) Industrial espionage; and

(f) Pirated computer software.

The Public Switched Network (PSN) provides services that are essential to US citizens and government agencies. Disruption or intrusion would clearly represent a serious threat to public safety and security. Similarly, Computer Network intrusion basically constitutes the malicious activity in the Network. Various Intrusion Detection and Prevention

Systems (IDPS) are in the offing to check the menace. Unexpected disturbances can cause widespread network 'outage' often described as' brown-out'.

Based on the above classification, there are certain new crimes that exist or occur only because of computers. These include hacking, cracking, spamming, pumping and dumping. Hackers are people who are intentionally interested in the arcane and recondite workings of any computer system. Computer users who break into other persons' computers without permission and modify any information in the server are called crackers. Crackers break into or violate the integrity of remote machines with malicious intention. Spamming is the sending of unwanted Email- an extreme form of which is denial of service caused due to the crash of the system. Pumping and dumping are perpetrated by unscrupulous investors who own a company's shares and publish fake/false information about company's prospects in the Internet.

From law enforcement angle, there are three generic cyber issues which constitute the major sources of cyber-crimes. These issues are:

(a) cyber-trespass (including cyber-espionage & cyber terrorism);

(b) cyber-theft; and

(c) cyber-obscenity.

The cyber trespass generally includes intellectually motivated trespassers or criminally motivated ones such as terrorists and others. The motive of the trespasser rather than the act of trespass weighs more when police and other agencies deal with these crimes. Basically there are four types of activities which are more relevant from criminal angle. The first one is deliberate planting of viruses that could be designed to disable a particular function or would be sleeping viruses designed to be neutralized only after a ransom has been paid. During the last one decade a number of such highly dangerous viruses had hit the cyber-space and caused huge loss to the computer system and network throughout the world. Anna Kournikova (a virus named after glamorous Russian Tennis star and spread in record-breaking speed in the Internet), Love bug (spread in Email and hit home pages and personal computer), Naked wife (high risk virus which spread quickly in E mail), Magistr (infested through E mail), VBS, VBSWG Zmm (hit the Windows-Outlook), Lion (infested the system of stealing passwords and installing hacker-tools) Goner (file detecting virus) Saddam Hussein and Bin Laden in Love (infested through Internet) etc were some of those worst devastating viruses that badly hit the cyber space. The second type of activity is deliberate manipulation of presentational data such as 'Home pages' so that they misrepresent or discredit the organizations which they are supposed to represent. Instances of cyber intruders entering into the Home pages of reputed institutions or organizations and defacing the minutes of their meetings or adding various pornographic and objectionable images in order to discredit them have come up in many countries.

Cyber espionage and Cyber terrorism are two major areas of concern for police, intelligence and security agencies. Cyber spies very discreetly enter and exit computer sites to gain access to specific secret or sensitive classified information without the knowledge of the actual user. A unique example was the busting of a West German Spy network which was operating in the cyber space. For more than a year, three members of the network were able to access data regarding Nuclear weapons and Strategic Defense Initiative (SDI) by breaking into 430 computers. They rifled at will through more than 30 of them linked in a network set up by Pentagon's Advanced Defense Research Project Agency. These spies were detected only after a Computer system Manager at Lawrence Berkeley Laboratory noticed 75% discrepancy between two files. Cyber espionage had also gained momentum with the increasing demand for industrial, economic and corporate intelligence mainly by MNCs and Mega Corporate houses'. 'Designing a chip can take hundreds of labor days and millions of dollars. Simply copying it is both cheap and faster' writes John D Halanka in 'Espionage in Silicon Valley', explaining why companies have encouraged such operations in the present century.

Cyber terrorism results in the deliberate destruction of material and raising considerable concern within the Military circles. In the information warfare terrorists resort to such strategies to break into the official propaganda net in order to fan out disinformation among people. They break into such computer systems and tamper with National Insurance Numbers or Tax codes or weapon Licenses. An act such as this could not be detected immediately and would cause irreparable damage to the relations between the public and the State. The Indian web sites especially those relating to Kashmir have been under frequent attack by Pak hackers since the last couple of years. NASSCOM had estimated that there had been over 1200 hack-attack on government sites since the country conducted her second nuclear test in May 1998. Away from the borders, other sensitive establishments such as Bhabha Atomic Research Centre, Mumbai, Atomic Energy Regulations Board and All India Institute of Medical Sciences (AIMS) are defaced with hackneyed breaks and missive, scribbled across their Home pages.

Another major generic type of cyber crime is cyber theft which is of two types. The first type is appropriation of intellectual property for which highly sophisticated modus operandi is used by the offenders to out beat the police and other investigation agencies. For example, various pictures of a popular Movie or sports or pop star may be appropriated from Internet images or scanned from physical sources. They were then repackaged in a glossy and professional format and sold on via a cyber shopping mall to the interest parties in good faith. The Mall could be one site in the Gulf, but its payment made to Swiss bank account. The whole operation would be of short duration and by the time the deception was detected, the proceeds would have been removed from the Bank account and the perpetrators gone. Another derivation of the appropriation and exploitation of the intellectual property currently taking place is the production of counterfeit product, direct copies of the original being made and sold through the cyber Shopping Mall. Thailand, Taiwan and Singapore have become the major centers of such organized activities. In the middle of 1980s the American Movie Industry alone had incurred an estimated loss of 750 million dollars annually due to such organized piracy. The situation is also not different in India where pirated CDs of popular Hindi and Regional language Movies flood our cities and town ships causing nightmares to the producers of such films. In spite of an array of laws and regulations governing Intellectual Property Rights, Patent Rights, Copy Rights, Stock-markets, Trade and Commerce etc. violation of such laws goes unabated with cyber-pirates playing an upper hand in such offenses.

The second type of cyber theft is the appropriation of cyber cash. The cyber cash concept has developed along with the global electronic banking network which creates a balloon of Stateless currency-money or credit- outside the control of any individual government. The developers of this banking system envisage the eventual establishment of a self contained money system linking cyber cash to credit cards. Thus there is no wonder that some leading Credit card firms like VISA International had an astonishing number of around 200 million card holders who used their credit cards at some 7 million retail stores, gas stations, restaurants, hotels, air booking counters and other business and running bills at the rate of around 600 million dollars per day, 365 days a year, during the beginning of this century. These figures have now almost doubled in the first decade of this century. Visa is only one Credit Card firm. There are other well known types of Credit Cards like Smart Cards, Super Smart Cards etc with millions of customers through out the world virtually making paper currency near total obsolescence. A very common form of cyber theft is the fraudulent use of appropriate credit cards to buy goods over internet from cyber shopping mall. For that the offender actually does not require credit card but only a discarded credit card with name number and expiry date. The wide spread use of cyber cash with Automatic Currency

Tellers (ACTs) and the extensive online banking facilities have paved the way for other offenses like bank swindles, Telecom/ Insurance Frauds etc. Through attractive and unexpected financial offers like Winning lottery or Charity aid intimated by E-mail from Websites, appear to be genuine, the gullible net-users are asked to furnish their personal information like Credit card numbers or Bank Accounts which are used by offenders for cyber cash theft. The Nigerian Chain Group is in the forefront of such frauds through out the world.

The wide use of Internet for the consumption of pornography has developed as a major issue in the West with moral and legal implications. The menace is fast spreading to developing countries like India because of the commercial exploitation of Internet by corporate giants. There are many impediments for the law enforcement agencies to check this offence. Basically, the definition of pornography and legislative norms to contain it vary from nation to nation. For example, in UK individuals regularly consume images that may be classified as obscene in many Middle Eastern countries. At the same time what individuals considered to be obscene in the UK is acceptable to many Scandinavian countries which have legalized homo-sexuality or gay movement. The formulation of general guidelines concerning cyber obscenity particularly child pornography has become an important agenda among the comity of nations. The European Commission' s Green paper on the protection of minors and human dignity in audio-visual and information services emphasized the need to distinguish between illegal acts such as child pornography which are subject to penal sections and children gaining access to sites with pornographic content that is not illegal but deemed as harmful for children's development.

As the population of cyber space increases and the range of human activities carried out there expand, the incidence of cyber crime will increase For example, a survey conducted by National Computing Centre of UK in 1996 revealed that the proportion of respondents reporting computer-related crimes rose by 60% during a period of two years. The situation is not different in countries like India where cyber crimes have shown an upward trend during the last three years. Unfortunately, there was no corresponding improvement in the professionalism or computer literacy of the police. Some studies indicated that as much as 85-90% of the law enforcement machinery at the cutting edge level have absolutely no knowledge or understanding about new generation of cyber crime.

The present limitations of the police or their dilemma to meet the challenges emanating from the cyber space need a closer look before working out changes within the force. Basically the legacy and heritage of police had been based upon locally organized policing model that was furnished by Sir Robert Peel in early 19th century. Many countries including India adopted this as role model with some cosmetic changes. One of the dominant characteristics of the police organization since its inception was its adaptation to the demands of the modernity. But this has not happened in the case of new technologies in the cyber space which in many respects were alien to the police occupational culture. Ironically the police response to the crimes occurring in this field was somewhat contradictory. On one hand they appear to have not the capacity to respond quickly at organizational level where as on the other hand, the police practices have been molded by the time honored traditions and practices of police and not in accordance with rapid developments in the cyber space. In short, the principles of policing remained static where as unprecedented changes had occurred in the nature and complexion of crime. Even in offences such as cyber-theft, the police follow the traditional investigation methods and canons of criminal law such as the apprehension and prosecution of the perpetrator and the restitution of the goods to the owner but seldom attaches any consideration to the value of the contents/data stored in the electronic devices. Such aberrations in police occupational culture blunt the professionalism of the force to face new challenges in the cyber space. In fact this dissonance between the existing police occupational and operational culture is the main root cause for the present police dilemma in combating cyber crime. This emanates from a phenomenon commonly found in the studies of police culture, whereby the police tend to change the meaning and common understanding of the area in which they become involved. So, when police operate in the 'cyber-space', they interpret the issues there in terms of the traditional police functional culture. Thus Sterling in his most influential work upon the policing of hackers had rightly commented;" they (police) want to believe that all hackers are thieves" Similar interpretations are common in the case cyber-obscenity especially the misuse of Internet. It is no surprise to see statements by police which describe the Internet News Groups as libraries of pornography etc. While anticipating what they see as the problem, the police draw from their experience of terrestrial world conceiving of cyber space as a new world without police.

The level of ignorance of the police personnel on cyber crimes and lack of appropriate skills to deal with them are other two areas of concern. Thus on many occasions, the police forces are shying away from even attempting to investigate these crimes. Even the special groups or experienced detectives are not keen in pursuing these cases. The reality is that the police personnel are far behind the cyber criminals in their various operations, Police can catch them only when they become complacent or keep using old technology. As long as the cyber-criminals update their technology and adopt novel modus operandi for the commission of crimes, they remain far ahead of police and safe. One major reason for this discernible trend is that the police responses to cyber-crimes are under-resourced and they suffer from lack of support or co-ordination from other agencies which are equally less enthusiastic in vigorously pursuing cyber offences. Besides, cyber crimes are under reported though their incidence is comparatively high. Such under-reporting of these offences incapacitate the police to enhance their investigation skills by involving in a wide spectrum of cyber crimes.

Police, no doubt cannot maintain their exclusive domain or jurisdiction over the cyber-space; nor they can be fully involved in cyber space patrolling. The success of fighting cyber crimes depends much on the co-operation that police receive from the community and the users of the new technology in the cyber-space. Three main groups which can assist police in fighting cyber-crimes are State funded non-police organizations/Non-governmental organizations; Internet Providers and Internet users. The strategies employed by these bodies provide a spectrum of policing models which depending upon the nature of cyber space evolve a system of security or preventive mechanisms concerning privacy, authentication, integrity and non-repudiation of communications transacted through electronic media particularly Internet and Email. Such bodies have come up on a big way in many advanced countries like USA, UK etc with the active support of government and police. For example, the Internet Watch Group Foundation (IWF) formed with governmental support in UK 'polices' Internet and other technologies in the cyber space in order to check their misuse for a wide range of offences like child pornography. At the same time leading Internet providers are engaged in efforts to develop anti-virus software by introducing different mechanisms. For example, certain 'hi-tech' firms in Israel had developed a system that cuts off the main route used by many Internet hackers when they try to break into Company's network. The new technology is aimed at safeguarding the business interests of E-commerce firms that offer goods and services to customers who sometimes are wary about providing Credit card information over the Internet Similarly, Microsoft Corporation had released a security tool that includes Internet printing, advanced search functions and scripting technologies that are intended to reduce the impact of viruses/worms that rapidly spread in the computer net work.

Another area of significance is the enactment of proper legislations to deal with cyber crimes. A comprehensive list of cyber crimes constantly updated should go in the Statute Books. In countries like USA, a number of such laws have been enacted with the spread of Information Technology (IT). The Computer Misuse Act (1990) of UK included three new criminal offences namely unauthorized hacking; unauthorized access with Internet and unauthorized modification of the contents of any computer system. However such laws have inherent weakness of tracing or identifying the hackers or bringing them before the courts and awarding conviction for their offences. One major lacuna is that many of these laws are based on the traditional concepts of physical property and its protection. These laws are inadequate when the nature of crimes that individuals are increasingly falling victims, is moving from physical to virtual reality. This explains another issue that police are not the only criminal justice agency which is experiencing problems with cyber crimes, but also other institutions like Legislature, Judiciary etc. The Courts have currently having some difficulty in ascertaining the relative seriousness of cyber theft or similar crimes when the victims have-not experienced much loss, but a dilution of the value of original property because of its duplication. Such ambiguity in laws and connected procedures concerning cyber crimes lead to a large number of acquittals in such cases. However the governments are conscious of such lacuna and appropriate corrective measures are being taken up to augment the legal machinery. For example the government of Singapore in 1999 had enacted a legislation bringing the contents/data in the Internet under the purview of Copy Rights Act with a view to protecting the knowledge disseminated through the cyber space. India has also enacted new Acts in respect of Intellectual Property Rights, Patent Rights, Money laundering etc to deal with the issues in the cyber space and to enhance the policing potential of the State apparatus.

The governmental and legal initiatives to deal with the challenges in the cyber space should be supplemented by functional and structural changes in police organization. The various aspects of police occupational culture which breed dissonance between police operational culture and cyber culture should be re-institutionalized through personnel and organizational mechanisms so that police can involve in cyber crimes at right time with right strategies. Certain encouraging signs helpful to accelerate such changes have been noticed in the police. Unlike in the past, now-days, the personnel recruited to the police come from a broader social and educational background than their predecessors. More than that sizeable percentage of the present day personnel are not only receptive to new ideas but also enter the police organization with high degree of computer literacy. Despite high demand for technocrats in global market, a number of IITans and graduates/post-graduates from different Engineering branches like Electronics and Communications (EC), Computer Science (CS) and Information Technology (IT) join Indian Police Service (IPS). Their knowledge, skills and aptitude in tune with the new police culture and essential to meet the challenges in the cyber space can be enhanced through proper training and in-service courses. It is significant that premier Training institutions like the National Police Academy (NPA) Hyderabad have been imparting such training/courses in cyber crimes to IPS Probationers since 1998 with a view to preparing future generation of police leaders to effectively deal with the issues of policing in cyber space. Many States like Karnataka, Tamil Nadu, Kerala, and Andhra Pradesh have introduced computer technology in a wide range of police operations and functions. Needless to mention, such Human Resource Development policies should be supplemented through better organizational resources in order to equip the force to meet the sophistication attained by the perpetrators of cyber crime. The Government of India has already initiated some major steps-in this direction. The Union Home Ministry in 1999 constituted six Policy Planning Groups (PPGs) with important agenda like Modernization of Central and State police Forces in order to enhance their professionalism and competence to meet the new challenges in the internal security field. Substantial funds have been allocated to the State and Central Police organizations under Modernization of Police Program (MPP) during the last one decade in order to improve the efficiency of the forces through procurement of more infrastructure, logistics, weaponry, communication/transport facilities and computer devices. It is a debatable point as how far the Modernization and procurement have helped to improve the competence of these forces. The cardinal truth is that the success of any such policy decisions or connected developments in respect of the organization and manpower viz-a-viz the performance and competence of the forces depend on their implementation at cutting edge level; which unfortunately is totally lacking in police organization. The subjective decision of a set of leaders at the helm of affairs and the subsequent utilization of governmental funds without any accountability or transparency in the name of infrastructure and facilities have become a boon to the senior hierarchy and a curse to the organization and the large majority of personnel at grass roots level. The Political Executive instead of soft-pedaling such organizational aberrations should deal them with an iron hand. Then only there will be real salvation in our police forces!

8

Police, Society, Law and Accountability:

The Myth and Reality

"We expect him (policeman) to be human and yet inhuman, we employ him to administer the law and yet ask him to waive it. We resent him, when he enforces the law in our case, yet demand his dismissal, when he doesn't elsewhere. We offer him bribes, yet denounce his corruption. We expect him a mentor of society, yet not share its values. We admire violence even against society itself, but condemn force by police on our own behalf. We tell the police that they are entitled information from the public, yet we ostracize informers. We ask for crime to be eradicated, but only by the use of 'sporting methods'. The above excerpts from Mr. Ben Whitaker's classic work on police in United Kingdom as early as in 1964 are relevant for police-public perceptions in the present century. Eminent Novelists and fiction writers of UK portrayed such scenario of public visualizing police men with distrust and disdain. Charles Dickens' police characters were not looked upon as friends of society or the poor. Colin Mac Inns, a suspense Novelist and student of police through his famous work "Mr. Love & Justice" effectively portrayed the dilemma of police men in the streets and at home. Ironically, such impressions on police and dichotomy of the public on their expectations and the actual role of police emanated from the homeland of famous "London Bobby" considered to be an epitome of model policing in a civilized society.

Such dichotomy in respect of society's approach towards police prevails in almost all countries. Many factors contribute to this trend. The first and foremost one pertains to different perceptions of people on the exact role of police. Peter K Manning, who made extensive study on police work and their social obligations had rightly commented; "the absence of clear, unambiguous and universally agreed upon statement of the police mandate in our society creates confusion among the public as well as the police". Just as Society's expectations, different perceptions exist among Political Executives, Police leaders, sociologists and intellectuals on the exact role of police in a democratic society. From conventional or traditional angle, police are duty bound to protect the life and properties of citizens through the effective enforcement of law and order and prevention and detection of crimes. A number of legal luminaries and criminal justice experts like Lord Delvin (UK) and Richard A Myron, Dean of the School of Criminal Justice for President's Crime Commission, USA strongly propounded and favored the crime control role of the police. On the other hand, others like Michael Benton, Jerome Skolnick, Lehman etc through their works interpreted that modern police organization is the most wide spread government sponsored social service agency. A third category of police experts described them as 'ombudsman for the weak and exploited in the society'. There is yet another school of thought who strongly argue that police is 'public's agent' whose authority may never exceed the authority of the society. Just like the wide diversity on the role and core functions of the police, the people's perceived notions on policing lack objectivity and often lead to unrealistic expectations from police. Neither have they appreciated the limitations of the police in controlling crimes nor the criminogenic factors on which the police have absolutely no control. Three major myths dominate their perception. The police devote preponderance of their time and a resource for combating crime is myth number one. The second myth is that there is fairly fixed, definable and measurable thing called crime. The third is that police work can some how lower crime rates regardless what other institutions do. In all these three cases, the reality is entirely different. In fact, crime per-se consumes only a microscopic percentage of the working hours of police personnel. For example, a research study by Thomas A Johnson and Gordon E Misenor on "Police accountability & Public" in USA revealed that general duty police officers spent about 70-80% of their time for dealing non-crime related tasks. The situation is also not much different in India where only 1% of the man hours are actually utilized by police for investigations and processing criminal cases (A Training Mannual for Police on Human Rights by N.R. Madhava Menon). Similarly crime is neither measurable nor the police alone can ensure zero-tolerance on crime. In fact police is one of the key players of criminal justice system along with other institutions such as Judiciary, Executive etc. Thus, in a society in which such myths on policing camouflage realities, the general expectations of the public on police will be highly exaggerated or unrealistic. On many occasions such expectations clash with the concepts of accountability to law which is the basic principle of good policing.

Such issues are more glaring in heterogeneous democratic societies with cultural pluralism and diversity. Unlike the centripetal societies which generally have one standard, one norm and one set of values etc, in centrifugal societies its diverse elements are being forced outward thus forming smaller groups with their own local pool of experience and culture. This leads to the formation of congeries of 'sub-cultures' which are at times at logger heads with the larger culture. Recently in February 2011, David Cameron, the British Prime Minister used his speech at an international security conference in Munich to declare that time had come to bury "State multiculturalism" mainly from security and law and order angle. Cameron highlighted that "Multiculturalism or cultural pluralism had encouraged different cultures to live separate lives with segregated communities behaving in ways that run counter to our lives and common system". We, in India now face such a unique situation in which these sub cultures appear in the form of religious, linguistic, ethnic, tribal, minority, caste or regional groups whose perceptions and expectations are always at variance or sometimes diametrically opposite to that of the society in general. More rabid or radical sub-cultures will soon attain 'sub-nationalist' tendencies and open new frontiers of conflicts and tensions with the slogans of 'self determination' or sovereignty. Added to this is the dilemma created by political parties as part of the democratic process. It is regular practices of all political parties, cutting across ideologies or policies, come out with tall promises on the eve of all major elections. The improvement in law and order would prominently figure in the long list of such promises which would be seldom fulfilled by any of these parties. But the hype and hoopla created by these promises intensify their expectations in the law and order front, beyond the contours of reality and rationality. Thus the reality is that police can never fulfill the expectations of all sections or sub-cultures in a pluralist, fractured, fragmented or highly politicized society.

When such an array of factors influence society's expectations from police, the crucial question is what role do we want the police to perform in the society? The primary objective of an efficient police emphasized by Charles Rowan and Richard Mayne, the first two Commissioners of Robert Peel's Metropolitan Police in UK "is prevention of crime, the next that of detection and punishment of offenders if crime is committed". But much water had flown through River Thames and the revolutionary changes sweeping across the world coupled with the new challenges that had taken place in the world of crimes and criminal offences have radically changed the perceptions and expectations of the society in respect of policing. Apart from the maintenance of public order and the enforcement of rule of law, the police are required to protect the weak, unorganized and poor from oppression and exploitation; to promote communal harmony and gender justice; to assist the functioning of democratic institutions and to safeguard the unity and integrity of the nation. Besides, as a well knit, disciplined and regimented body with grass roots level spread, operating with good communication and twenty four hours of a day, the police have proved useful as general providers of assistance during natural calamities/disasters, domestic conflicts, missing of persons and properties etc. In short, the society expects that the police should play a more crucial and significant role closely intertwined with the wide spectrum of human activities.

The omnipresence of police with multidimensional role as envisaged by the society leads to role conflicts on a number of occasions. As the police with their minimal manpower and scarce resources are engaged in a plethora of tasks, their performance would not come up to the expectation of the people. Then there would be much hue and cry and bad publicity and propaganda against the police. Very often the society is not clear as what exactly they expect from police? Do police enforce all laws in letter and spirit or ignore some violations? This dilemma always confronts the society and police. There are any number of situations in which the legal action of the police goes contrary to the expectations of people or particular sub cultures. For example, police can legally fire at a fleeing young felon, but many people dissent such action. The patrol officers face more conflicting situations. There are sub-cultures of people having licentious life style and vices like gambling, mild use of drugs and narcotic substances, who expect the police to ignore laws regulating such activities. Once the police try to enforce the relevant laws against such offenders, they may face stiff resistance from such groups. We should not forget the hard reality that even the most barbaric and inhuman practices like 'Sati' or 'honor-killings' of young brides have sacrosanct among sections of society which oppose tooth and nail of policing efforts to bring the perpetrators of such dastardly crimes, to book.. In the case of order maintenance particularly civil disturbances or riots, such conflicts become more vocal and vociferous. We very often hear about 'over-reaction' of police whenever there are any lapses or use of mild force to quell such disturbances. Their 'action' or 'inaction' comes under criticism. For example, when police resort to strategies like Preventive arrests under 109 Cr.Pc or impose curfew in order to defuse brewing tension in a particular area, they are accused of curtailment of civil and democratic rights. On the contrary, they are blamed of 'inaction' when they fail to contain such disturbances either due to the dearth of manpower/resources or due to the intervention of Political Executive. Even in more serious organized crimes such as insurgency, extremism, terrorism and communal riots, the perception and expectations of the society in respect of police seldom show any unanimous approach. Such trends are more glaring in multi cultural societies. While the worst affected people of such organized crimes expect that the police should totally eliminate such threats even by adopting 'extra-judicial' or apparently illegal methods, intellectuals and strong advocates of human/civil rights are against any dilution of the 'due process of law" in dealing with such extra-ordinary law and order situations.

The role and role-conflicts of police vis-a-vis the expectations of the society often pose a pertinent question whether police can deviate from the core concept of accountability to law especially while dealing with major law and order problems? Should they switch over from the concept of 'rule of law' to 'rule of order' or 'due process of law' to 'crime control model'? Naturally such questions do create dilemma to police leadership. Basically, law is the substitute for force in human governance. In primitive societies, jungle law prevailed with the mighty and powerful deciding the matters of life and death. With the advancement of these societies, a set of customs and traditions based on moral or ethical codes or belief had come into existence to regulate human life. The emergence of State paved the way for the enactment of laws which legitimized the use of force by the State under very limited circumstances and made the governments accountable for any infractions. Police as the main instrumentality of the State is the creation of law and their authority is limited to what is vested in them by specific laws. Moreover, laws regulating their role and functions are laid down on the basis of certain desirable normative standards. In short, the police are vested with cognitive features like discretion and authority by virtue of these laws on a hypothesis that the human situations that the police are required to deal with are highly ambiguous. But it is equally important that while exercising these features, the police should adhere to laws and legal process to ensure that 'justice is not only done but shown to be done'. Thus, literally also in the expression of law and order, the word 'law' takes precedence over order. The Anglo-Saxon Common law which we .adopt for the administration of Criminal Justice System in the country, through a number of historic judgments in its homeland, unequivocally upheld this position. The best example is the First Blackburn Case in which Lord Denning M.R. rightly observed; "I hold it to be the duty of the Commissioner of Police as it is of every Chief Constable to enforce the law of the land. He must take steps so as to post his men that crime may be detected; and that honest citizens may go about their affairs in peace. He must decide whether or not suspected persons are to be prosecuted and if need be bring the prosecution or see that it is brought, in all these things, he is not the servant of anyone, save of the law itself. No minister of the crown can tell him that he must or must not keep observation of this place or that, or that he must or he must not prosecute this man or that nor can any police authority tell him so. The responsibility for law enforcement lies on him, he is answerable to law and law alone".

The Indian Constitution and various other statutes have unequivocally upheld that the Police are totally accountable to law. The Law Commission in its 14th Report observed; "The greater is the need for the ceaseless enforcement of rule of law so that Executive may not be under the mistaken belief of monopoly of wisdom and its zeal for administrative efficiency, overstep the ends of its power and spread its tentacles on the domain where citizens would be free to enjoy the liberty guaranteed to them". Thus for all purposes, the law is the 'dharma' of the police which they cannot compromise for fulfilling society's expectations. Despite such constitutional provisions, the ground reality is that majority of police leaders violate the rule of law or the 'due process' of law mainly under political intervention, but not on the lines of the aspirations and expectations of the society. The need of the hour is that such bottlenecks in the force which tarnish police image in the society should be overcome through sound organizational and personnel reforms and policies.

In fact, proper definition of police functions and a set of standards for fulfilling them without any extraneous or other influences are the basic requirements to overcome such lapses. Mr. Herman Goldstein, who made extensive studies on police and society, formulated some worthwhile concepts in this direction. According to Goldstein; Police functions in two worlds. They play an integral part along with Prosecutors, Courts and Correctional agencies in the operation of criminal justice system. This is a highly structured world defined by statutes, and court decisions and subject to strict controls. The second world is less defined. It comprises all aspects of police functioning that are unrelated to the process of an accused person through criminal system. Within this world, a police department seeks to prevent crimes, abates nuisance, resolves disputes, controls traffic and crowds, furnish information and provides a wide range of other miscellaneous services to the citizens. In carrying out these functions police officers frequently make use of authority which is there by virtue of their role in the criminal processes-the first of their two worlds. The above 'two world theory' on police functions can be co-related to their accountability to law through a simple equation: P is equal to M+D (P=M+D) in which 'P' stands for the totality of police functions whereas 'M' and 'D' stand for 'Mandatory' and 'Discretionary' functions.

The mandatory role especially the enforcement of law makes the police totally accountable to law and no compromises are allowed. In this regard, the police leadership should guard against the 'organizational deviants' or extraneous influences which on many occasions try to dilute the rule of law or procedures of good policing. For example, there is a general tendency among many police functionaries not to register First Information Report (FIR) of cognizable offences, which they are legally bound to do. The main reason for this illegal and discernible trend is the over enthusiasm of police personnel to keep the crime statistics at moderate level to please the Political Executive or the government in power. In that process not only the police are violating the law but also denying justice to aggrieved citizens. More over, such wrong tactics by police and the dull, dry and distorted statistics on crime which the public will come to know through the convulsions in the society adversely affect credibility and image of police. It is high time that effective measures should be initiated by police leadership to ensure free and fair registration of crimes in all police Stations. Measures such as designating more and more reporting centers for registration of complaints, introduction of E-complaint format in police stations and strict action against police personnel violating procedures in respect of registration of FIRs etc are to be initiated by police leadership. Similarly, proper detection and investigation of crimes are other two sensitive mandatory functions of the police. Conventionally and legally, the police should be guided by three principal standards namely 'fairness, impartiality and acceptability' while performing these tasks. The Constitution and the penal and procedure laws such as IPC, Cr.Pc, Indian Evidence Act etc have laid down a number of provisions-rights/obligations, checks and balances and control mechanisms-on all aspects of investigation such as arrest, search and seizure, collection of evidence and formation of opinion on prosecution. Apart from these constitutional and legal provisions, another crucial aspect is the independent character of the investigation agency. The Royal Commission on Police in UK as early as in 1962 emphasized that investigation of cases is part of the judicial process and that the police must be entirely independent in the discharge of functions which are judicial or quasi-judicial. In India, way back in 1968, the Apex Court in 'Abhinandan Jha' case clearly laid down that the investigation is the exclusive domain of police who is to form an independent opinion on the result of investigation without any intervention from the Executive. But the crucial question that stares at us is whether police could insulate their independence during investigations? And to what extent they remain accountable to law and procedures while performing this mandatory tasks? While searching answers to these questions, one can easily find that the overall record of police in the area of investigations is far from satisfactory. Time and again the Courts have come down heavily upon the police on their omissions and commissions in the investigation of a number of sensational cases. Similarly, the less told, the much better on the adherence of police to rule of law or due process of law during investigations. The increasing incidence of 'custodial deaths' and 'custodial violence' reveals that the police resort to 'third degree methods' and other illegal means during investigation of crimes. The Annual Reports of the National Human Rights Commission (NHRC) since 1993 showed steady increase in the number of custodial deaths.

The above facts are clear indicators on the need of police leadership working out strategies to improve the performance of the force in their mandatory tasks especially the field of investigation of crimes which very often evoke public interest and expectations. The success of investigation of crimes depends mostly on professional training, competence of personnel and judicious application of science and technology. For equipping the personnel on above lines, they should be imparted special training in police interrogation techniques, Finger-printing and other modern scientific aids of investigations so that many unhealthy trends and illegalities like use of 'third-degree methods', padding of evidence etc during investigations can be dispensed with. It is equally important that professionally competent personnel with proven integrity should be entrusted with the investigation of sensational cases. The separation of investigation wing from the law and order wing will enable the personnel of the former to concentrate more in their tasks. Similarly, the effective insulation of police from political or other extraneous influences is prerequisite for ensuring impartiality in investigations. The police leaders should work out proper organizational mechanisms to effectively monitor the investigation and prosecution of sensational cases leading to conviction. For that purpose proper interaction and co-ordination among various stake holders of criminal justice system especially the police and prosecuting agency should be ensured. The present acquittal rate of over 90% is a matter of serious concern to the society and also exposes the weakness of the entire system. The law and legal provisions cannot be blamed for this trend as rightly observed by Justice V.R. Krishna Iyer of Supreme Court; "Deterrence against crime is defeated not because the penal law is impotent, but law becomes lame because the investigation is insouciant and procrastinatory and court-proceedings are so paper-flogged, flabby, dawdling as to lose public credibility and exhaust patience and pockets of victims".

On the other hand a lot of freedom is allowed to police for the exercise of their discretionary role, which to a great extent, is influenced by society's expectations. A unique feature is that personnel from top to bottom engaged in policing have the power to use their discretion. This enables the lower ranking personnel to exercise powers of discretion on a number of situations such as prevention of crimes, order maintenance, social service etc. Simultaneously, it imposes certain obligations on the part of police leadership to exercise supervision over the personnel so that they would not misuse the power of discretion detrimental to the interests of the organization. Very often police leadership confronts dilemma when some personnel influenced by caste, community or political sentiments exercise discretion in a discriminatory manner causing much animosity against police from the affected. Ironically such attitude of section of personnel during communal conflicts or caste disturbances had blurred the secular credentials and image of Indian police on a number of occasions. In any ideal concept of policing, discretion should not pave the way for discrimination. This aspect had been succinctly highlighted by the National Police Commission as; "Every police officer should normally be left free to exercise the discretion on his own judgments, but there may be situations, the disposal of which have repercussions beyond the jurisdiction of one police officer and it will become necessary in such cases for the supervisory ranks to step in and exercise discretion at their level".

The natural question is how the discretionary role of police is exercised to the full advantage of the organization and the society. Basically, among the various functions of the police, the power of discretion is all the more important on the issue of order maintenance. James Q Wilson who made extensive studies on police role and functions in a democratic society, had rightly highlighted; "the order maintenance function necessarily involves the exercising of substantial discretion over the matters of greatest importance (Public or private mentality, honor or dishonor, life and death) in a situation that is by definition, one of conflict and in an environment that is apprehensive and perhaps hostile". Truly speaking, the police have to deal with any number of such situations; hostile and apprehensive such as student agitations, labor troubles like 'gherao', inter-religious disputes, unlawful mob etc. There are also areas of conflict between private and public morality with sections of people endorsing minor vices like gambling, liberal sex, gay-movement etc and laws prohibiting them. In many such unique situations, police will be forced to adopt 'watchmen-strategy' and refrain from enforcing many controversial laws. What matters much is the proper understanding of the problem in the backdrop of society's expectations and rational handling of the same using discretion, without resorting to use of force or formal arrest etc.

The Police leadership needs to work out such strategies in order to strengthen the relations between the police and society. The concepts like' Community policing' or 'problem -oriented policing' which have gained considerable momentum in modern policing can be largely attributed to the efforts by police administration to develop better police - community relations. These concepts work on the main hypothesis that 'police might become partners with the people in the community so that together they can address local priorities related to crime, social and physical disorder and neighborhood decay'. The National Police Commission (NPC) had highlighted this point in uncertain terms and called for "increasing involvement of the public in law enforcement work in general and getting of their co-operation in day to day police work in particular". An added advantage of such schemes is that police diagnose longer term solution to the recurrent crime and disorder problems and mobilize community resources to implement them through pro-active role. This will help to enhance public security, safety and order and in turn society's confidence over police. Once this crucial element of confidence is built up in the community and people, much of the dichotomy and confusion on society's expectations from the police could be fulfilled or sorted out. However, the mere conceptualization of such new areas of policing will not in any way help the police or the public. What is required is their effective implementation at grass roots level so that a new culture would be developed in the police and the society. Significantly, modern police organizations utilize their resources and expertise in this direction. For example, the idea of 'civilianization' of policing has become a reality in USA where a number of innovative schemes and mechanisms have cemented the relations between police and public. Formation of 'Para-police' in all the Metropolitan areas; 'Police Cadet Crops' (body of students inducted from Colleges and used for policing tasks after proper training and motivation) and Civilian Review Committees (aimed at evaluating police performance and help to shape police policies) are some of the important moves in this regard. In Great Britain, Police Community Liaison Committees with the representatives of police, local authority, and ethnic-minority groups are in existence in all the Provincial Police areas in England and Wales along with Metropolitan Police in London. In Canada and Japan regular Police Commissions chaired by serving or retired, Judicial functionaries with a few public men and retired executives operate with the aim to strengthen police community relations.

We have also initiated a number of community policing schemes which are yet to make decisive impact within police organization or on police-community relations. Unlike in the West, the people in India lacked proper understanding on the constraints of the police in combating various offences. Majority of the people are either ignorant or indifferent on the limitations of the police for their effective functioning or the mosaic of socio-economic and political factors influencing policing in a democratic polity. In fact, the expectations of the society from police have been molded on the basis of such perceptions and ignorance of the people on policing. Thus the real challenge before the police leadership is to remove the darkness of ignorance on policing constraints from the minds of the masses through better police-public relations.

9

Training and Development of Subordinates:

A Challenge Before Police Leadership

Organizations adopt a number of mechanisms for the development of their human resources. Training is one of the most important inputs for human resources development. Training is defined as conscious effort to improve the professional knowledge, proper skills and right attitude of an individual in a desired direction. The main objective of training is to enable the personnel to perform various tasks and functions associated with their present and future role and develop an organizational culture with better superior-subordinate relationships and teamwork and collaboration among sub-units. In organizations like police institutional training assumes considerable significance as the personnel acquire the required professionalism and talent for the effective performance of various tasks mainly through such programs. More over "police department have a special property (as compared with few other organizations) that within it discretion increases as one moves down the hierarchy". Thus even the lower ranks in the force have a major responsibility in maintaining the image of the organization by properly exercising their power of discretion and authority, while performing their diverse duties. The fact that more than 80% of the force constitutes such lower ranks (Constabulary) explains the vital role that they play in the organization. Unless the performance of Constabulary and other subordinate ranks in police is improved through training and other institutional reforms, no perceptible change in the professionalism or image of the police is possible. Thus, former Union Home Minister L.K. Advani rightly observed; "the success of police training will be judged by the change in the attitude and behavior of junior police officers, constabulary and upwards in dealing with the general public".

The crucial question is whether the present training curricula and other Human Resources development strategies in the police are adequate in effecting such change of attitude of the personnel especially at cutting edge level? What should be done to improve the training/development of subordinates so that there would be qualitative improvement in the professionalism and performance of the force? And what role the police leaders can play in this regard?

While discussing these questions, one can easily find that the militaristic orientation of police training which was adopted by police training institutions, both by design and circumstances was the main impediment in changing the attitude of the personnel or bringing them closer to the public. The British who adopted the Irish colonial model of policing for the Indian Police envisaged an organizational structure partly military and partly civil within the organization. Thus, the police training institutions established for the training of Constables and officers of and above the rank of Sub Inspectors in early 1890s and in the first decade of last century followed a military model of training for the personnel. The same trend continued even after independence. The more complex and difficult law and order scenario as manifested through increasing accent on turbulence and violence in different parts of the country forced the police to exhibit the characters of vertical organization and hierarchy with more and more tendencies of regimentation and centralization of powers. Thus the Gore Committee which was constituted by the Government of India in1971 in order to review the existing facilities in different police training institutions and recommend measures to improve the quality of police training rightly commented; "the syllabi of police training institutions are heavily weighed in favor of outdoor activities". The Committee which made a series of well thought out recommendations for improving the police training shifted the focus of training from the drill and regimentation to the development of proper attitudes through the study of social and behavioral sciences and modern management norms and techniques. Though many of the important recommendations of the Committee were accepted by the Government of India and concrete steps were taken to tune up the functioning of these institutions, the quality and nature of training in many States have not registered any noticeable improvement after nearly four decades after the publication of the report. The training and the knowledge and skills imparted through such training appear to be totally out of sync with current realities and challenges. This, according to M.K. Narayanan, the former National Security Advisor (NSA) has created a unique situation in which; "as much as 80-85% of the law enforcement machinery specially at the cutting edge level has little of any understanding of the contours of militancy, the nature and content of terrorism, insurgency, sectarian violence, the shape of organized violence and possibly nothing at all about the new generation of cyber crimes". Levels of ignorance even at higher formations remain high in such areas which have become the thrust areas of policing. For example, some mediocre IPS officers shunted to innocuous Transport/traffic section or Police Battalions and languished there for years appear as odd men out while posted to sensitive law and order or intelligence wings in trouble-prone States. The case of some others, who were forcibly sent from States on Central deputation and occupied cozy assignments for long, is not different as they remain totally cut off from ground realities of their cadre States. Thus, it is high time that we should review training objectives and evolve more consistent and appropriate training/HR development strategies so that personnel at all levels should be imparted professional knowledge and skills, technical know-how etc in line with the new challenges confronting the police in the present century.

While re-orienting the framework of training strategies especially for lower and subordinate ranks, the police leadership should consider certain basic parameters such as the present character/complexion of the force, nature of new entrants into the organization and the anticipated role and tasks of the force in the changing environment. On the basis of these parameters, the training modules for various subordinate ranks should be formulated and implemented. Basically, the image of police as an oppressive instrument of a colonial power during the British Raj had undergone considerable change because of the organized efforts of the democratically elected governments to reform the police in line with the aspirations and expectations of the common people. The bourgeoning role of the police especially their tasks to implement a plethora of social legislations and the various proactive schemes have made the police closer to various cross sections of the society. The above developments have considerably helped the police to attain many qualities of a horizontal organization with less regimentation and more flexibility. But, the growth of terrorism, Left Wing Extremism (LWE), militancy and insurgency with violence, blood shed and destructions in different parts of the country has forced the police organization to retain its paramilitary profile/ character with more regimentation. This has accelerated the alienation of police from the public. Similarly, the complexion of personnel joining the organization has undergone subtle change. Now-a-days more and more highly educated young women and men with professional qualifications and skills join Indian Police Service and the subordinate ranks including the constabulary. The problems and challenges that the police would be confronted .in the changing environment are unique and not accustomed to the law enforcement machinery. Cross border terrorism, Narco-terrorism, gang-wars, cyber crime, organized and syndicate crime, use of high explosives and detonating devices, are a few examples in this regard.

Ironically, the police leadership is not much keen to ponder over such parameters during the formulation of

Mission Statement or Training philosophy and in the preparation of training curricula for Police training institutions. On the contrary obsolete training modules and schemes, which in many respects carry the legacy of the British, dominate the indoor and outdoor curricula of training. For example, except a couple of States, there had not been any significant change in the training syllabi for police force which was followed during the last 60 years. And whatever changes were effected, they were peripheral and cosmetic and not capable to create positive attitude or imprints among the personnel. In many Police Training institutions, the outdoor instructors with their illiterate or semi-literate background and oppressive style and barking orders kill the initiative and self confidence of many trainees who develop negative 'imprints' in their outlook and attitude towards people. This in many respects is akin to the crude and cruel ragging methods in academic campuses where the victims of the exercise repeat the same with more venom and vigor against the new-comers. The only difference in police is that those probationers who developed negative imprints during the training carry on the same during their entire career. Unfortunately, their future victims are the poor citizens! More devastating are the adverse impact of certain indoor classes and subjects in which the Faculty members with dubious background and immersed in corruption and malpractices try to glorify and inculcate vices and traits like 'third degree methods', violation of human rights etc in the minds of new recruits. Thus a challenging task before the police leadership is the proper balancing of outdoor and indoor contents in the training curricula in consonance with the character of the force, complexion of the new entrants and the changing environment in which police have to operate.

While we discuss this balancing act, our main focus on outdoor content should be on physical endurance and stamina building for which the present emphasis on infantry or lathi-drill or equitation would not be of any use. Police force in India, are no longer meant for ceremonial parades or colorful and extravagant shows, but for undertaking major challenges like terrorism or Left Wing Extremist violence or the threats emerging from the cyber space. What matters more is their physical and intellectual well-being devoid of stress or strain even during the most tiring situation of prolonged combat with the dreaded extremists in the deep forests of Chattisgarh or Jharkhand or with the insurgents in the North East. Thus the outdoor curriculum and schemes are to be reoriented and primarily aimed at:

(a) physical fitness of personnel on a continuing basis;

(b) proficiency in handling various weapons of use;

(c) acquisition of skills of various forms of unarmed combat;

(d) counter-insurgency and Jungle warfare;

(e) crowd control and dealing with riotous mob;

(f) wearing of uniform, bearing and deportment;

(g) four wheeler and two wheeler driving with basics of automobile mechanism;

(h) swimming;

(i) use of water canons, tear gas shells;

(j) search and surround;

(k) mobile and foot-patrolling; and

(l) response to sudden ambush and assault.

The indoor curricula should also be reviewed and emphasis should be on subjects that will help to improve the professional skills and knowledge of the personnel. Criminal law which is the basic of police work should be given precedence over all other indoor subjects and should be taught in detail. Similarly prolonged local issues having a bearing on law and order should also be taught. Some of the subjects of importance are:

(a) Police Manual of the State and relevant procedures;

(b) Scientific aids to investigations;

(c) Arrest and custody;

(d) Bail, Remand and Search;

(e) Preventive and Security action;

(f) Area Beats;

(g) Public Relations;

(h) Handling of women, children and weaker sections;

(i) Fundamental rights and their protection;

(j) Human Rights-International and National Covenants and Guidelines to law enforcing personnel;

(k) Tradecrafts like observation, portrait building, crowd control, surveillance, collection of criminal intelligence, interrogation/ police questioning, search and seizure;

(l) Application of computers and modern gadgets;

(m) Use of wireless and other communication channels;

(n) First Aid/Lego-Medical jurisprudence;

(o) Cyber crimes, Economic offences;

(p) Bombs, Explosives, Explosive devices, Remote control mechanisms;

(q) Community/Pro-active policing etc are Police ethics and police public relations and approach to media;

(r) Personal protection schemes and threat assessment.

Mere change in the training modules/ curriculum will not help to improve the quality of training. There is urgent need to change the present methodology of training which now focuses more on the conceptualization of knowledge and ideas than giving them practical orientation for the real benefit of trainees. Instead of functioning as Alma -centers imparting knowledge to trainees on a wide range of subjects, the endeavor of police training institutions should be to familiarize trainees as how their knowledge could be applied to the tasks that they have to perform on the ground. Class room lectures and discussions should be accompanied by a number of role-play scenarios. But such exercises should not fall to the level of mock drills undertaken by the trainees within the four walls of the institution. Instead they should be performed by the trainees in the actual field with due seriousness. Significantly, some premier Police training Institutions like National Police Academy, Hyderabad and Training Establishments in certain States like Punjab, Delhi etc have taken initiative to streamline the training on the above lines. For example, NPA has recently introduced the scheme of IPS Probationers participating in actual field exercise in the jungles of Sathyamangalam (Veerappan fame) or in the citadels of LWE elements in Andhra Pradesh, along with 'Grey-hounds' personnel. Earlier, Magasasay laureate Kiran Bedi in her capacity as Joint Commissioner (Training), Delhi Police, introduced such practical modules in which trainee Sub Inspectors of Delhi Police were assigned the task of completing investigations into 100 simulated cases in their two years stint in the police training school. The aim of this scheme was to orient them to 'Metropolitan Policing'; make them conversant with the critical areas of policing such as maintaining case diaries and labeling forensic samples etc.

Periodic review of training on the basis of proper evaluation is essential for the improvement in the training system. The Gore Committee in their report emphasized this aspect as; "in order to ensure that trainees are developing properly, the system of evaluation which can serve as the basis of further improvement in teaching as well as training should be introduced. It should be continuous and comprehensive enough to cover both the academic and non-academic areas and related to the objectives of training programs". Unfortunately, in most of the institutions, there is no proper evaluation system. The institutions which undertake such exercise fail to assess trainees frank views to the training programs by adopting any well laid out scheme. Instead their main endeavor is to project the 'everything is fine attitude'. Such statistics-oriented fake and artificial evaluation schemes seldom serve any purpose to re-orient or improve the training programs. More over the present scheme of in-house evaluation of training by the training institutions will not help to make any objective assessment as how the training programs equip the personnel to effectively perform their tasks in the field?

The most important reason for the present unhappy state of affairs in respect of police training is the attitude of the political Executive and police leadership towards the very concept of training. Ironically, Police training is coming palpably very low down in the priority of Government approach, whereas the police organization underrates its values and significance, as compared to other priorities of the force. Thus in many States, Police training institutions are ill-equipped in terms of infrastructure and other amenities; most are also handicapped due to the poor level of Human resources. In fact, Gore Committee had gone into these aspects and made specific recommendations to improve the resources and the quality of Trainers. For example, the Committee recommended suitable incentives including rent-free accommodation, special pay, and recognition in the form of accelerated promotions or choice postings to the trainers with a view to attracting the best human resources to the training schools. However, majority of the States have not seriously taken these recommendations, but made paltry incentives for the Faculty and other staff of these institutions. Thus, very few professionally competent and experienced personnel join such institutions. Very often, posting in Training institutions is viewed as punishment. Those unwilling personnel who join these institutions under compulsion hardly take any interest in the training curriculum or the personality development of the trainees. The more frustrated and disenchanted among them try to subvert the minds of the trainees by spreading distorted or colored version regarding the functioning of the institution or police leaders who head the force. In fact, the sad plight of the majority of Training institutions can be attributed to the steady decline on the quality and caliber of the trainers. Unless conscientious, experienced and highly committed officers are inducted into the faculty of these institutions, the present scenario would be continued without any perceptible change or improvement in police training.

Another equally important area for the proper development of subordinates is the in-service or refresher courses which are basically aimed at providing the personnel with sufficient inputs about the changes that have occurred in their sphere of activity and thus to keep them abreast of the latest happenings. Unfortunately, many of these courses are designed on bureaucratic style for statistics sake to justify the existence and huge administrative and other expenses of the training establishments. The situation is not different in respect of Central training establishments which occasionally organize such in-service courses for the State police forces. These courses are designed neither to improve the professionalism and skills of the personnel in the light of the new challenges and threats in the policing front nor to give new practical insight on the ground level issues of policing. On the contrary, the professionally incompetent Faculty members of such institutions teach them obsolete theories and concepts on tradecraft and intelligence or National security issues which have no relevance to grass roots level policing or the contemporary law and order scenario in their States. In fact, many Special in-service courses conducted by Central Training institutions run by CBI, IB, ITBP, NSG etc for State police personnel could not create adequate response because of the nature of modules, methodology of training, language problem etc Interestingly, many State police forces show reservations to nominate the personnel to such wasteful exercises on the plea of financial crunch or inadequate manpower, whereas the majority of personnel who get nomination utilize the exercise as a pleasure trip to the location of the institution, sometimes with their better-halves and kids!. The establishment of Regional Training Centers (RTC) at the instance of the Centre and directly under the control of Intelligence Bureau (IB) to impart special training to police personnel of the States having almost the same nature of law and order problems or graver issues of internal security could not help to change the scenario. Ironically, these Centers (RTC) have become a safe haven for a set of age old retired hands of IB, hand-picked by their bosses for their sycophancy and incompetence! These timid, senile faculty imparting lessons on age-old concepts and theories on security and intelligence fail to create any new insights or practical skills to police personnel attending such courses. On the contrary, such ventures expose the short-sightedness of the Political Executive and police-security hierarchy and reconfirm the truth that they are not at all sincere in building up professionally superior force through effective training schemes/mechanisms.

However, the importance of in-service or refresher courses, for the development of the subordinates cannot be undermined especially in the light of the ever changing law and order and internal security scenario in the country. But the tragedy is that the Political Executive/Governments are less concerned on such matters particularly in formulating long term sound strategies for police training and development of human resources. They leave everything to the whims and fancies of a handful of serving or retired higher echelons of police/security organizations, having their own narrow vested interests. The implementation of their recommendations/proposals which on many occasions are utopian or far away from ground level realities seldom make any positive contributions in enriching the professionalism or competence of the force or proper development of the human resources. Now, time has come for real introspection, as how the training of police personnel at various levels should be restructured and re-modulated so that the police organization can effectively meet the new challenges in the law and order front. A Committee on the lines of Gore Committee of 1971, comprising police leaders of proven integrity, sociologists/ educationalists, intellectuals, Management and HR professionals, cyber-experts etc should be formed to review police training curriculum and to make recommendations to improve various aspects of police training and in service courses/personality development mechanisms. The States can initiate their own mechanisms to strengthen their training strategies instead of looking upon the Central or Regional Training Establishments. The reality that almost all State Police forces have dozens of outstanding police leaders excelled in the most difficult and challenging policing tasks with ground level practical knowledge and skills along with well structured Training institutions should not be forgotten while such initiatives are being worked out. With the Modernization of Police Programs (MPP) majority of the State police forces have drastically improved the infrastructure and facilities of these Training institutions. The only thing is that the Political Executive should show the wisdom to properly utilize these institutions with competent Faculty under the command of a couple of police leaders of the State with proven excellence. The Training institutions should design several short term courses for specific purposes so that every personnel spend fifteen days or one month in the institution every three years after fifteen years of continuous service. There should be special courses in order to equip the personnel with the necessary talent or professional skills to meet the new challenges in their respective areas of operation.

Initial induction training or the subsequent in-service courses alone are not sufficient for maintaining high standard of professionalism by police. There should be supporting environment built in the work culture of the force. The police leaders particularly of and above the rank of Superintendent of Police (SP) have to play a crucial role in this connection. The real challenge before the police leadership is as how should they motivate the officers and men under their command to heights of great success, valor and dedication? The first and foremost is the proper understanding of the psychology of the personnel. The complex psychological factors involving policing in diverse social conditions and social imperatives of a policeman's life require dexterous handling to promote morale and high motivation. This has become more applicable in the case of new breed of police personnel who are eager to demonstrate their efficiency, initiative, intrinsic knowledge and innovative ideas. Such personnel can be better motivated and developed by factors like achievement, recognition, satisfaction in work, personal advancement and growth etc. For working out suitable strategies, drastic revision in existing norms of discipline, command and control, promotion criteria etc is highly essential. Instead of regimentation and highly centralized functioning, police leaders should encourage flexibility in the organization so that personnel at various levels can fully exploit their talents to the optimum advantage of the organization. The subordinates should be involved in the decision-making process, though the power of taking final decision would vest with the leader. Time and again it has been proved that subordinates having best experience, ingenuity and enterprise have proved to be more successful in achieving specific results while working under the able leadership and command of senior police officers.

In motivating the subordinates, the police leaders should imbibe better qualities of manpower management, personal integrity and professionalism. In many cases, the present trend is to treat the grain and chaff in the force on par in matters of duties, promotions, rewards or medals or other financial and non-financial incentives. Unfortunately, on many occasions, the decayed and degenerated chaff get preponderance over solid glittering grains! Personnel known for corrupt practices, inefficiency, disobedience, lack of professional skills or leadership qualities, in the absence of any objective assessment of their performance appraisal come up in the ladder and occupy sensitive positions in the hierarchy of the organization. On many occasions, caste-communal considerations and sycophancy play a crucial role in such unhealthy practices in the force. Such police leaders deviate from the path of impartiality and involve in controversial organizational decisions. Thus, personnel who have never done any outstanding work or successfully investigated any important case, but survive by mere sycophancy and lip-service would be recommended for Police Medals for meritorious and distinguished service, whereas actual performers are sidelined. Slowly and steadily a process of degeneration sets in motion and competence and professionalism take a nose dive. Unfortunately, a section of the new generation of police leaders who carry the legacy of the police in pre-independent

India and greatly influenced by material gains, come under the influence of such corrupt and incompetent personnel. Such unhealthy trends in the organization which are mainly the fall out of the weakness and aberrations of police leadership erode the faith of subordinates over their superiors and strain officer-men relations.

Just like the partisan behavior and biased decisions, the failure of police leaders to stand by the subordinates for their just and lawful actions during their official duties and the opportunist trend of sacrificing the subordinates in the altar of expediency are the other factors adversely affecting police morale. On many occasions, subordinates are given oral orders which may be ambiguous or unlawful; but are complied by them on good faith. But when any serious controversy erupts, some police leaders conveniently wash off their hands and make the subordinates scapegoats. Their pleas of having carried out the orders of their superiors are never heard. Such actions show the leadership in poor light and lead to the deterioration of the relations between the subordinates and superiors much to the disadvantage of the organization.

The 21st century has opened unprecedented challenges to the police. Undoubtedly the existing resources of the police and the professional knowledge and skills of the personnel are inadequate to successfully combat these challenges. In fact, the knowledge, skills and techniques of the police have hardly kept pace with the exponential growth seen in crimes and organized violence. Thus, the immediate task before the police leadership is to prepare the police to deal with the future challenges for which the training and other human resources development mechanisms assume considerable significance. However, the existing training schemes and in-service courses which in many respects are the continuation of the training curriculum framed by the British over two centuries ago are inadequate to professionalize the police to meet the new threats. Thus there should be radical changes in the training modules, methodology and the functioning of training institutions. The need of the hour is that the State police forces should develop the training institutions as centers of excellence with better infrastructure/facilities and highly competent and professionally efficient faculty members instead of depending on Central/Regional Training Establishments which really lack the expertise to train the police personnel to take up challenging policing tasks at ground level. The State Political Executive should take initiative for such moves that should be supplemented by police leaders with excellent and proven track record in the States. Needless to mention that training is not the only input for the proper development of subordinates in line with the core tasks of the police. Equally important is the conducive and congenial organizational climate and work culture. Basically this task falls on the shoulders of police leaders who should show personal integrity, initiative, impartiality, imagination, drive and leadership qualities in achieving this task. Inevitably, police leaders of the 21st century should not only be successful professionals in law and order front but also dynamic and vibrant HR mangers.

10

Human Rights and Policing Issues in India

The very concept of Human Rights derives from the 'dignity and worth of human person'. Thus, the United Nations and other international organizations through a number of Covenants and Declarations have broadened the scope of human rights so as to protect the dignity and worth of human person in the fast changing world. Three major generations of rights now constitute the wide spectrum of human rights. The first generation of civil and political rights covers individual rights such as right to life, security, freedom of movement, right to association, right to conscience and freedom of religion and the right to participate in the political decision making. The economic, social and cultural rights which include health care, education, food security, housing, employment with equal pay for equal work, freedom of ethnic groups and minorities to maintain their cultural identity etc constitute the second generation of human rights. The third generation or the collective/solidarity rights include issues or questions of global nature such as arms-race, disarmament, protection of environment, development and security etc.

The mere conceptualization or crystallization of human rights is not a guarantee for the protection of these rights. Thus, R.H. Dworkin, a human rights expert of early 1970s rightly observed that; "the concept of human rights presupposes that the States have duty to advance or protect these basic rights". Many countries initiated efforts to enforce these rights by ratifying UN Covenants and Declarations without jeopardizing national interests. As a founder member of the UN and a party to the Universal Declaration Human Rights (UNDHR) in 1948, India always upheld the concept of human rights. The Fundamental Rights guaranteed under Part-III of the constitution substantially cover wide range of rights enshrined in the UNDHR and the two UN Covenants namely, International Covenant on Civil & Political Rights (ICCPR) and International Covenant on Social, Economic &Cultural Rights (ICSECR). Side by side, a number of social legislations which were enacted during the last six decades coupled with a plethora of judicial pronouncements by the Apex Court had widened the horizons of human rights in India. These conceptual traits have found expression in the definition of human rights as incorporated in the Protection of Human Rights Act, 1993; the first major legislation in India in the direction of the protection of human rights. As per the Act, "human rights are the rights relating to liberty, equality and dignity of the individual guaranteed by the Indian Constitution and embodied in the fundamental rights and international covenants".

The law enforcing agencies, designed to safeguard the safety, security, dignity and liberty of human beings have pivotal role in the protection of human rights. The UN and various other international organizations have unequivocally upheld this truth through various covenants. For example, a Resolution adopted by the General Assembly of UN Security Council, as early as in 1975 underlined that; "the obligation of the police force created by law is to maintain and protect human rights; in the principles of which police officers should receive proper education and training". Similarly a Committee of experts set up by the Council of Europe for the Promotion of Information and Education in the filed of human rights in the early1990s identified police of the member States as the most important and primary target for the attainment of the objectives and laid emphasis on the inclusion of human rights modules in the police training curriculum. The Supreme

Court in a number of judicial pronouncements highlighted the role of police as the protector of human rights. In Kishor Singh v/s State of Rajasthan (AIR 1981 SC25), the Apex Court made significant observation that the government should take necessary steps to educate police so as to inculcate the respect for human person. In short, Police is one of the major instruments by which the State seeks to meet the obligation of protecting some of the fundamental rights of the citizens-right to life, liberty, security of persons, right for fair trial, equal protection of law etc. In fact, effective order maintenance and enforcement of rule of law by an impartial and professionally competent police force would not only help to safeguard the political and civil rights of the people, but also their social, economic and cultural rights. On the other hand thoughtless, biased and illegal policing will lead to the suppression of these rights. Thus, one often witnesses the paradox that human rights are protected by the constitution and law and yet are often at risk, because of its non-implementation or mal-implementation by various institutions including police.

Perhaps it is this paradox that leads to the steep increase in human rights violations in India as manifest by the Annual reports of the National Human Rights Commission (NHRC). In fact, more than 80% of the complaints/violations arose out of the omissions or commissions of the police or other security agencies in their duties/tasks. This evokes certain pertinent questions. What are the major causative factors for the increasing violations of human rights by police? What should be done to make Indian police more human rights friendly?

A number of authentic studies on these aspects were undertaken by social and human rights activists. Maurice Punch, in his detailed study on police functioning captioned "Conduct Unbecoming" highlighted that the cause of police deviance are deep-rooted. It is the result of various factors such as 'ambiguous legislations, vulnerability to legal sanctions, occupational culture and the pressure to produce quick results'. Punch's findings are truly applicable to Police in India which operate in highly difficult situation The Amnesty International in its report on police in India had highlighted some of these factors such as; 'poor service conditions of police personnel, political interference in police work, over-loading of police personnel in crime-detection works, inadequate police training, lack of interest in the application of science and technology in police work, poor resources and public pressure to detect cases etc'. Though the successive governments had taken a number of steps to modernize the force by improving their service conditions and introducing welfare programs, the colonial legacy continue to dominate the organization as well as its style of functioning.

The vestiges of colonial sub-culture of 'total subservience to the authority' encourage servility to those in power and induce them not to say 'no' to the superiors or political masters regardless of the irregularity of orders or directions. The much elated' steel-frame' of Indian Civil Service has become a myth to large majority of police personnel , both at leadership and cutting edge levels. These traits in Indian police, according to the words of Ved Marwah, the former Commissioner of Police, Delhi and Ex-Governor of Manipur, have encouraged" cynicism in their conduct and character". The sub-culture allows the handling of law violations by lawless methods and encourages the trampling of basic human rights. This sub-culture becomes more vocal during emergency situations when police get draconian powers. The Shah Commission which was appointed to enquire into the excesses during the National Emergency (1975-77) highlighted this aspect as; "police was used and allowed themselves to be used for purposes some of which were to say the least questionable. Some police officers behaved as though they were not accountable at all to any public authority. The decision to arrest and release certain persons were entirely on political considerations that were intended to be favorable for the ruling party. Employing the police to the advantage of any political party is a sure source of subverting the rule of law". There is no exaggeration that such attitude and approach of police are not uncommon even during normal times when majority of police personnel are keen to grease their political masters by brutally violating the canons of rule of law.

The outdated legislations, rules and procedures and regimented organizational structure give enough scope for the personnel to deviate from the rule of law while enforcing law and order. The Police Act of 1861 which the British had actually drafted to constitute a civil force in order to safeguard their colonial interests in India by suppressing the freedom struggle continues to govern the structure and functioning of police in the present millennium. The Indian police system is not accountable to the people; it is not a service; it is a force and finally it is one of the most unfortunate British legacies that the democratic India had retained and strengthened with all catapult of a colonial or neo-colonial force. This archaic Act with colonial fervor is the sure source for human rights violations. The damage caused by this legislation to the Indian polity and system can be well assessed when we learn that in advanced countries like USA, UK and France, all the major legislations which govern the affairs of the people are periodically reviewed in order to ensure their social acceptance and legitimacy. This approach of legislation-making popularly know as 'sunset principle' underlines that every rule or law should have of limited life of three to five years, at the end of which they have to be reviewed before they are revalidated or rescinded. Another equally important concept is 'interactive- rule making" which stipulates that new rules should not be enacted without interacting with the users. We never follow such worthy concepts but blindly practice centuries old laws and regulations with immunity. Thus, ironically police in India is still governed by an alien act of 150 years old!

The interdependence of political authority and police creates a situation of 'quid-pro-quo' by which the political masters are unable to question human rights violations by police when quick and decisive results are demanded of police and no questions regarding the means are raised. 'When ends become important and means are not questioned, the human rights become the first causality'. Given the complex nature of crimes, mounting threat of terror and extremism in more and more parts of the country endangering the safety and security of citizens and the general failure of criminal justice system, more and more people, in their anxiety, quite often approve police excesses and human rights violations on the hope that such measures would restore peace and tranquility in the society. Very often, influenced by political or religious dogmas or convictions, they blindly endorse archaic concepts like 'eye for eye and tooth for tooth' and support inhuman practices by police against offenders. Ironically, political masters and their loyalist police leaders through illegal collusion exploit such misconceived notions to their advantage. The post Godhra developments in Gujarat are clear example in this regard. A series of illegalities such as fake encounters, custodial violence, biased investigation/ suppression of evidence, illegal arrest and detention, influencing of prosecution etc committed by police in Gujarat with political patronage as manifest in Shorabuddhin-Kausubi, Ishrat Jehan, Best Bakery and other cases, were approved by large sections of the people who were under the impression that the State and its political masters are under terror threat. Such social sanction and political patronage embolden the police to resort to extra legal means while enforcing law and order.

The human rights scenario further worsens due to the dominating behavior and 'psyche' of section of police personnel who are wedded to 'third-degree methods' and other illegal means in policing. The irony is that still there is a generation of police personnel who believe that the good 'old danda' is the ideal means for the successful investigation of crimes. Not only that they negate and discourage the modern concept of police investigations or application of scientific aids in investigation works, but also tries to influence the style of functioning of the new generation of police personnel. Even two Divisional Commissioners who deposed before Uttar Pradesh Police Commission as early as in 1971, strongly justified use of 'third- degree' methods holding that; dishonest steps of investigations, recovery, third degree method, creation of false evidences are social requirements of India. There is ample justification by police to use third degree methods with criminals as the latter were using it against the society. Much water had flown through Ganges, but the general psyche of overwhelming majority of police personnel are akin to that of these two Deputy Commissioners. In fact, the social requirements, the complexities in the collection of evidence under various penal laws, lapses in criminal justice system leading to large number of acquittals etc force the personnel to make compromises with the rules and procedures while undertaking law enforcement tasks. There is also lurching fear among section of personnel especially at middle level that once human rights dictates and directions enter into policing, their sweeping powers and authority would be undermined and "crisis policing" would be impossible.

Added to this are the plethora of organizational and personnel issues that influence their psyche and create negative 'imprints' leading to violation of human rights during policing. Within the organization, there are issues like pressure of work; lack of career prospects, authoritarian style of functioning of section of police leaders and partisan behavior etc that breed frustration and discontentment among the personnel. Similarly external factors such as growing criticism from media, political intervention, unending stream of Public Interest Litigations (PIL) and Court strictures/verdicts on police omissions and commissions make the personnel disgruntled paving the way for negative influences. Above all, police work itself is stressful and at times unbelievably thankless. A study conducted by the National Productivity Council a few years ago showed that in many police stations, a police man has to work almost 16 hours a day and seven days a week. The recuperation time is short and facilities for healthy recreation are non-existent. In such circumstances, a large number of personnel coarsen and turn cynical. The stress and strain and surrounding circumstances develop as ideal breeding ground for the violation of human rights during day to day policing. Ironically, there is no effective mechanism or platform in the police to identify such issues and work out remedial measures. Though Police Associations or Staff Councils were floated in many States, they are either inactive or operate as appendages of political parties/police hierarchy.

Let us examine the nature and common areas of human rights violation by police. In fact, there can hardly be any area of police functions whose values and principles that constitute the core and contents of human rights, can be deemed as insignificant. However, it is in 'pre-trial' areas, human rights volitions appear glaring and cause immense concern in the minds of right-thinking citizens. One such common area is the non-registration of FIRs/cases by police which is violation of section 154 Cr Pc. A large number of complaints received by National Human Rights Commission (NHRC) pertained to the non-registration of cognizable offences by police. The police adopt various tactics for committing such illegalities. Those includes:

(a) creation of an impression to the complainant that his or her complaint has been registered;

(b) registration of cognizable offence as non cognizable to avoid investigation;

(c) non-registration on the pretext of jurisdictional controversy; and;

(d) indirect intimidation coercion of the complainant.

The reason for non-registration of complaints can be mainly traced to political intervention or the undue influence exercised by the accused over the police through corrupt means. By non-registration of FIRs, police indirectly helps the proliferation of crimes. The offenders against whom cases are not registered get emboldened to carry on their criminal depredations with immunity.

The functional aberrations of police are another major area of violation of human rights. The fabrication of evidence by arranging fake witnesses is a common practice in police. In many States, there are any numbers of 'police witnesses' at the instance of police or investigation officers in particular. Too much obsession with .direct oral evidence and number of witnesses prompt police to pad up evidence with the help of false witnesses. What is actually required in professional and successful investigation is the right blend of scientific and oral evidence. However there are only a microscopic section of police personnel who follow such scientific methods / aids in the investigation of cases. Instead, majority of the investigators summon the witnesses to police stations and record their statements under intimidation or duress. Male persons below fifteen years or women, who otherwise are prohibited to be summoned to the police stations for recording witness statements under section 164 Cr.Pc, are not spared.

The police powers of arrest are grossly misused. The National Police Commission observed that; "nearly sixty percent of the arrests were unnecessary and as such unjustified". The Commission had also estimated that about 43 % of the expenditure in the concerned jails was over such persons who in the ultimate analysis need not have been arrested at all". The situation is now graver considering the fact that the arrest and detention of persons on the grounds of suspected linkages with terrorists or extremists has substantially increased after the spread of terrorism, militancy and Left Wing Extremism in more and more areas of the country. Ironically, majority of such victims are human/ civil rights activists. Through this process of 'liberal arrests", the police very often deny human rights to the accused and violate the various rights and privileges of the arrested persons as enshrined in the constitution and various International covenants ratified by the government. Some of these provisions are as follows:

(a) Article 22(1) & Section50 (1) Cr Pc- Right against Arbitrary arrest/right to be informed of the grounds of arrest.

(b) Article 22 (1) & Section 303 Cr Pc- Right to Counsel for the accused.

(c) Article 39A - Right to legal aid

(d) Section 56 & 76 Cr Pc- Right to be produced before a Magistrate within 24 hours of arrest.

(e) Section 50, 55 & 75 Cr Pc-Right to be informed of the ground of arrest at the earliest.

(f) Section 56 & 57 Cr Pc-Right against arbitrary and illegal detention.

(g) Section 54 Cr Pc-Right to have medically examined.

(h) Section 436, 437, 438 & 50(2) & 167 Cr Pc-Right to be released on bail on arrest.

(i) Section 51 Cr Pc-Decency while arresting female.

(j) Section 83 IPC & The Probation of Preventing incarceration of Offenders Act, 1956 Juvenile young offenders.

Apart from the above provisions, the Apex Court while disposing PIL by D.K. Basu, the Executive Chairman of Legal Aid Services, West Bengal laid down important guidelines to be followed by police in all cases of arrest and detention. These guidelines included:

(a) Proper recording of the particulars of the police personnel who arrests/interrogates the person.

(b) Preparation of Arrest memo with time and date of arrest, attested by witness and countersigned by the arrestee.

(c) Intimation of arrest to a person known to the arrestee as soon as possible.

(d) Notification of arrest through legal aid organization within 8-10 hours after the arrest.

(e) Informing the arrestee about his right to have someone informed of his arrest.

(f) Proper entry in the diary of the police station of detention with the details like the person informed and the name and particulars of police officials in whose custody the arrestee is.

(g) Medical examination of the arrestee and proper recording of grievous and minor injuries in his body

(h) Forwarding copies of all documents of arrest to Ilaqua Magistrate.

But the tragedy is that the police nakedly violate the Supreme Court's norms and keep the arrested persons in illegal custody till they are produced before the Magistrate. Such illegalities are more in the case of persons arrested for their suspected involvement in terrorist or extremist activities. Ironically, the Judiciary also adopts a lenient view on such matters and come to the rescue of police when such illegal arrest and detention are challenged before the Courts. Another serious matter of concern is the illegal collusion of police hierarchy with Political Executive in some States in order to implement their hidden agenda and to win over public support. In such illegal operations, innocent persons are clandestinely arrested and detained and some times executed in 'fake encounters' branding them as dreaded terrorists or extremists. Such fake exercises which are clear and brutal violations of human rights, on one hand are meant to bolster the public image of controversial political leaders whereas on the other hand are part of the professional ambitions and malpractices by a set of police leaders. Unfortunately, such political set up or the police leaders collaborating with them seldom pay any heed to the guidelines issued by the Apex Court in respect of the modalities to be followed by the police in respect of all 'encounter-killings' in the country. Many of these cold blooded killings are buried under the carpet in the name of fighting terrorism/extremism in the country. A series of such cases that have now come up from Gujarat are typical examples of the illegal nexus between the political executive and police in which the biggest causalities are the rule of law/ due process of law; democratic ethos, human freedom & life and the human rights,. A civilized world definitely would be ashamed of such dastardly acts perpetrated by law enforcers.

All types of custodial violence need to be condemned in the strongest words. The Supreme Court had rightly observed that; "custodial violence is one of the worst crimes in any civilized society governed by rule of law". Any form of Torture or cruel inhuman or degrading treatment of persons would fall within the ambit of Article 21 (Rights to life and property) of the Constitution, whether it occurs during investigation, interrogation or otherwise. Sections 330&331 of IPC prohibit harassment or ill-treatment of the accused during investigation, whereas Section 49 of the Cr. Pc underlines that accused should not be subjected to unnecessary restraint. The Article 5 of the UN Declaration of Human Rights, 1948 spells out that; "no one shall be subjected to torture or cruel inhuman punishment" and the same spirit can be seen in Article 10 of International Covenant on Civil & Political Rights1996 as; "all persons deprived of their liberty shall be treated with respect for individual dignity of human person". The UN General Assembly as early as in December1975 adopted a similar Declaration on 'Protection of all Persons from being subjected to Torture or other Cruel, Inhuman or Degrading Treatment or Punishment' in which torture had been defined as" offence against humanity". The General Assembly adopted a similar Resolution in 1975 which contained a Code of conduct for Law Enforcement Officers. Article 7 of the Resolution lays down that, "in the performance of their duties, law enforcement officers shall protect and respect human dignity and uphold human rights of all persons". In India, based on the recommendations of the Conference of Director General and Inspectors General of Police the Union Home Ministry framed a Code of conduct for the police officers which enshrines that police officers should respect and uphold the rights of citizens as guaranteed in the constitution. In spite of UN guidelines, International Covenants & Declarations, Constitutional and legal safeguards and series of Executive directions, custodial violence is on increase in India. This had prompted NHRC to recommend for the compulsory judicial enquiry in all lock up deaths and the Law Commission to make a suggestion that compulsory prosecution proceedings should be launched against all those responsible for custodial deaths. The Apex Court had whittled down the 'doctrine of sovereign immunity' making the police personnel personally responsible for paying compensation to the victims of custodial offences.

There are other areas of human rights violations during police investigations. For example, surveillance of persons of suspicious grounds which amounts to denial of privacy is violation of Article19 of the constitution. Similarly, the extensive monitoring of telephone or other channels of communications of citizens is another area of infringement on privacy and violation of human rights. The illegal search of premises, denial of the right of female accused during searches (Section 100(3) of Cr. Pc), implicating persons in false cases or under wrong provisions of law or the denial of Right against Double Jeopardy etc are other major areas of human rights violations by police.

In the sphere of public order maintenance, violation of human rights by police is more rampant and serious. In a developing country like India, the widening gap between the haves and haven't coupled with the rising expectations and aspirations of the masses kindled by the enunciated constitutional ideas and the ground level realities opened a flood gate of heightened tensions and conflicts leading to organized struggles and movements The disparities of development and socio-economic issues have compounded the situation. All these factors pave the way for agitations and disturbances of a wide variety. The maintenance of public order is the sole duty of police. Non-adherence to various rules and procedures, misuse or improper use of police discretion and authority in such situations etc lead to human rights violations especially when police has to deal with violent mob, frenzied caste-communal groups, industrial workers, student agitations etc. Some of the common natures of violations are:

(a) Using force blindly against the individual members or collectively against an assembly while dealing with unlawful assemblies. In fact, the powers given to the police to regulate and control the mob are to be used strictly to achieve the objectives mentioned in Article 19(3). One major guideline to be followed by police is that the fundamental rights as guaranteed by the Constitution should not be interfered with. It should be ensured that the personnel should use their discretion without making any compromise with the established procedures and the rule of law.

(b) Partisan or biased behavior while dealing with communal riots, or caste conflicts or delayed police action causing the death of innocent civilians and destruction of properties and adversely affecting the impartial image of the police. A typical example was the post-Godhra carnage in Gujarat in which police totally failed to protect the lives and properties of sections of people in the State. Similar organized violence and attack against Christians in Orissa also exposed the weakness of police organization in maintaining their integrity and impartial image.

The success or failure of many legislations meant to safeguard the social, economic, political and cultural interest/ development of weaker and underprivileged sections like Dalits, Adivasis, women, children and unorganized workers depends on the professionalism, unbiased behavior and commitment of police. Unfortunately, these sections of the society especially in backward areas continue to be the worst victims of human rights violations. Untouchability, discrimination of SC/ST, child and bonded labor, trafficking in women/prostitution, rape/molestation, archaic or inhuman practice like Sati or 'honor killing' of young girls, denial of minimum wages and atrocities against Dalits/Tribals continue in many States with police remaining as passive spectators. This speaks of the hard reality that Constitutional/legal safeguards or promises of Political Executive can never accelerate social change or safeguard the interests of weaker sections, unless there are effective mechanisms or instruments for the strict implementation of rules and regulations and the decisions of the Political executive. No doubt, police is such a vital instrument of the State empowered to enforce such legislations intertwined with the concept of human rights. But when the police collude with caste-communal forces or the underworld/mafia (who are the kingpins in organized crimes like prostitution, child/bonded labor) the biggest causality is not only the human rights but also the very right of individuals to live in society.

Apart from the major areas of policing, all facets of police work are interlinked with the very concept of human rights. The illegal or improper police conduct and behavior can seriously imperil the human rights. The Police Act of 1861, the substantive and procedural penal laws such as IPC and Cr.Pc together with Indian Evidence Act have comprehensively presided the way in which the police will have to fulfill their duties, commitments and meet their tasks with universal point of view. The Code of Conduct of Law Enforcement Officials has been well accepted by the comity of nations. Some of the common conduct or aberrations of police where human rights violations are indeed real and immediate relief may not be certain are:

(a) Minimization of the seriousness or enormity of the offence.
(b) Delay in investigation.
(c) Biased or perverse or poor investigation.
(d) Supporting unjustifiably the counter-parties in cases.
(e) Delay in execution process to harass the complainant.
(f) Exerting pressure on prosecution witnesses.
(g) Making perverse enquiries into the complaints.
(h) Favoritism while granting various licenses.
(i) Making mischievous entries or false records.

Besides, there are known categories of misconduct or misbehavior that tantamount to human rights violations such as:

(a) Rude and discourteous conduct.
(b) Refusal to entertain complaints.
(c) Overbearing attitude.
(d) Beating or other acts of harassment.

A pertinent question which is widely discussed and debated is whether the 'extra-legal methods' leading to naked human rights violations are effective or successful in criminal investigations or in controlling troubled situations? The answer is definitely 'no'. The high-handedness of police may create a temporary lull in the crime scene, but in the world of organized crimes, the illegalities or human rights violations have either no impact or have just opposite impact. Another reason as why such practices cannot put an end to crimes is that the criminals or their sympathizers who become the victims of police excesses, try to take revenge over the perpetrators of violations and embarrass the establishment. This is how resistance grows. This was what happened in Vietnam in 1960s and 1970s when mass resistance was built up by the natives after suffering brutal atrocities at the instance of colonial regime and their security forces. Another impact of human rights violations is the loss of fear and respect for the authority of the State. A State or political establishment devoid of moral authority cannot survive long. Ironically, organized human rights violations perpetrated by police or security agencies, on many occasion are in pursuance of a political or personal agenda, camouflaged under an appealing theme of fighting a national or social menace. In such an atmosphere of violence and tension, personnel from enforcement agencies and desperate elements spearheading the movements may take advantage of the situation and indulge in cold-blooded killings, rape and molestation of women, looting and extortion. Moreover, committing injustice in the name of justice cannot be called a service for the cause of justice. It can only be called as 'jungle justice' whom no civilized society can consciously promote.

On ultimate analysis, the law enforcing agencies in democratic countries should strongly stick to the rule of law and 'due process' of law, upholding human rights In the backdrop of increasing incidents of 'fake encounters' and custodial violence there is urgent need of transforming Indian police human rights friendly, for which a number of structural, organizational and legislative initiatives have to be taken. The first and foremost task is the enactment of a new police Act to replace the archaic act of 1861. The new act should redefine the role of police and categorically affirm that the duties of police should cover proper protection and safeguarding of the rights of the people. A draft police act prepared by the National Police Commission in 1977 giving more emphasis to make the police more 'service-oriented and humane, free from extraneous influences and yet accountable to the people' was a major step in this direction. Though many of the recommendations of NPC had become out of context or obsolete because of the sweeping changes in the law and order front, the implementation of some relevant recommendations would help the police to remain neutral and non-political with better professionalism. The implementation of certain recommendations such as formation of State Security Commission, fixed tenure for Police Chiefs and insulation of the investigation wing from any sort of political or extraneous influences etc would help the police to overcome many of its human rights issues. The attitude of the police masters matters much. If the top- brass in the organization does not show any leniency towards the violators of human rights and does not allow them to go scoot free, in the name of police image and morale, a strong message would go down the lines that deterrent action be initiated against the violators of human rights. The heart of the matter is that if the senior echelons of the force sincerely desire to curb illegalities such as human rights violations among subordinate personnel, they can definitely enforce the same through carrot and stick metnods especially in view of the regimentation in the force.

But the disturbing trend on the functioning of police in the country is the liberal use of "informal system" by which every Tom, Dick and Harry in the society dictate terms or issue instructions directly to police functionaries at various levels circumventing hierarchy, departmental norms and statutory and delegated powers of police. Ironically, many of these orders or instructions are apparently illegal or unethical relating to core areas of policing such as maintenance of law and order, criminal investigations and prosecutions. The overwhelming majority of police personnel especially at higher level, who have their own axe to grind with the patronage of such extraneous forces obediently concede such 'informal orders' and make the entire process of law enforcement a mockery by violating the basic canons of rule of law and human/civil rights. In order to curb such unhealthy tendencies in the organization, the police leadership should truly uphold the code of conduct for law enforcement officers and adopt an unbiased approach on all issues of human rights and promptly hold impartial investigations into all instances of custodial violence and torture and bring the perpetrators to justice. Through such measures, the police leadership can send a clear message to the entire force that custodial violence of any type will not be tolerated in the organization. But a genuine question arises what should be done when the fence itself eats the crops? Here comes the role of vigilante public and Judiciary. The Apex Court in State v/s Ramanandeo Yadav (AIR 1985SC416) made an observation that burden of proof should be shifted to police functionaries against whom human rights violation are made. However the Apex Court directions and other judicial pronouncements on issues of custodial violence and human rights have lost much of their teeth in view of the enactment of a number of Special legislations like TADA, POTA etc which give draconian powers to police and other security agencies to curtail the various provisions of rule of law and due process of law. A re-look on such legislations is the need of the hour especially in the light of the exposure of a number of cases of misuse of such Acts.

Reforms and structural changes are imperative to transform the Indian police more human rights- friendly. Greater emphasis should be laid down on the training of personnel especially those operating against terrorists and extremists under the ambit of Special laws such as Armed Forces Special Powers Act, Disturbed Areas Act etc. The personnel operating in such areas under considerable stress and strain should shun their 'psyche' that they are operating as if in an alien territory and are free to do anything dastardly like killing the civil population on slightest provocation or raping/molesting the innocent women and girls there. For changing their 'psyche' they should be imparted special Training schemes or in-service courses that will make them more humane and human rights friendly. More over, the general curriculum for all categories of police personnel should be re-oriented in such a way that the new generation of police personnel would become more sensitive to human/ civil rights and social justice especially those of women, children and weaker sections. Simultaneously, the personnel should be kept abreast of various Constitutional and Legal safeguards on human rights as well as the International Covenants and Declarations upholding these rights. The more they learn and convince about these rights, the better be their approach while dealing with these rights. The heart of the matter is that any number of Statutes, Covenants or declarations on human rights would not make police human rights friendly unless there is a real change of heart on the attitude of personnel. This reality prompted the learned Judge Hand to rightly comment "Liberty lives in the heart of men and women. When it dies there, no Constitution, no Law, no Court never do much to help it. When it lies there, it needs no Constitution, no Law, and no Court to save it". Perhaps, such beautiful concept motivated London Metropolitan Police to declare their motto as "We must be compassionate, courteous and patient dealing without fear or favor or prejudice to the right of others. We should respond to the well sounded criticism with a willingness to change."

11

Myths and Realities of Corruption in Indian Police and Coping Mechanisms to Counter Them

Corruption is a complex problem having its roots and ramifications in society as a whole. The Santhanam Committee Report, 1964 defines corruption as "improper or selfish exercise of power and influence attached to a public office or to a special position one occupies in public life". Infact corruption in one form or other had always existed in the country. During the last one decade several cases of corruption and scandals have come to the public notice due to vigilant media, efforts of public spirited individuals and a pro-active judiciary. The Bofors, HDW Submarine deal, Airbus deal, ABB Loco deal, Jain Hawala Racket, Sugar Scam, Security scam, Urea Scam, Fodder scam in Bihar, Tehelka tapes, Adarsh Housing Society scam, Commonwealth Games scam and last but not the least the mammoth 2 G Spectrum scandal are a few instances. These scams which surfaced were only the tip of the iceberg and we are sure that more and more heads will roll if the details of the black money depositors in Swiss and other foreign Banks are formally released by Government of India. Majority of these scams related to "public expenditure" by the Central and State governments. Equally alarming are the cases of corruption in the collection of public revenue and arrears thereof. The corrupt practices in the realization of direct and indirect taxes, non-recovery of loans from industrialists, money-laundering in the banking sector etc have resulted in the loss of thousands of crore to the national exchequer. Thus Transparency International, the Berlin based NGO has rated India as the 22nd most corrupt country in the world in its year 2010 corruption perception index. Over the years, the tentacles of corruption have spread to the system of governance-civil, political and military. No institution can honestly claim that it is totally free from corruption. Even the shadow of scandals has eclipsed the image of Judiciary when legal luminaries themselves have come out with allegations of corruption and irregularities against the higher echelons of Judiciary. Majority of citizens find corruption practically at every level and every sector of life. One can undoubtedly say that corruption is not a myth but has become a way of life in the country. But mythicising corruption by camouflaging the real from the unreal and exploiting the emotions and psychic energies that were dormant in the collective unconsciousness of the masses has the inherent danger of people forming false or distorted impressions on the image of organizations. The Santhanam Committee had also referred to this trend and observed; "we heard from all sides that corruption in recent years spread even to those levels of administration from which it was conspicuously absent in the past. The general impressions are unfair and exaggerated. But the very fact that such impressions are there, cause damage to the social fabric. In the words of Gunnar Myrdal, it is the "folklore of corruption".

Unlike the other executive wings of the State, the police which have maximum visibility in the society are a pet theme for such folklore. Their omissions and commissions rapidly attract public attention and spread like a wildfire through gossip and heresy. As the police wear the mantle of defensiveness and many of their functions are shrouded in secrecy, there is tendency to mythicise or sensationalize such lapses like corruption. The image of police so created in the minds of people always remains poor and sullied. For example, studies carried out by the Banaras Hindu University in 1972 and Indian Institute of Public Opinion, New Delhi in

1978 on the public image of police revealed a very unattractive image in the minds of people. These studies disclosed that those who had personal experience or some interaction with the police had a better impression on police than those who formed their opinion on heresy without any personal knowledge. Another recent sample survey conducted by 'The Statesman' in Delhi also demonstrated the above trend. Though the main conclusion of the survey was that "police are power drunk, corrupt, immoral without any professional ethics" more than 90% of the respondents denied even having given bribe to any policemen; nor did they ever see a policeman beating an alleged offender. Another research study by UNB Rao, IPS was more revealing in this regard. Out of 2071 respondents (adolescent students from nine different Mega/metropolitan cities of India) who responded to a question" whether they have ever met a policeman and talked to him? 72% replied in negative. The overwhelming majority of these students had negative impressions on the style of functioning and image of police. For example 75% of them spoke ill of police and policing mechanisms;61-71% stated that public are afraid to lodge complaint with police;60-90% held that police are corrupt and 32 to 56% disagreed that police are sympathetic to public (percentage indicated pertains to different questions). The basis for such impressions of young adults was mainly the media (63 to 70%) while 21 to 30% of the respondents stated that they heard about police from others. Significantly only 13% of them confirmed that they have had personal experience and interaction whatsoever with the police. Thus one of the major findings of the study was that the lesser the awareness about police work and police constraints, the greater is the mistaken impressions of students or public about the police.

The reality is that majority of the people especially of the rural areas do not have any personal or specific knowledge on issues like corruption in police. But their impressions on such matters have been crystallized mainly at the instance of media or hearsay. The visual media with their effective network throughout the country plays up such factors detrimental to the image of police. The instances of corruption and other misdemeanors of police personnel and their stories of prosecution and conviction are frequently given prominence by the media. All too frequently facts are overtaken by fiction, built around speculative characters or instances and it becomes difficult to determine where the true stories end and the fiction begins. No doubt public awareness on policing has tremendously risen, but issues like corruption are such hidden areas where facts, fiction, myth, perception, impressions and reality are intricately interwoven. The defaulting policeman becomes a symbol of the entire organization and his misconduct would be used as powerful weapon to tarnish the image of the force. Many people adopt the infamous "guilt by association" technique of Senator McCarthy and smear the police with the failings of a few personnel.

The paramilitary orientation and general regimentation in the organization are the major contributory factors for the galvanization of such impressions on police by the public. There is a general tendency at police hierarchy not to admit the lapses of the personnel. On many occasions, they consciously try to cover up or whitewash these omissions and defend the delinquent police personnel on the pretext of safeguarding the morale and image of the organization. Lord Delvin had rightly observed "it is the general habit of police not to admit the slightest departure from correctness". But, this approach instead of protecting the image of the organization, causes more embarrassment to the force when the media or the detractors of police come out with highly exaggerated, speculative 'stories' on the misdeeds by the personnel. This underscores the need for fostering a more candid, transparent and open door and fulfilling police-public relationship based on mutual respect and understanding of each other's roles and responsibilities.

Police leadership should defeat the efforts to mythicise corruption by adopting sound organizational strategies and innovations; especially attitudinal change of police managers towards the media and the society. They have to develop a realistic approach towards endemic corruption in police which no longer can be buried under the carpet or kept away from the eyes of vigilante public by enforcing the canons of the culture of secrecy or regimentation. In fact corruption in police is not a new phenomenon, but the irony is that the issue has seldom been seized by the organization with a sense of seriousness. The British government appointed Police Commission namely the Second Police Commission (1902-03) that looked into the working of the police observed; "one of the strongest proof the commission had received of the corruption in police is the testimony of responsible parents, teachers and other gentlemen of the difficulty experienced by an young man in accepting one of the direct appointments as Sub-Inspector and Inspector which are sometimes offered. He finds himself a member of corrupt service, he is surrounded by influences that forbid his acting uprightly; the evidence provided is that the canker of corruption affects the force in greater or less degree from Constables to Inspectors".

The First Police Commission of free India (1977-1981) headed by late Dharma Vira also found rampant corruption in police and commented; "in the perception of people, the egregious features of the police are politically oriented partisan performance of duties, partiality, corruption and inefficiency, degrees of which vary from place to place and person to person. What the Police Commission said in 1903 appears more or less equally applicable to the conditions obtaining today". More than three decades had been passed since the submission of the report by the Commission, but not much appears to have been done in combating corruption in police.

As the popular adage goes that "power corrupts and absolute power absolutely" two cognitive features of police namely power and discretion give ample scope for the personnel to indulge in corruption. They enjoy wide powers while discharging the core functions of police namely maintenance of peace and order and prevention and detection of crime and criminal activities. Similarly police discretion is a double edged sword that can be used or misused by the personnel on a mosaic of law and order situations. Though the personnel are bound to exercise these unique features in accordance with the procedures that lay down processes and formalities, those intoxicated with tremendous powers and dominated by selfish motives can misuse them with a view to attaining private gains. Such "deviant behavior" of the personnel appears in different forms in many areas of policing. Basically, these personnel behave rudely and are overbearing towards ordinary citizens who approach police in distress. They refuse to register FIRs of hapless citizens who otherwise should carry a recommendation from political middleman or be prepared to entertain the concerned personnel. Even if FIR is lodged, investigation or the other follow up action as per law would proceed only if the subordinate police functionaries are greased by way of payment of bribe in proportion of the gravity of complaint. Further periodical payments are to be made to ensure that paper work is completed without any lapse. A slip up in the bribe payment schedule would result in immediate dropping of the case from the priority list and inordinate delay in investigations or prosecutions. Influenced by corruption or other extraneous factors, police resort to illegal practices and procedures such as use of 'third degree' methods, fabrication of evidence, false implication of innocent persons in criminal cases, padding or concoction of evidence to buttress or weaken the cases, illegal detention, "burking" of cognizable crimes, delaying arrest of persons and allowing them to avail anticipatory bail thereby avoiding arrest etc. In the case of more serious offences like murder, rape, dowry deaths, accident cases etc, in which the accused are poor or underprivileged, the corrupt personnel exploit them and their relatives monetarily to the maximum extent on the pretext of helping them and bailing them out of trouble. But, ultimately, they land up in jails after trial and conviction. Most of the sensational murder cases involving the rich and influential as accused are simply hushed up and closed. Thus, K.F.

Rustamji, IP commented years ago "the age old belief that if you kill anyone, you will be hanged is now giving way to the new belief that if you kill anyone, you can bribe your way out or be acquitted for lack of evidence".

Over the years, the corruption has spread to other areas of police as well. This was largely due to the steady expansion of the role of police in view of the enactment of a number of social and other legislations that are to be enforced by the police. Aparna Sreevastava who has exclusively dealt with the subject in her work *'Role of police in changing society'* commented; "the success of any social legislation depends on the effectiveness of its enforcement and police have a protective as well as promotional role to perform in this sphere. "However police have many limitations on the effective enforcement of such legislations. The ambiguities in many of these legislations coupled with the police discretion "to act or not to at" in respect of certain offences under them give ample opportunities to the personnel to resort to corrupt practices during the enforcement of such acts. For example police discretion would prevail upon all other factors when a question is to be decided whether the provisions of The Prevention of Sati Act, 1987 can be attracted against the relatives of a widow who committed Sati at her own will. Same is the case with a number of other offences like child labor, untouchability, immoral traffic on women and indecent representation of women etc which are brought under the ambit of a plethora of social legislations. An equally disturbing trend is the mounting incidence of corruption in police while dealing with gender issues such as dowry deaths, exploitation of women etc. Hundreds of unnatural deaths which fall under the above category of offences are closed without proper investigations. For example, a survey conducted by 'The Deccan Herald' daily in Bangalore city during 1999, revealed that out of 714 unnatural deaths of married women below the age of 40 reported in Bangalore in 1997, 455 were death by burning. These cases were routinely classified as 'stove burst' or 'kitchen accidents' and subsequently closed as accidents without investigations. Situation is not different in other mega cities where offences against women on issues like dowry, inter-caste marriage, domestic discord, sex and extra-marital relations are on increase whereas police response against offenders is lukewarm.

The misuse of police powers and discretion in contravention of the established procedures and practices with ulterior motive to gain illegal gratification is only one aspect of police corruption. The open instances of corruption by lower ranks that are in direct contact with the public have wider implications on the image of the police and police public relations. P.E. Somaih of Bangalore University who undertook a research project *"Bangalore City Police: A study in Organization and Personnel problems"* has given a panoramic account of some of these unhealthy practice as Civil rules in our cities and towns are not specific and definite, several types of criminal activities are carried out on pavements and open places The police personnel especially the Constables harass and extort money from the people many times a day. In most of the places there is a deal of understanding between the street vendors and police regarding the "Mamool amount" (bribe) to be paid to the police. According to the grapevine in the police circles money extracted from these people also reaches the higher levels. Many of the night beat constables in all the Bangalore city police station limits immediately after reporting for duty at 2100hrs rush to snack vendors and cart sellers to extort mamools which range from just one rupee to 20 rupees and even more. Small shop-keepers, groceries and stationery marts are not spared either. Lower ranks take away stationery items like pens, refills, white-paper, carbon sheets, ink, torch batteries and newspapers from the shops that fall in the proximity to the police stations for their regular official use. On the eve of festivals or a new officer takes charge of the jurisdiction or any personnel retires from service, the constables go on a spree of collecting money or house-hold items from certain people and shops which fall within their jurisdiction. The city of Bangalore is not an isolated case from the point of view of police corruption, but it symbolizes the earthly realities of corruption that are glaring among the police personnel in almost all mega/metropolitan cities and urban agglomerations in the country.

The increasing nexus between police personnel at various levels and mafia operators is yet another disturbing trend in most of the cities like Mumbai, Delhi, Kolkota, Lucknow, Ghaziabad, Hyderabad, Vijaywada etc. These mafia syndicates bribe the police and the organized crimes such as periodic extortion, kidnapping for ransom and "supari killings" committed by them go undetected. Similarly some personnel connive at smuggling; blink at alcohol induced crimes and wink at ant-social offences like trafficking in women, peddling in drugs, sale of spurious liquor etc. Ironically .the infamous red light areas in mega cities like Mumbai, Delhi, Kolkata etc operate with the tacit support of a section of police personnel who not only collect bribe from well-established brothels but also enjoy free sex. The Dancing girls of Mumbai and the chain of hotels and bars engaging them are another major source of such activities for these personnel. The criminalization of politics and the political patronage coupled with money and muscle power enjoyed by the underworld prompt many police personnel to collude with such forces in order to make material gains. More shrewd and smart personnel tacitly associate with powerful mafia gangs in their inter-gang wars and emerge as 'encounter specialists' and become affluent overnight. In majority of such instances, pliable police leaders and opportunist political leaders patronize them till these specialists themselves turn against their mentors or involve in serious controversies or offences. N.N. Vohra Committee which was constituted by the Government of India in 1993 in its report highlighted that there had been rapid spread and the growth of criminal gangs, armed senas, drug mafias, smuggling gangs and economic lobbies which have over the years developed an extensive network of contacts with police, bureaucrats, government functionaries, politicians and media persons. However much could not be done yet to free polity and governance from the unholy nexus of such groups. On the contrary, the new culture of consumerism and material gains as an offshoot of fast growing market economy, devaluation of institutions and rampant corruption have led to further growth and consolidation of such forces which on many occasions could successfully use religious and political cards to influence and neutralize police.

On issues like corruption, here is dichotomy on the approach of police and public. The general public aspire an honest, impartial and professionally competent 'people's police' whereas the general psyche of many police personnel is that if the public wanted the policemen to behave like 'London bobby', then they too should be honest, transparent, refined and helpful as the public there. Very often, police leaders put forth apparently convincing arguments such as police is a mirror of image of society or the behavior of policemen living in a corrupt society would be the same and the honesty and integrity spring from the community in which he lives and works etc. But on a closer look, we can find these arguments as emotional. As the very popular dictum goes that "chastity begins at home", it is true that reforms or changes can be easily initiated in a small (as compared to society), definite, compact and disciplined organization such as police than in society as a whole. A person not less than Lord Denning said that between the police and the public the former had a duty to change first.

When we discuss the coping mechanisms to counter corruption and organized efforts to mythicise it, the first and foremost task should be implementation of reforms/changes especially on organizational and personnel levels. However, such reforms should start from grass-roots level ie the recruitment and training of police personnel. It is regrettable that in our country there is no uniformity in the recruitment of constabulary and middle level police personnel such as

Sub-Inspectors. In some States like Kerala, the constables are recruited by the Public Service Commission while in other States like Tamil Nadu, a Uniformed Service Recruitment Board headed by Director General of Police or Additional DGP with all the members drawn from the Police force and co-opting one or two members like psychologists or sociologists from outside. The problem lies not in the status or complexion of the Recruitment Board, but the transparency and the integrity of the persons undertaking the whole exercise. The exposure of the Punjab Public Service Commission Recruitment scandal, some times in the past, in which the Chairman himself was involved in corrupt practices in the recruitment to State Civil Service including the police creates genuine doubts on the integrity of constitutional bodies like Public Service Commissions which are now under greater political influence. The case is not different in respect of Uniformed Recruitment Boards (of Police).which also resort to unethical practices during the recruitment of the personnel. In the past such Boards in Gujarat, MP, and Rajasthan etc came under cloud for irregularities and malpractices in the recruitment of Constabulary and other junior ranks. In Gujarat an upright IPS officer launched decades- long legal battle against the perpetrators of such malpractices. Unfortunately, those personnel who get appointment in the force by paying the highest bid (of bribe) to the Recruitment Boards or their agents strive to recoup the bribe money from the very day they join the service. Such unhealthy trends which breed corruption in police organization can be countered only by ensuring transparency in recruitment process, for which the police hierarchy and government should work out joint strategies. Improving the image of Public Service Commissions (PSC) by inducting persons with proven integrity and honesty, inclusion of retired Judges or management experts in the department level Recruitment Boards, outsourcing selection test/examination to independent Agencies etc are some viable mechanisms to ensure transparency in the recruitment process.

Another equally important area is training which inculcates proper attitude and modifies undesirable ones among new recruits. But police training is in a pathetic stage in the country. Except a few premier institutions like National Police Academy of Hyderabad, majority of the police training establishments in the States are ill-equipped in terms of infrastructure and resources and also handicapped due to poor level of human resources. An unfortunate trend in respect of these institutions especially those imparting training to lower and middle ranks in many States is that they cannot inspire and motivate the new recruits in line with the mission and objectives of the organization. Instead the adverse 'imprints' that are created in their minds during the training period due to the lethargic, indifferent and overbearing attitude of some Training instructors reappear in the form of unhealthy traits such as lack of integrity, corruption etc during their active service.

It is often said that general working environment, poor salaries and lack of financial incentives force public servants to adopt corrupt practices to make both ends meet. Though there is some truth in the argument, corruption basically is" habit-forming" and once an officer starts taking bribe, he develops this as permanent habit and explores all modus operandi to amass wealth by hook and crook. Moreover, higher echelons of civil service including police who have excellent working environment and heavy pay packets and perks are more inclined to amass wealth by bribe and other corrupt practices. The craze for money and power is more among higher echelons of the force. However, as large number of lower ranks in police, bereft of ideal working climate, become coarsen and turn cynical due to stress, strain and law enforcement profession, the improvement in their working and living conditions would have positive impact in curbing corruption. Thus, it is necessary to take a new look at the work environment and style of management for the police organization and see how it can be molded into a more humanistic professional and service oriented organization. A number of innovative mechanisms can be thought of in this regard. The human resources development in the police units through 'micro-economic governance' by involving police personnel and their families in sustainable development schemes such as Police Public School, Banking/Co-operative institutions, IT kiosks, Housing Societies, Horticulture and production units like police garments, Bakery, etc would help to enrich the quality of living of the members of police organizations. Most of the police units in Madhya Pradesh have successfully implemented such schemes. A Police Hospital with all modern facilities and staff in all the State capitals on the pattern of Military Hospital for the treatment of serving and retired police personnel and their dependents and Police Departmental Sores in all district headquarters to supply provisions and house-hold items at subsided rates would help to improve the police morale. Similarly, the Police Housing Corporations/Co-operative Housing Societies need to play a pro-active role in extending housing loan/other assistance to lower and medium level personnel without any dwelling places. A system of monetary incentives like rewarding the police personnel an amount of money equivalent to 5-10% of the total value of the recovered stolen property will motivate the personnel to give their best during investigations leading to greater professionalism and reduction in corruption.

The success of such innovative mechanisms depends on the attitude of police leaders who wield substantial powers in the organization. Two aspects are vital in this regard. Firstly, there should be effective decentralization of powers and functions at various levels of police administration. Secondly, the organization should be transformed into a horizontal one with more flexibility and individual innovativeness and initiatives so that there would be meaningful deliberations and interaction at all levels of the force. Simultaneously efforts should be made to redefine the core areas of policing and identify and de-link those duties and tasks that give ample scope for the lower rungs of police to resort to corrupt practices. Very often there are allegations of rampant corruption among traffic police personnel in booking false cases and slapping fines on motorists especially two-wheelers, taxies, Rickshaws etc. The function of Traffic management may be de-linked from the police department and an exclusive traffic management department can be constituted with thorough overhauling of existing rules and regulations. Similarly, the police can be dissociated from other duties like passport verification, enforcement of local laws such as Excise Act.

Delay is attributed to be one of the main causes for corruption. The Santhanam Committee noted that administrative delays are one of the major causes of corruption and quite often, delay is deliberately contrived so as to obtain some kind of illegal gratification. "Speed money" is reported to have become a fairly common type of corrupt practice particularly in matters relating to granting of licenses, permits etc. Police organization is not an exception to this general trend. For example, in many police stations registering a complaint especially by a poor or less privileged person has become a big problem. In such cases, the complainant will receive due attention only if he pays a bribe. Another disturbing trend is the improper or delayed investigations in respect of major offences like murder, rape, dacoity etc. This will not only destroy vital clues and evidences but also lead to a large number of acquittals of cases. The innovative schemes such as encouragement for registration of maximum number of cases, departmental action against those officers encouraging" burking" and introduction of special rewards or medals to those personnel who conduct maximum number of investigation of cases with conviction in the Court will help to improve the overall functioning of the police. For example, Punjab police who had introduced such mechanism in Patiala district could achieve spectacular results with regard to free registration of cases and their speedy investigation. The total number of cases in the district which was 2978 in 1998 had increased to 5752 in 1999 as a result of the introduction of this scheme. Another notable achievement was the greater involvement of Constables and Head constables in the investigation/enquiry tasks under the close supervision and monitoring of Sub-divisional police officers. The empowerment of police constables who constitute more than 80% of the total force would help to improve their motivation and productivity level. Similarly, introduction of' single-window' system at Circle, Sub-divisional and District Police establishments for the public who approach the police for multifarious requirements like Police Clearance Certificate (PCC), Arms License, Identity certificates etc would help to minimize delay and demand of 'speed-money'.

The police leadership should take firm steps to eliminate corruption in the force. The process of cleansing has to be started at the top echelons that should not only be honest but also should ensure honesty at lower level. In a disciplined organization like police, the basic responsibility of curbing corruption vests with the senior officers. In the current scenario, they should seriously exercise this task. They should ensure active functioning of internal vigilance to a greater extent. It is important in this context, to reiterate the statutory guidelines which are already in existence and issue new ones wherever necessary. These guidelines should be practical and sacrosanct. The self-regulatory mechanisms which have become dysfunctional have to be strengthened after successfully identifying and updating them. Another concept which needs consideration is that a graded scale of punishment be meted out depending on the status of policeman found involved in the corruption. Some State police organizations have already introduced mechanisms in vogue in this regard. For example, Kerala police have recently initiated steps to link up transfer and posting of personnel with their attitude, behavior pattern and professionalism. Adverse traits like involvement in corruption, rude and indecent behavior towards the public etc would be incorporated in the Annual Performance Appraisal of personnel which would form main criteria during posting/transfer etc. A move is also in the offing to constitute a Police Review Board with the inclusion of members outside the police with a view to objectively assessing the professionalism of the personnel and work out remedial measures to refine the police.

There is some misconception in certain quarters that effective anti-corruption drive would demoralize the personnel and adversely affect the police image. But, the reality is that prompt action against the corrupt personnel will have wholesome deterrent effect. The 'anti-dote' to the prevention of folklore of corruption lies in such stringent action to put down corruption at all levels. This would also help to contain the conscious efforts by organized groups or critics of police to mythicise corruption with a view to discrediting and demoralizing police at cutting edge level. The police leaders should take initiative to demolish the walls of the "culture of secrecy" in the force without prejudicing the investigations and subsequent judicial proceedings. In fact the "closed mouth" and "no comment" policy of the police organization has been exploited by the media and the public for "police-bashing"

The National Police Commission had examined these issues at great length and made a number of recommendations to harmonize the relations between the police and the media. The Commission had strongly advocated the sharing of as much information as possible (by the police) with the media so that the tendency of the latter to come out with highly exaggerated stories on every omission and commission of the police can be effectively curbed. It had also recommended that District Superintendent of Police (DSP) should be empowered to deal directly with the media, while the police stations should be permitted to furnish routine statistics such as number of cases registered, arrests made etc. In the current scenario, the endeavor of police hierarchy should be to establish 'mutual code of honor' between the police and the media by appreciating the role and responsibilities of the both so that their interests and of the public that are ultimately served by the both, would be well protected. Side by side efforts should be made to bring the police closer to the public.

Public talks, seminars, symposia and workshops on different aspects of police administration will help to project the real image of police with more transparency. Reputed local NGOs and Community Liaison Groups should be involved in such programs. They should be used as effective channels for sensitizing the general public on various aspects of police functioning and their constraints. The concept of Community Policing (CP) becomes relevant in this context. As the concept is basically a philosophy of client-oriented service delivery aimed at improving the accountability and effectiveness of police by focusing on problem-solving, experiences and perceptions of the citizens on policing issues such as corruption should be properly assessed while formulating long term strategies and planning as part of problem-oriented policing. Such pro-active decentralization approach with the active involvement of citizens at grass roots level would act as major deterrent against corruption and other maladies in police organization.

Corruption seems to have become a way of life in this country. Though the quantum of corruption in police is not as high as that in several other departments, its extent is quite wide spread and the consequences are more serious. The cancer of corruption in police very often jeopardizes constitutional governance and acts as catalyst in the violation of civil and human rights of citizens. The fact the bribe giver is always in distress and the capacity of the personnel to use or misuse their powers and discretion to extort bribes leads to wide spread propagation of the image of police as the most corrupt wing of the State. The lack of consonance between the empirical existential reality of police and its cognitive perceptions in the public mind also contributes to the crystallization of such an image which to a great extent is the product of hearsay and media built stories. A police force whose image is corrupt and partisan is bound to evoke negative feelings among the public and cannot effectively enforce the rule of law in a democratic set up Thus, a major task of the police in the new millennium is to refurnish its image for which reforms at organizational and personnel levels are imperative. A number of innovative mechanisms focusing on the attitudinal change of personnel especially the constabulary and pro-active schemes to harmonize the relations between the police and the public/media are vital to combat corruption in police vis-a-vis organized moves to mythicise it. The success of these programs depends on the attitude of police managers who wield considerable powers in the police organization.

12

Policing in 21st Century: *Role of Information Technology*

The invasion of 'microchip' or the information revolution is perhaps the most significant event of human advancement in 20th century. Thus, Zbigniew Brzezinski, the Polish-American political scientist, who served as US National Security Adviser to President Jimmy Carter (1977-81) rightly described this age as "technetronic" characterized by scientific and technological revolution in which the Information Technology particularly the Electronics/communication and computers enabled us to reach beyond the gross features of time and space. Hardly any area of daily life is left uninfluenced by the new technology which is getting more and more innovated by the day. This had created a "third wave rhythm" (Alvin Toffler) which paved the way for "new family styles, changed ways of working, loving and living, new economy, new political conflicts and beyond all this an altered consciousness". Individuals, institutions, organizations and society in general have undergone radical transition in their roles during this process. Admittedly, the impact of IT was more glaring in technologically advanced nations of the 'South' whereas the developing nations influenced by globalization and domestic socio- economic compulsions opened their space for such technologies/industries. In countries like India, the IT based industries have occupied major space during the last two decades. Initially, the spread of this technology in relation to the geographical areas and various cross sections of the society was a slow process. Once the Y2K uncertainties were over, IT and related fields made rapid strides and epoch-making changes in all areas of life. We can make an attempt to identify the major role of IT and related advancements in augmenting the law and order edifice of the State and fortifying police efforts to build a peaceful and safe society. Any such exercise in determining the application of IT in policing should necessarily start from an assessment on the anticipated role, tasks and challenges of the police in 21st century.

The Indian police in the present century are in the midst of a mosaic of challenges and problems which unlike in the last century, are greatly influenced by global developments/ trends. Besides the traditional police functions of prevention and detection of crimes and maintenance of public order, the police have now the additional responsibility of safeguarding the sovereignty and integrity of the nation against the organized efforts of hostile neighbors to disintegrate and balkanize the country by using the tools of aggression such as subversion, sabotage and "proxy wars". The attack on Parliament House, 26/11 (2009) Mumbai terror strike and series of bomb blasts on the length and breadth of the country from East to West and North to South, clearly demonstrated the gravity of such threats and policing challenges. These 'clandestine wars' or the Low Intensity Conflicts in which the enemy is clearly hidden among the civil population are by their very nature are to be fought by the police and not the defense forces. Even in the traditional areas of policing, the police would have to deal with newer and serious tasks involving weapons, highly destructive explosives and explosive devices and even chemical or biological weapons in the light of increasing possibility of mercenary groups or terror outfits procuring and using them for evil purposes. Added to this, there is growing sophistication in the modus operandi of criminals and mafia-gangs. Similarly, the technology-based ingenious crimes like white-collar, computer-manipulated, drug-related, Bank/Insurance/ Telecom frauds, Money laundering etc had shown an upward trend especially in view of economic liberalization and circulation of huge amounts of black money in Indian Economy. Prevention, detection and investigation of such crimes can be expected to prove it an uphill task. Above all, keeping in view of the past trends as reflected in the sociological studies and the Annual publications of the Government of India such as "Crime in India" crime in general will increase and spread to new areas such as global terrorism, international drug-trafficking, trafficking in women and children and white collar crimes with the involvement of more and more sections particularly youth and women. Correspondingly, the society's expectations from the police in respect of their performance and professionalism would remain high. All the above trends clearly manifest that police in the present century should reinforce their organizational set up with major structural and personnel changes in order to combat the new challenges knocking at their doors.

The widely disparate law and order problem in different areas and regions of the country is the main challenge to the nation and the police. Terrorism, political extremism, insurgency, religious fundamentalism/communalism, mafia operations etc are some such major issues which threaten the unity and integrity of the country. Time and again it has been proved that each of these problems is required to be dealt with not only with professional dedication but also by employing right techniques and appropriate technology. For example, LICs abetted or patronized by belligerent neighbors with sinister designs cannot be handled by police as routine law and order problem or like the ethnic struggles or movements built up purely on the sentiments or emotional demands of a section of people. There would be much disparity on the intensity, strategy, ultimate goals, ground level tactics and local support in the case of such conflicts and struggles, which initially emerge as basic law and order problem. In the case of Left Wing Extremism (LWE), there would be yet another different scenario in which ideologically committed trained cadres open domestic war-fronts against the State through 'guerilla war fare' with series of violence and killings. Routine policing would be ineffective to contain any such movement. Thus the precise diagnosis of the nature and contents of the problem or issue and formulation of right strategies to deal with them are of paramount importance for the police to effectively tackling such crimes. The relevance and application of IT is more in such areas of policing particularly in Low Intensity Conflicts, insurgency and terrorism in which terrorists or mercenaries heavily depend on clandestine channels/techniques to carry out their operations. It has already been established that some of these groups have developed highly sophisticated communication net work by intercepting satellite channels; remote control/detonating mechanisms and other innovations in cyber space by using IT/Computers. To meet these challenges, the police have to upgrade their IT potential. The new technology provides Police and other security agencies a wide range of invincible capacities such as "electronic surveillance", monitoring of Internet/communication network, sensitive sensory devices, Acoustics, clandestine photography etc which can generate vital tactical intelligence enabling the police to launch operations striking the targets with much accuracy and precision. The police leaders and the field operatives have to determine as how to make use of these sophisticated systems and tools of trade to the maximum advantage of the organization.

In public order policing which emphasizes on the covert and preventive policing, the IT has an equally important role to play. The rapid urbanization, the presence of sprawling slums and urban agglomerations with an ocean of floating population in our major cities, the pressures of poverty and unemployment and above all the emergence of too many pressure groups comprising politicians, students, youth, workers and farmers have made the order maintenance task more complex and intricate. The traditional system of police beats and patrols have become obsolete in many areas because of the proliferation of high-raise structures in our environs and the collapse of traditional way of living. It is not an exaggeration that in the modern 'flat culture' one may not know his or her immediate neighbor or their activities. Nobody has time to ponder over the affairs of others; nor to develop cordial social bonds or friendship. Life in modern cities has become totally mechanical. Preventive policing with conventional methods becomes more arduous in such situations. The alternative definitely is the technology in which IT has a crucial role. A number of covert and technology based operations are getting popular in such areas of policing. The surveillance system and intelligence gathering mechanisms are clear examples. The use of Closed Circuit Television (CCTV) at open and public places to identify violators of law, clandestine monitoring of Internet to intercept mails having security implications etc which have become part of policing in the West, are now getting popular in India. The application of such technologies facilitating better evidence gathering process helps to lessen the risk to police personnel from 'mafia' and other organized criminal syndicates.

Another major area of policing which is subjected to serious stress and strain is personal protection especially of VIPs and other dignitaries. Added to this is the safety and security of vital installations and strategic establishments. The extent of threat to such targets has assumed serious dimensions in view of the revolutionary technological innovations in the form of communication net work, invisible gadgets, remote control mechanisms, concealment and detonation devices etc which the terrorists and extremists have easy access. The ideologically indoctrinated and subverted 'suicide and human bombs' have the potential to break any 'fool-proof access control mechanisms' or security system as manifested in Rajiv Gandhi's assassination at Sriperumbudur (Tamil Nadu) on May 21, 1991 and other dare-devil acts of terrorists such as Parliament attack, Mumbai terror strike etc. These realities speak of the necessity of constantly upgrading and updating our personal protection schemes and security to vial installations. Significantly, a number of advanced technology based devices like electronic gadgets, bugging devices, clandestine photography, electronic alarm systems and communication net work etc have been introduced in these fields. The proper application of such technologies by our elite and specialized forces such as National Security Guards (NSG), Special Protection Group (SPG) will help to improve the existing personal protection mechanisms.

The upgradation of technology, infrastructure and resources coupled with better professional knowledge of the personnel on the new areas of crime is essential for the police to improve their performance in the traditional area of the prevention and detection of crime. Any lacunae or indifference of the police leadership in equipping the personnel on above lines adversely affect police professionalism, leading to increase in the number of offences, lop-sided and unsuccessful investigations and above all abnormally low percentage of conviction in cases. A number of mechanisms are in the offing to make the police tech-savvy. Almost all State police forces have opened separate 'cyber cells' which are engaged in tracking down the criminals and offenders through the analysis of communication data, e-mails, etc. The Information Technology Act have incorporated special provisions empowering police and other security agencies to have accessibility to Call data from Telecommunication Department and Private Service Providers, besides monitoring the calls of persons on the grounds of suspected terrorist or anti-national linkages. Ironically, such provisions are not properly used by Police and other agencies which have to adopt a more professional approach in the use of such technologies. The present practice of police using such technologies in the investigation of all routine offences including petty thefts or pick-pocketing without following security guidelines should be dispensed with. Similarly, the tendency of Security/ intelligence agencies vying with one another to go for large number of interception/monitoring of calls on flimsy grounds or pressurizing the Service Providers to furnish bulk call data of long periods would not serve any major purpose. Basically, it should be understood that technology is only an aid to investigation or intelligence probe and not all and whole of the entire gamut of policing/investigation or intelligence collection. They can seldom be a replacement to professionally competent, trained and unbiased human resources. We cannot vouch for certain that technology-oriented evidence or intelligence is cent percent correct; their margin of error is more depending upon the nature of interpretation and analysis of data- be it call data analysis or the inputs from monitoring. Perhaps this reality has prompted the Judiciary to spell out in clear terms that technology-oriented evidences like Narco-tests, video-cassettes, etc would not be taken as conclusive evidence.

In order to overcome such difficulties and to give better direction and orientation for the proper application of IT and related technologies in policing, the Police leadership should develop a "Crime-Criminals Information System" with the facilities to analyze crimes on the basis of which police can formulate and display special skills and attitudes to make improvements in the techniques and methodologies in their crime prevention and detection tasks. The IT, particularly the computers are potential to properly equip the police in this regard. The computer technology has opened a new era of information system in which such data/ statistics on crime and criminals can be computed and analyzed for the benefit of the organization and other stake-holders. Proper formatting and parameters should be developed so as to include useful data which should inter alias include the nature of offences, key players of offences particularly terrorists, extremists, communalists with their identifying particulars, their modus operandi, sources of finances and funds, inter-linkages and nexus with drug-mafia, underworld, shady politicians, bureaucrats etc within the country and outside. Much of such information can be collected and collated from the existing police records or the questioning/interrogation of suspects or criminals belonging to such groups. Infact the State Intelligence units which fizzle out much of their energy and time for routine and insignificant tasks should utilize their personnel for collection, collation and building up of comprehensive crime-criminal data in their jurisdiction. Another equally important task is the better co-ordination among the States and various agencies for the proper dissemination of such data on need or job basis. Though general concepts and consensus on above lines have been formulated at higher levels, real co-ordination efforts on sharing of information still suffer from turf battles among agencies or the dominating career aspirations of higher echelons of police/other agencies. Such issues need to be sorted out by policy-makers.

The significant strides in the field of IT have created unprecedented advancement in the field of communications which led to the convergence of the world into a "global village". It is paradoxical that criminals first lay their hands on such technologies in pursuance of their evil designs. Now it is possible for criminals to travel thousands of kilometers in the least of time by air for taking asylum or safe sanctuaries after completing their operations. He can use Internet or E-mail or other quick electronic channels for the speedy transmission of messages relating to "hawala transactions" or the delivery of weapons or explosives. The attack on WTC in USA by Al-Qaeda demonstrated all these trends when their operatives from different nationalities drawn on a common plank due to highly fundamentalist and puritan ideals; got training at different nations; sneaked into USA; by using ingenious communication channels and network to finalize their action plan and executed their most dreaded operation surpassing the ever watchful eyes of US security and intelligence agencies. Such extensive networking and application of technology by terrorist and extremist organizations is really a matter of concern to nations and law enforcement agencies fighting international terrorism and trans-national crimes. In fact, since the early 1990s the whole world was reeling under the threat of such organizations and groups but could not avert the tragedies like the attack on

WTC. For example, the IX International Crime Prevention &Criminal Justice Conference of UN held in Cairo in 1995 called upon the member States "for harmonization of relations, training of able personnel, exchange of information, mutual assistance in extraditions and enactment of effective legislations" in order to combat the growing challenge of transnational crimes. Ironically, such sound signals given by the international organization to the member countries to prepare themselves to face the serious challenge of global terrorism could not create any major impact among the comity of nations because of foreign policy relations or internal issues. Thus, catastrophes like terror attack and killing of innocent civilians go unabated in different parts of the world.

Co-operation between the public and law enforcers is vital to face the growing threat of various crimes. A partnership should be forged on the basis of mutual anticipation and perceptions on social change. In forging such an alliance, IT has a crucial role to play. Very often the public assess the competence and effectiveness of the police on the basis of the speed, urgency and readiness of the force to respond to their calls or the speed at which police detect sensational crimes. The public perception on police crystallizes mainly on the basis of the response or treatment that they receive from police stations or police control rooms which are virtually the focal points of the entire gamut of police-community relations. The better the functioning of these centers, the better would be the impressions of the public on police. Unfortunately, the basic facilities and resources in these centers are rather inadequate. However, the modernization of police Control Rooms and police stations have now found prominence in the various structural and organizational reforms in police. The expertise and financial support of international organizations such UN, DIFD (UK) etc have also been made use of by the government in this regard. IT has also made significant contributions in such endeavors. For example, an ambitious program of interlinking all police stations in the country with the help of satellite network has been recently launched. The computer net working/ programming have also been extensively used in various projects like Police Station automation, Automating Police Control Rooms, Automatic Finger Print Identification System (ANGULI) etc. With such technology oriented modernization and improvement in facilities especially the faster communication and transport, the grass roots level policing has attained noticeable refinement.

As the society is becoming more and more dependent on technologies like IT, professionalism or professional ethics has gained focus on organizations like police. 'Professionalize or perish"-that has become the buzzword in the modern management system. For organizations like police which basically functions with a built-in-element of regimentation and wide powers of discretion and authority, the index to their public acceptance mainly depends on their professionalism. Increased professionalism would indeed be the hallmark of efficient policing in any democratic society. It warrants that each policeman should have professional background and professional attitude. He has to develop intensive knowledge, high degree of proficiency in multifarious skills and proper orientation and attitude related to his area of work. The 'Information revolution' and 'knowledge explosion'-the main facets of 21st century have opened new horizons in these areas, hitherto unknown or unfamiliar to police". In many threat areas like terrorism, militancy, religious fundamentalism or political extremism, the present level of knowledge of personnel at cutting edge level needs improvement. Unless the police improve their understanding on their ideology, strategy, techniques, inter-linkages, sources of economics, communication channels etc, the police efforts to neutralize or eliminate such threats by formulating suitable strategy and developing appropriate skills and attitudes, will attain only limited success. The IT has opened a flood-gate of innovations which are helpful to improve police knowledge and skills in such fields. For example, "Information Technology Parks" have come up through out the world with the objective to build up centralized infrastructure, resources and information pools that can be shared by organizations for updating their knowledge, information and skills. Such parks and related technologies like Internet-cafes have created revolutionary changes in the computation and sharing of data and information of professional value among organizations. Significantly, there is much consensus among the comity of nations in the effective dissemination of such information and knowledge by law enforcement agencies of various countries, especially while dealing with transnational crimes.

The police personnel develop professional knowledge, better skills, right attitude and approaches mainly through training which needs to be up-graded or reoriented with the application of new technology and innovations. The Gore Committee which was appointed by the Government of India in 1973 emphasized this aspect. But, when the Committee made their recommendations, many of the challenges/threats confronted by the police today never existed or not felt/ experienced by the police organization. Domestic and international terrorism with new forms of Narco and Eco-terrorism, Low Intensity Conflicts, 'Cyber crimes", Chemical and biological weapons, highly destructive explosives and explosive devices with sophisticated concealing and detonating mechanisms and economic offences like money laundering and frauds are a few examples. The existing training mechanisms have limitations to impart adequate professional knowledge and skills to personnel and thereby effectively countering such challenges at cutting edge level. Taking cue of the situation, a number of police Training institutions have extensively used IT and other technology to restructure and re-orient training curriculum for police personnel at various levels. Some of these innovations are:

(a) Simulators,

(b) Virtual reality,

(c) Micro-computers,

(d) Video-conferencing and net working through LAN & WAN,

(e) Internet/E-mail,

(f) Computer-based Finger Printing,

(g) Digital Resource Library and;

(h) Tele-teaching/Electronic lectures.

However, there should be clear cut parameters and norms in respect of the category of personnel who should be imparted with advanced IT modules, infrastructure and resources available with the Training institutions, cost factor etc. These matters should be properly dealt with by the police leadership through appropriate Policy, Planning and development strategies instead of encouraging ad-hoc arrangements or adjustments which the police hierarchy is accustomed to.

An A3 Chart based on the Area, Application and Advantage of Information Technology in major areas of policing will explain the position in nutshell.

Our basic approach should be that the IT oriented input inculcation to the personnel may be based on job needs and must be on most scientific manner. The heart of the matter is that our endeavor should be to practically prepare the personnel to undertake IT-oriented policing tasks instead of merely enriching their conceptual or theoretical knowledge of IT/ computers. Moreover, the specialized cells or units that exclusively deal with organized crimes like Terrorism, cyber crimes, LICs need to be imparted with advanced knowledge and skills based on IT innovations. Another equally important aspect is the role and leadership of police training institutions in developing IT-oriented modules or innovations in the training curriculum. For example, Training Institutions like National Police Academy have excellent infrastructure, vast funds and outstanding track-record of over 50 years; but the institution has seriously ventured to launch IT-oriented Training modules only during the beginning of this century. Now we can imagine the fate of Police Training Institutions in the States which suffer from many odds such as inadequate infrastructure and funds, poor or indifferent administration and

A3 Chart on IT *vis-a-vis* Policing

Area	Application	Advantage
Organized Crimes	Electronic surveillance, Interception/Call data analysis, sensitive sensory devices	Generation of specific tactical intelligence/ inputs for various operations
Public Order policing	Electronic surveillance, CCTV, clandestine photography	Evidence gathering with less risk, identification of trouble-makers
Personal protection/ security of vital installations	CCTV, Electronic gadgets, Bugging devices, Electronic alarms etc	Fool proof security of VIPs and vital installations with less manpower
Prevention &detection of crimes	Crime-Criminal Information System, Computer-based finger printing, Simulators, Crime-mapping	Major investigation aids , successful investigation of complex and ingenious crimes
Communication Infrastructure	V-SAT, Video conferencing, LAN/WAN, Optical fiber cabling &high speed brand width, encrypted E-mail	Speedy and timely response by police over offences
Community Policing	Virtual reality &image building exercises, better interaction with public through media	Better police-public relations helping crime prevention &investigations.
Police Control Rooms &Police Stations	Automation, Automatic Response system, satellite networking of police Stations	Better response from public &strengthening police public relations
Professionalism	IT Parks, Internet/ Email, E cafes	Better professional knowledge, skills helping overall functioning of the force
Training	Simulators, Electronic Library, Tele-teaching/ Electronic lectures, Computer Finger Printing	Developing better skills and attitude and professionalism to deal with new challenges

above all intervention by immature political masters at the helm of affairs. Further one single institution like NPA cannot cope up with the demand of imparting intensive knowledge and skills in diverse fields. Added to this is the cost factor. Thus, the police leaders should think of alternate strategies. For example, many institutions like IITs, National Informatics Center (NIC), DRDOs, etc have highly advanced infrastructure and resources in the field of IT. The selection of some of these institutions/organizations and establishing net working with them for training of police personnel on IT modules would be prudent and practical especially from the point of view of quality and cost factor of such training.

The rapid expansion and wide application of IT in various fields have posed new problems and issues to the police. Such threats mainly arise from the organized efforts of mafia and criminals to exploit these technologies for perpetration of all types of crimes. On every day, we hear lurid stories from "cyber-space", about bank swindles, espionage, Credit card manipulations/frauds etc Movies like 'Wage games" have dramatized the dangers from the unauthorized entry to the computers and net work communication that even control nuclear weapons. Adam James have immortalized such stories which predict that any Third world war would be fought in "cyber space" with computer-manned Missiles and nuclear weapons and computer viruses that can control or wreck economy, Power-distribution system, or the normal life of the people!, The official reports on IT related crimes are equally revealing, According to a published report in France, as quoted by Alvin Toffler, the mafia kidnapped an IBM executive and cut off his finger because they needed his finger-print to break a computer security system, Similarly, the US Department of Justice defined a dozen different methods used in computer-based criminal activity. They range from switching and altering data as they 'enter' the computer, to putting self concealing instructions into the software for tapping computers. And in India, 'hackers' from our hostile neighbors made efforts to enter into cyber-network of strategic establishments like Indian Defence Forces, Scientific Research Institutions, DRDO, Atomic Research Bodies, Stock Exchanges, etc. Mafia/criminals use e-mail and other channels to organize 'supari' killings in big cities.

All these trends emphasize the need of police evolving an 'information security system' which should ensure privacy, authentication, integrity and non-repudiation of communications transacted through electronic media. Such a system assumes more importance in organizations like police in which security breach of communications involving criminals or crimes or hacking can endanger National Security and lives and properties of common people. Many innovations are in operation to counter the IT-related crimes. They include card system, which generates pass word in synchronization with those demanded by host-computer, finger prints or other physical or behavioral traits to confirm the identity of the user or encryptions to protect the integrity of messages and the data transacted through Internet/E-mail. The anti-virus software is growing at an alarming rate. In countries like UK, where IT has made significant advancemen; watch groups such as "Internet Watch group Foundation have been formed with governmental support to 'police' the Internet and other electronic communication channels. Such groups with the co-operation of police could effectively check the misuse of IT for a wide range of offences like Child pornography and 'hacking'. Needless to mention that only by developing security systems and watchdog Committees, the police in 21st century can ensure the safe and secure application of IT in their wide range of operations.

13

India's National Security and Police Response: *Past, Present and Future*

The Indian concept of National Security has for long focused on military aspects especially the protection of the country's territorial integrity and sovereignty from external assault or internal disruption. Thus, India's foreign policy objectives and defense strategies were greatly influenced by these aspects particularly maintenance of peace in the region. The initiative for Non-Alignment Movement (NAM) during Nehru-era and the neutrality of the country without aligning with any superpowers etc were clear manifestations of the above trend. The end of cold war era, growing egalitarianism in the international sphere with diffusion of democratic idea, emergence of a uni-polar world after the disintegration of Soviet Union and globalization of world economy etc have brought radical changes in our concept of National security. Now Security is an inclusive term which transcends beyond the contours of strategic and military factors and encompasses political, economic, technological and environmental factors. Besides, the non-conventional sources of insecurity such as demographic movement due a variety of issues constitute serious threat to national security. So are the transnational threats such as international terrorism with its seminal links to arms, explosives and drugs-smuggling, money laundering, information warfare etc. Similarly, internal problems like domestic terrorism, insurgency, secessionism or socio-economic issues like poverty, economic exploitation, unequal distribution of wealth, population explosion, exodus of people from rural to urban areas, growing corruption etc have added new dimensions to the current scenario of national security.

In the context of National security, police is the most important instrument of the State. The police in India was established during the British rule. At that time, the main mission of the police was to protect and perpetrate the interest of British rule in India. The Statutory base of the police was the Police Act of 1861 which still governs the Indian police in the new millennium. After independence India was besieged by several national security issues of all possible types and dimensions. The post-partition riots which witnessed large scale macabre killings and destruction and exodus of people from different parts of the country, were perhaps the most tragic and bitter episode of the free India. The police responses to various challenges and their efforts to enforce rule of law by ensuring the safety and security of the citizens and the integrity and sovereignty of the nation, to a great extent, had been generally acknowledged and acclaimed by the major segments of the Indian society. The fact that more than 25000 police personnel have laid down their lives at the altar of duty after independence is an eloquent testimony to the gravity of these issues and the innate capacity of the force to give their best in a crisis or exigency. In fact, during the last six decades the police had operated in a highly complex and difficult security environment which was a volatile mixture of external threats and internal problems.

Though 'Public order' and 'police' figure in the State list in the 7th Schedule of the Indian Constitution and States have exclusive control over their police forces, the major issues of National security fall under the domain of the Centre. Article 355 of the Constitution requires the Union to protect the States against external aggression and internal disturbances. The Union Defense forces are constituted, trained and equipped to meet these challenges. In order to assist the States in serious law and order issues, the Centre has also raised paramilitary forces like BSF, CRPF, Assam Rifles, ITBP, besides the intelligence organizations like Intelligence Bureau. The Central Paramilitary forces along with police operate as the front line defense against external aggression or organized infiltration by enemy forces/terrorists into the country across our international borders. Thus the first brunt of any attack will be on border police which should counter and hold the attack till the Army steps in. But on many occasions, the border police or the State police forces bereft of adequate manpower or logistic support such as modern weaponry, surveillance/observation equipments or communication network demonstrated their weakness in effectively countering the challenges from across the border.

The ill-equipped State Police forces had to face the intruders from Pakistan in1948 in Kashmir. The Army had to be summoned to beat back the raiders. Same was the case with Chinese attack in 1962 in North East Frontier Agency (NEFA) where the border police and paramilitary forces could not resist the attack of Chinese Red Army. Again the police forces had made supreme sacrifices in their brave efforts to check the onward march of mighty Chinese forces into the Indian Territory. The internal security tasks such as anti-sabotage and anti-subversive operations and deterrent measures against' agent-provocateurs or anti-national elements especially in the border and sensitive areas had fallen on the shoulders of police forces during the Indo-Pak wars in 1965 and 1971. The 1971 Indo-Pak war was a major landmark in the security scenario of Indian sub continent. In the case of Pakistan, it was the beginning of its serious search for alternate strategies to confront India. General Zia-ul-Haq, the supreme head of a 'battered and bruised' Pakistan, was the architect of the new strategy which was nothing but "proxy war" or Low Intensity Conflict (LIC) against India. With the formulation of self-styled operation 'Topac', the Pakistan declared an unconventional war against India. The main objective of this operation was the disintegration of India by utilizing the spy-net work for acts of sabotage/infiltration and by exploiting the porous borders with Nepal and Bangladesh.

Punjab was the initial testing ground of Pakistan's 'covert-warfare' against India. The disclosures made by Lal Singh, a terrorist belonging to Khalistan Commando Force (KCF) who was arrested by Indian security forces in early 1990s had given specific indications that Pakistan had been vigorously pursuing its self-styled 'K2 Plan' since 1980s as part of its long term strategy of the destabilization/disintegration of India with the help of terrorist and insurgent groups operating in the border States of Kashmir and Punjab. During the course of a decade long terrorist violence in Punjab which resulted in the killing of more than 12000 persons, Pakistan provided covert support to major terrorist groups in terms money, training, hide-outs and sophisticated weaponry. In spite of such external support and the appealing ideological and religious orientation of the movement during the early years, the police and Para-military forces in co-operation with the army could wipe out Sikh militancy to a great extent, by the end of 1992. Certain major lessons relevant to internal security, can be drawn out of the success of police and other security forces in combating terrorism in Punjab.

The success of any counter-insurgency operation by police depends on the extent of public support and good will enjoyed by the forces. In the case of Punjab, the police could get tremendous response from the people in the form of intelligence and co-operation when the militancy had lost its ideological base and degenerated into simple criminal activities. When the instances of random killing of civilians, looting of their properties and assets and raping and molesting girls and women, continued unabated, the public despite their ideological sympathies with the movement were forced to look towards the police for their safety and security. It was this 'mass-psyche' rather than the operational skills or professionalism of the police, helped the security forces to contain the militancy. The spine chilling atrocities and brutalities committed by the police in fighting terrorism went unheeded in the light of this mass-psyche, except in the case of a microscopic minority of human rights activists/ intellectuals who bore the brunt of police hierarchy. Secondly, the political leadership - both at the Centre and in the State-showed considerable political will and acumen in fighting Sikh terrorism. The police and security agencies were given a free hand which on many occasions went beyond the contours of rule of law and due process of law. Many laws were amended and new laws were enacted to plug the loopholes that could adversely affect the operational efficiency of the police. Another important factor which improved the professional capabilities of Punjab police was their re-orientation, modernization and re-organization after a detailed assessment of the ground level requirements of the force to fight terrorism. These reforms in their working modes, re-orientation of training system and syllabi, motivational techniques and large scale expansion of its armed battalions and upgrading of their weaponry helped the force to meet the challenges of terrorists. Thus, there is no rationale behind the moves from certain corners to glorify the individual contribution of the then head of Punjab police in eliminating Sikh militancy and terrorism. More over the 'questionable strategies' and 'modus operandi' adopted by Punjab police to eliminate Sikh Militancy are still a matter of debate. Perhaps these strategies led to two most unfortunate tragedies of independent India, namely the assassination of then Prime Minister Indira Gandhi and the subsequent genocide of Sikhs in Delhi and other parts of India. Despite such tragedies and controversies, the role played by police in fighting Sikh Militancy could not be belittled.

The professionalism and competence of police and other security agencies in combating' proxy-war' and cross-border terrorism were tested in Kashmir. Since the early part of 1988, Pakistan and her intelligence agencies showed active interest in aiding, abetting and arming various terror groups which with the support of secessionist and anti-Indian forces in the

State established their strong bases in Kashmir valley. Infiltration and ex-filtration of trained terrorists continued across the border. So was the case of smuggling of arms and explosives into the State. Initially, the State police in spite of their grassroots level organizational network could not do much to check such organized activities of terrorist groups which enjoyed considerable goodwill and support of larger segments of local population due to decades of major aberrations in the proper democratic governance and development in the State. There were also conscious efforts from the part of terrorists and fundamentalist groups to wean away the people from national mainstream through orchestrated propaganda highlighting the issues of discrimination, development, corruption and right to self determination. A popular feature of the situation in many places in Kashmir was the repeated attacks on security pickets and patrols in town areas provoking retaliations in which large scale civilian causalities would occur in cross-fire causing further resentment and hostility against police and security forces. The transition of insurgency/terrorism in Kashmir valley into a full-fledged 'proxy-war' aided and controlled by Pakistan and non-State actors/ foreign mercenaries had brought new serious problems for the police and other security agencies. Large number of foreign terrorists and suicide squads from Afghanistan, Sudan, Egypt, Algeria, Yemen, Libya, Bahrain, etc were infiltrated into the State with sophisticated weapons and explosives. These mercenaries sponsored by Al-Qaeda and other Islamic terror groups along with local militants from various 'Jehadi' outfits such as Lashker-e-Toiba, Harkat-ul-Mujahideen/Hizbul Mujahideen, Harkat-ul-Jehad-e-Islami, Jaish-e-Mohammed and many other self styled Islamic outfits resorted to large scale killing and explosions. They had demonstrated better planning and sophistication in laying of ambushes, effective use of communication equipments, explosive devices, land-mines and ingenious remote control mechanisms much to the embarrassment of police and security forces. The "Fidayeens" fighting for Kashmir cause had dare-devil attack of Kashmir Secretariat, Srinagar Airport and Army Cantonment areas, besides their regular confrontation with police and security forces. Such large scale violence and killings led to steady migration of people from Kashmir valley, resulting in major demographic changes in the border areas with inherent national security implications. During the last one decade more than 22,000 people including around 2,000 security personnel were killed in the State. In spite of such large scale causalities to the civil population and security personnel, Kashmir continues to be a seething cauldron of terrorism with serious national security implications. The Kashmir tangle demonstrates a cardinal truth that highly motivated insurgent or terrorist groups often with cross border connections and having the goodwill and sympathies of sections of indigenous population can play havoc with the life of a nation and her people. The police or security forces find it extremely difficult to eliminate such terrorism/insurgency.

The Pak Intelligence agencies particularly the Inter Services Intelligence (ISI) have become a serious threat to our National security. ISI which was formed as early as 1948, during its initial years was mainly engaged in espionage and subversive activities targeting defense/strategic establishments especially in border areas. This was part of their strategy to furnish specific inputs to Pak defense forces to select and strike strategic locations/ installations during any conflict with India. But over the years, ISI sponsored activities and ISI modules have dangerously proliferated across the Indian land mass. Apart from its involvement in militancy and terror activities in Punjab and Kashmir, ISI hands were suspected in a number of serial bomb attacks in different parts of the country. ISI also played a major role in the well planned infiltration of soldiers and mercenaries across the Line of Control (LOC) in Kargil sector and the hi-jacking of Indian Airlines flight IC 814 on December 24, 1998 from Katmandu much to the embarrassment of Army, Police and other security forces. While ISI's involvement is suspected in the attack on Indian

Parliament House on December13, 2001, the outfit is fully involved in Mumbai terror strike on November 26, 2008 as confirmed by the disclosures made by David Headley and Thahawur Hussein Rana before the US Courts/Juries.

The geographical spread and clandestine operations of ISI in India is a serious matter of concern to police and other security agencies. Delhi is a focal point of ISI activities. The Tarai region of UP has become a hot bed of ISI activities. Same is the case with high reaches of Himachal Pradesh which harbor ISI operatives and have become sanctuaries for ISI backed militant outfits. Parts of the North East- Assam, Manipur and Tripura in particular have become important from ISI point of view. Siliguri corridor into West Bengal has been used for systematic infiltration into the region. In the recent past, a number of ISI modules which were engaged in espionage on sensitive defense establishments in the western sector have been unearthed in Rajasthan. Gujarat is yet another sensitive State where ISI is quite active. A Pak spy plane "Atlantique" was intercepted and shot over Bhuj area bordering Pakistan, Hyderabad in the South and pockets in Andhra Pradesh, Kerala, Karnataka, Tamil Nadu and Goa also figure quite prominently in ISI's designs. Another equally disturbing trend is the growing nexus between ISI and underworld/mafia and Narco- terrorists and arms dealers. On a number of occasions ISI utilizes such elements to carry out their operations such as killing/kidnapping, smuggling in of arms and explosives, circulation of counterfeit currencies and Hawala transactions for clandestinely channelizing funds to terrorists and militants in India. Nepal, Bangladesh, Sri Lanka, UAE and Maldives have become the main bases where such underworld syndicates operate in tandem with ISI operatives. The genesis of Al-Qaeda and spread of Islamic terrorism to various parts of the country have given an impetus to broaden their network and to launch targeted operations against India from different transit bases. With the killing of Osama Bin Laden in Pakistan territory, it was established beyond doubt that Osama and Al-Qaeda enjoyed the tacit support of ISI sleuths. Though the police and security agencies could unearth and neutralize a number of ISI modules in different parts of the country, the extent of damage caused by the outfit to the social and democratic fabric of the country and its economy, development and infrastructure through various operations was huge. Two specific examples are Mumbai blasts of 1993 and the Mumbai terror attack in 2008. In 1993 Mumbai blasts, 500 persons were killed and property/infrastructure worth over Rupees 10000 crores was damaged where as in the 2008 terror attack, persons lost their lives and assets/ properties of around were damaged.

India's fights against the 'covert war' by ISI and other foreign agencies in the past and present bring out certain major trends which are indicative of the need to develop future strategy to effectively deal with such challenges. Firstly, our police and security agencies are yet to develop proper expertise and acumen to unearth such clandestine operations. Basically, the State Special Branches/intelligence units which have grass roots level spread have not been properly trained or tasked for such purposes. The situation is not much different in the case of Central intelligence agencies which accord low priority for counter-intelligence operations in view of their dominating interests in the generation of political intelligence. More over, except in Delhi and other metropolises, these agencies have not got adequate manpower or resources to undertake systematic operations to unearth the 'modules' of foreign intelligence agencies. Their over-dependence on technical operations on many occasions leads to major aberrations resulting in wrong conclusions and findings. Another disgusting aspect is the unethical practices resorted to by these agencies to detect the 'so called modules' in order to make their records straight and thus to justify their huge spending in the name of operations and projects. Ironically, the Political executive at the Centre are keen only on the number of 'modules' busted by the intelligence and Security agencies so as to enable them to blunt the criticism of their detractors in the parliament and outside on the issue of national security. Interestingly, one former Union Home Minister was in the habit of quoting such numbers after every serial bomb blast in the country purportedly conspired and executed by ISI! So long as Political Executive are ignorant or 'acting ignorance' on the ground realities and blindly parroting the inflated and distorted' findings and statistics' of security and intelligence agencies, the fight against 'covert war' becomes a mockery and national security is the causality. Thus, the need of the hour is that the intelligence and security agencies assigned with such tasks should be made accountable to the Parliament and their operations having implications on national security need proper scrutiny and review so that chaff from grains could be properly separated. Meanwhile, the State Police forces should re-structure and re-orient the functioning of their intelligence/Special Branch apparatus so that they should play a key role in counter-intelligence operations. To begin with these agencies should catalogue the background and activities of suspected individuals and organizations of their area, who pose a threat to national security by way of links with militant/subversive organizations or contacts with foreign agencies. The heart of the matter is that proper decentralization of the police/intelligence network with trained and sensitized personnel alone will help to effectively face the challenge of 'covert-war' by hostile neighbors to disintegrate our nation.

The North East is another major area of security concern. Over the last six decades, the police forces in the region were engaged in their fight against different shades of insurgency, ethnic or linguistic conflicts or secessionist movements. The 1950s saw Naga hills going up in flames when Nage insurgents spoke for an 'independent Nagaland'. In the 1960s the fire spread to Mizoram, Manipur and Tripura which turned into "traditional killing fields". Assam has been in perpetual turmoil since the last three decades. The seeds of militancy that were sown in the State during the six year long (1978-83), Assam movement on 'Foreigners issue' sprouted and grown up into full fledged insurgency in 1980s when United

Liberation Front (ULFA) virtually took over the reign of administration in the larger areas of the State under the canopy of a pro-ULFA State government headed by the protagonists of Assam Movement. The emergence of extremist outfits belonging to Bodos and other ethnic/ tribal groups in the State made Assam a fierce battle field. The successive joint operations by Army, Police and Para military forces against insurgent groups including ULFA, National Democratic Front of Bodoland (NDFB) and Bodoland Tiger Force (BLTF) failed to yield expected results. The situation in Manipur and Tripura is equally grave from internal security angle. The outfits like All Tripura Tribal Force (ATRF) and National Liberation Front of Tripura (NLFT) had taken the path of violence and blood-shed since long in order to protect tribal interests. Of late these groups have vastly extended their sphere of activities by attacking security posts, police Stations and non-tribal population, kidnapping of VIPs etc. The Meitei extremism in Manipur which took different shapes and shades during the last four decades and resulted in large scale violence, killings and blood-shed had later assumed the character of inter-tribal conflicts between Naga and Kukki tribals, especially after Government of India's efforts to work out a negotiated settlement with NSCN (Issac-Muivah) faction. Some sort of 'ethnic cleansing' was obviously underway to buttress the Naga demand of re-drawing State boundaries particularly between Manipur and Nagaland. The major insurgent and separatist movements of the North East have undergone different pattern and configurations which make the policing response more arduous and difficult. Outfits like ULFA, NDFB (Assam), NLFT & ATTF (Tripura) have established their strong bases in Bangladesh, Bhutan and Myanmar and are aided and abetted by external forces. Side by side, some of these North Eastern militant groups have been rapidly upgrading their weaponry, training, organizational structure and inter-linkages and found targeting the security forces in more and more areas and thereby eroding the credibility of local administration. As the State police forces lack in effective cohesion, refinement in training techniques, modern weaponry, communication network and motivational drive, they continue to be relegated to the background and the armed and paramilitary forces dominate the counter-insurgency scenario in the North East. Another discernible feature is that sections of State police personnel influenced by the highly emotional parochial or ethnic slogans and ideologies become soft towards some of the incipient militant/ethnic movements which soon attain dangerous potential threatening national security. Thus, much has to be done in reforming and motivating the personnel at grass roots level so that they will turn into front-line soldiers in fighting militancy and terrorism in their own home States.

The steady exodus of refugees and infiltration from erstwhile East Pakistan (Bangladesh), Nepal and Bhutan to the North East across the porous borders have now become a multi-dimensional problem affecting national security. Besides the fluid socio-economic and political issues in these countries, the ineffective border management coupled with corruption and malpractices by various forces/agencies associated with it, led to large scale infiltration of migrants to the region and their escalation to hinterland areas of the North East and neighboring States like Bihar and West Bengal, over the last six decades. The exodus, no doubt, had created major demographic changes in the North East and opened a Pandora's Box of socio-economic and political issues which no longer is confined to the North East alone but the whole country with national security implications. Ironically, while the Political parties tacitly encouraged infiltration as part of their' vote-bank' politics, the State/Central forces handled the issue as one of the best sources of' illegal income generation' which intensified the gravity of infiltration issue which no longer is confined to the North East. Hordes of poor, unemployed Bangladeshis, disguised as citizens from West Bengal and Orissa migrate to various States especially Southern States like Kerala in search of job and establish their colonies. So long as they have identity documents such as voter's identity cards, Ration cards (fake or otherwise) issued by the competent authorities from these States, the police and other agencies have reservations to legally act against them. Keeping apart the rhetoric of political parties on infiltration, the "infiltration issue" is yet another example of the deep-rooted corruption and malpractices that the sensitive departments/agencies of the Central and State governments are accustomed to jeopardizing National Security.

Among the various other internal threats to national security, the most dangerous one is the ideologically oriented Left Wing Extremism (LWE) whose early signs were noticed in the socially and economically backward Telengana region of Andhra Pradesh which witnessed armed uprisings by peasants against landlords and feudalist elements immediately after independence. The violence and killings that continued for four years (1948-51) were ultimately contained with the help of police and Army through ruthless repressive measures subsequently known as Sardar Patel (SP) measures. But, Left Extremist movement in its present form took genesis in early 1967 when a section of Communist Party (Marxist) cadres who were inspired by the doctrines of Mao-Tse-sung and Chinese Communist Party broke away from CPM and resorted to the path of armed struggle against landlords and upper class in Naxalbari area of West Bengal. The movement later spread to other States like Andhra Pradesh, Maharashtra, Punjab, Bihar, Tamil Nadu, Kerala, etc and attracted a large number of youth, intellectuals, workers and educated sections. In pursuance of their ideological line and strategy, the Left Wing Extremists committed a series of violent actions particularly against their 'class enemies' like landlords, police, corrupt officials etc. However, strong measures adopted by the police and other security agencies coupled with ideological differences in the movement leading to splits, led to the disintegration of the movement in many States like West Bengal, Kerala, Tamil Nadu etc. In fact, much credit goes to the State police forces of these States in eliminating the first phase of the upsurge by Left Wing groups. Though there are now over thirty LWE groups in the country, only half a dozen of major groups like CPI (Maoists), CPML (Liberation), etc pose major threat to national security. The newly formed group rechristened as CPI (Maoists) after the merger of People's War Group (PWG) and Maoist Communist Centre (MCC) in September 2004 has become a major threat to the internal security of the nation through their repeated depredations against security forces and destruction and sabotage of governmental assets etc. Their formation of a Compact Revolutionary Zone (CRZ) comprising parts of the forest tracts of Adilabad (Andhra Pradesh) to Nepal traversing through the forest areas of Maharashtra, Orissa, Chattisgarh, Madhya Pradesh, Bihar and Jharkhand has led to the entire area vulnerable from security and law and order angle. Over 180 districts in the country are now affected by the violent activities of CPI (Maoists) which strictly adhere to the strategies and tactics employed by Mao Zedong during the Great March, has developed fraternal links with revolutionary Communist groups from other countries. The State police and Central paramilitary forces engaged in 'anti-Maoist operations' suffered heavy causalities in Chattisgarh, Jharkhand and Maharashtra demonstrating their lack of preparedness and expertise in 'guerilla warfare' which the Maoists are accustomed to. This emphasizes the need to chalk out alternative strategies by the police to effectively deal with the Maoist threat. Basically, the mistaken notion of the political Executive and police leadership that Left Wing extremism is a law and order problem should be shelved. On the other hand, the reality is that the issue is closely intertwined with socio-economic factors, aberrations in development, malfunctioning of government institutions and above all serious flaws in governance. The ongoing process of liberalization, the entry of Multi Nationals into rural India with their mega projects leading to the displacement of indigenous people from their traditional home land and the economic and cultural exploitation of marginalized and under privileged sections etc have given new impetus to the growth and consolidation of resistance- movements with the patronage of these groups. The violent movements in Singur, Nandigram and Lalgargh in West Bengal and in other States like Orissa and Chaattisgarh, backed by LWE, were clear manifestation of the protest and resentment of rural and marginalized sections against the entry of Multi Nationals and Big Corporate groups into their traditional land. Thus an integrated approach of development with social justice, better governance and effective law and order will only help to find a permanent solution to the growing threat of Left wing Extremism in the country.

In the area of collective violence that endangers internal security, the communal riots are of special significance to India. The venom of communal hatred and frenzy that had led to large scale violence, killings and bloodshed during the immediate post-partition years had spread to more and more sections of people and large scale communal riots broke out in almost all States, resulting in heavy toll of lives and properties of citizens. Thus to name a few, we had serious communal riots in Udaipur and Ahmedabad (1965-1966), Bhiwandi (1970), Jamshedpur (1973), Moradabad (1980) Delhi (1984), Bhagalpur (1989) and in a number of cities like Mumbai, Kolkata, Ahmedabad, Kanpur, Meerut, Surat etc following the demolition of Babri Masjid in 1992. The communal genocide in Gujarat during 2002 that had killed thousands of innocent people, raped, molested and murdered hundreds of women and destroyed properties worth thousands of crores and put an indelible mark of shame on the secular face of India was the latest of such series of riots. But the tragedy is that the communal fire instead of extinguishing itself through a process of social and cultural assimilation of people as part of national integration, spread to more and more areas and posed major challenges to police forces which on many occasions failed to put out the fire in time. Thus in almost all the major communal riots, there were anguished appeals by the victims for the deployment of Army or paramilitary forces leading to the erosion in the credibility of police. The various

Commissions which probed into major communal riots in Moradabad, Bhiwandi, Bhagalpur etc came out with startling revelations about the active collusion of sections of police personnel with rabid communal elements who were the perpetrators of most dastardly crimes during such conflicts. The Gujarat carnage of 2002 also demonstrated a disturbing trend of tacit collusion of the senior echelons of police with known communal elements backed by the ruling party in power. The situation was not different in States like Orissa, Karnataka and Madhya Pradesh where sections of State police including the senior hierarchy maintained passive approach while dealing with communal violence and conflicts targeting Christians and other minority communities. Moreover, the conscious efforts by the Political Executive and police leadership to give clean chit to the rabid communal organizations/elements behind such violence have exposed the increasing nexus between police and communal outfits.

The above trends evoke a pertinent question as where we went wrong. What happened to the solemn pledge of police personnel that they would safeguard the life and properties of citizens irrespective of caste, color or community? There are many reasons for the changing trends. Unlike our earlier conviction that communal feelings are confined to a microscopic percentage of fringe elements in various communities, the reality is that the communal venom has spread to more and more sections of people including the elite and educated. The orchestrated propaganda and campaign effectively carried out by communal organizations and political parties linking up caste/communities with religious practices/customs, socio-economic-educational-employment issues, culture and traditions etc greatly influence the line of thinking of people and attune their subconscious mind to be pro-active on communal or related matters. Such 'psychic imprints' act as 'prime-movers' and influence their sphere of activities-whether they may be in the field of law enforcement, judiciary, administration or politics. In the case of police, such camouflaged and submerged feelings break the barriers during communal violence and conflicts and quickly identify with their own flock, disregard to the canons of rule of law or the concept of impartial policing. Thus one major challenge before the police leadership in the country is the selection of persons with known secular credentials; wean away them from the influence of caste/communal forces and propaganda and professionally empower them to perform their tasks without any bias or prejudice to any particular community or class.

A police force with such an image alone can win over the support of the masses especially in rural areas where policing has become more arduous due to new issues. The process of resurgence of rural India and the awakening of the backward and under-privileged sections of the society especially after Mandal Commission Report in late 1980s had aggravated social and caste tensions. The Sachar Committee recommendations and the proposals by Ranganath Misra Commission focusing on the socio-economic and educational advancement of minorities particularly Muslims have added new dimensions to the entire issue. No doubt, casteism became a vibrant factor in Indian society and polity, but in its resurgent form, it has acquired some negative and divisive fall out which are reflected in the law and order scenario in the form of caste conflicts and killings. One disturbing trend is the formation of 'private armies' on caste lines. These 'senas' floated by rival castes and equipped with illegal weapons operated as parallel police set up and resorted to mutual killings, arson and atrocities. Many rural areas of Bihar in 1980s and 1990s had virtually become a battlefield in which such private armies floated by various powerful caste groups and the cadres of LWE groups were engaged in brutal killings and large scale destruction of properties. In many cases the police failed to act against such private armies which enjoyed the patronage of political leaders and caste- communal forces.

Large scale violence, killing and blood-shed which have become part of national scene since 1980s led to another dangerous trend of targeting VIPs by terrorist and extremist outfits with the ulterior motive to create chaos and political instability. For example, the assassination of former Prime Minister. Indira Gandhi by her own security personnel on October 31, 1984 led to large scale killings and violence in different parts of the country. In 1991, the LTTE planned the assassination of Rajiv Gandhi. After, September 11 terror attack in USA and the retaliatory offensive by US administration against international terrorism the looming threat against VIPs has become serious. Many Islamic terror outfits like Al-Quaeda openly preach the cult of violence including the killing of State Heads and dignitaries and destruction of sensitive installations/establishments. Even after the killing of Osama Bin Laden by US forces, such threats still persist in India which is in the hit list of Islamic terror groups, notably Al-Quaeda.

The country's score-board in respect of its responses to the challenges in the national security scenario, during the past six decades tells us its own tale of flaws and lacunae in the vital area of national security. The 'Kargil episode' of the intrusion of Pak soldiers in to the Kargil sector exposed the weakness of our Defense forces and security-intelligence agencies. Thus, the Kargil Review Committee rightly observed; "there were grave deficiencies in India's security management system, in so far as there had been very little change over the last 52 years and despite the 1962 debacle, the 1965 stalemate and the 1971 victory, the growing nuclear threat, the end of the cold war, continuance of proxy war in Kashmir for over a decade and revolution in military affairs." The Kargil enquiry report which emphasized the need for a major re-structuring of the national security management system, specifically identified four major areas namely higher defense organization, internal security, intelligence and border management. Four tasks forces which were constituted by the Government to make recommendations on the restructuring-needs to be undertaken in these areas, made a number of recommendations to the Group of Ministers. Though some cosmetic measures were initiated to strengthen Security-

Intelligence agencies like IB, Navy, and Coast Guard etc through better synergy and co-ordination, the overall scenario especially the functioning of these agencies remain far from satisfactory. The post-Kargil tragedies especially the November 26 terror attack in Mumbai and the serious flaws in counter-Maoist operations leading to the gruesome killing of a large number of Security personnel speak volumes, that much has to be done in the areas of intelligence, internal security and border management to avert such incidents. In fact, any attempt to revamp our intelligence machinery with certain cosmetic packages of incentives to the personnel or schemes like re-employment of dead-woods of personnel will not help to produce real time intelligence on National security matters. What is required is thorough overhauling of intelligence organization with the formation of a separate cadre; selection of right personnel with right aptitude through transparent recruitment process; proper training in tune with the new challenges and threats; proper motivation of personnel through long-term career planning and above all the accountability and transparency of the organization in their functioning. The thousand dollar question is that how an Intelligence/Investigation agency which cannot compile a fool-proof list of wanted extremists and terrorists, can contribute to National security in the backdrop of a plethora of challenges and threats that encircle the nation? The Political Executive or the heads of these Agencies can come out with any number of explanations which will never help to refurbish the image or credibility of the Agencies or the political set up that shields them. What is needed is a thorough review of the present functioning of these agencies and revolutionary measures to ensure their accountability and transparency. Similarly, instead of ad-hoc arrangements and mechanisms, internal security needs to be strengthened by introducing radical changes in the police set-up. Formation of bodies like National Investigation Agency (NIA) with a bunch of discarded personnel from Central police organizations or State police forces will not contribute much in unraveling the intricate networking of terrorists or extremists or the offenders of transnational crimes. Induction of professionally competent tech-savvy young blood and their proper motivation through sound human resources development strategy will alone help bodies like NIA to undertake serious internal security related tasks.

Thus, there can be no better time to revisit our understanding on the future responses of the police to the challenges in the national security scenario. As rightly commented by Daniel Bell; "future is not an overleaping leap into the distance, it begins in the present. Planning for the future thus does not become a gaze into the crystal ball, but actively grounded in the past" Taking cue from the words of Bell, the major threats to country's security during the first few decades of the present millennium would be a continuation of the past and present challenges with certain changes in line with the developments/trends in the international/regional security scenario and domestic policies. Among the sources of external threat, Pakistan will continue to be the most serious challenge to national security especially after its entry to the nuclear club. Moreover, for any military junta or theocratic set-up in Pakistan which is in the turmoil due to regional/ethnic strife, anti-Indian line is the best opium to appease the people. ISI is the best tool for the political establishment in Pakistan to whip up such sentiments among the people through their 'silent war' against India. Though there is a thaw in Sino-Indian relations, China's nuclear weapon capabilities coupled with its ambition to become a superpower, the still unresolved boundary dispute and Sino-Pakistan defense co-operation are matters of concern to India's long term security. Another area of considerable concern to national security is the proliferation of international Islamic terror groups especially after September 11,2001, terror attack in USA and the subsequent US policy of protracted war against global terrorism by building up 'anti-terror coalition' in which India is a key player. In the backdrop of open threat of 'Jihad 'on India by Osama Bin Laden as early as in 1999 and the country's painful experiences of Jihad- onslaught in Kashmir valley and terror attack in Mumbai (November/2008), the global terrorism will continue to haunt the nation.

The internal security scenario is unlikely to show any major sign of improvement. Despite attempts for a negotiated settlement, Kashmir issue still remains volatile with Pakistan keeping their options against any settlement adversely affecting their strategic interests. Same is the case with the major insurgent and secessionist movements in the North East which are yet to come across the negotiating table for discussions/ settlement. Though section of ULFA leaders has established initial contact with the Union government, there are many hurdles in initiating formal negotiations between ULFA and Government of India on the vexed issue of 'Assam's sovereignty'. There is no let off in CPI (Maoists)- violence in their citadels where police have to bear the brunt of their depredations. The advent of 'hi-tech' terrorism in the national scene which is an offshoot of 'Third wave rhythm' created in the cyber space will pose major challenges to the police in the coming years. Terrorists/extremists, underworld/mafia, militants and fundamentalists are in the process of developing new techniques for their operations by using the innovations in the cyber space. It will not be long before these groups get to lay their hands on nuclear materials or the chemical or biological weapons.

The crucial question is whether the police with the existing resources, manpower or professional skills are competent to effectively confront these future challenges? The answer definitely is 'no'. The police and other paramilitary agencies, to a great extent, are ill-equipped to deal with national security issues of major dimensions. The overwhelming majority of police personnel at cutting edge level have little if any understanding of the major threats to national security such as intricacies of trans-border terrorism, contours of militancy, insurgency, 'covert warfare' of ISI and possibly nothing at all about the new generation of cyber-crimes. Thus, to expect a well coordinated response to the future challenges that emanate from the external and internal sources to the national security seems to be like asking for the impossible. Further, police forces themselves suffer from ambiguities in respect of their future role as the concept of 'policy, planning and research' which should have offset their lack of vision on future still remains alien to police culture. This short-sighted approach incapacitates the force in the proper identification of major threats and formulation of right strategies to counter them. Similarly, the technology, trained manpower well versed with the sophisticated techniques of terrorists, weapons and other modern tools required to combat terrorist groups are not available with most police forces in India.

Thus, while preparing the police forces to combat the future challenges in the national security front, the first and foremost task is to make the force tech-savvy. The personnel at cutting edge level should be imparted knowledge, training and practical skills on the wide range of modern weapons, explosives, communication net work etc which the terrorists and other anti-national elements frequently use in their covert operations. This is more applicable in the case of border police whom is to be equipped, trained and armed like the Infantry Battalions of the Army so that they can counter the armed forces of the aggressor. In the hinterland areas, the augmentation of State Police forces has become imperative in view of the emergence of extremist and militant outfits with their direct or indirect cross-border linkages. Moreover, the concept that the States should equip and engage law enforcing agencies to deal with such groups operating inside the country instead of pleading for the constant deployment of Army and other Central forces in aid of civil administration is getting more and more acceptance. No doubt, the police forces which are familiar with the local issues and developments are the best bet to effectively deal with such threats.

Two areas that need immediate attention of the Political Executive and police leadership, while going for structural changes in police, are the revamping of its intelligence set up and mobilizing of community support in policing efforts to tackle national security issues. We have already discussed the issue of revamping intelligence machinery. On the second aspect of community support, the success of police efforts to tackle major internal security issues depends on the extent of public support and co-operation that the forces enjoy at ground level That is why Richard Clutterback rightly commented that; "the marriage between an uncorrupt police force and an alert and co-operative public is the healthiest guard against terrorism." The police should work out suitable strategies to constitute volunteer groups of civilians whose goodwill and co-operation should be made use of to nip in bud the activities of any organizations or movements that would endanger national security. This clearly demands a more proactive and people friendly approach from the side of police.

The Police in India which confronted serious issues of national security in the past and has been now passing through a highly complex and difficult security environment, occupy the central stage to handle the future threats to national security. The success of the organization in combating the future challenges depends much on its adaptability to the changing situations. Changes are inevitable in the organizational structure, their functional pattern and priorities, professional knowledge, skills and attitude, manpower management and relations with the community/public. Thus, the dictum' one who adapts the way he acts, according to the quality of time succeeds' is aptly applicable and relevant in the case of Indian police in the present millennium.

14

Innovative Organizational Initiatives in Promoting People's Respect for Police:

A Challenge Before Police Leadership

In the present era of globalization and liberalization when the concepts and ideas are revolutionizing the society and new ways of life and working styles are influencing all sections of people, innovations which introduce as something new, have become an inevitable component in the proper functioning of any dynamic organization. Police organization which operates in the midst of a mosaic of challenges and difficulties arising out of a complex web of socio-economic changes and incredible advancements in the field of science and technology is not an exception. However, as all innovations are not good or conducive for the ideal growth of an organization, police leaders should be selective in the introduction of innovations. Thus, P Hersey and K.H. Balanchard, management experts in the field of Human Resources and Organizational behavior, rightly observed; "to be effective to change process, the police Executives should have more than good diagnostic skills. Once they have analyzed the demands of their environment, they must be able to adapt their leadership to fit the demands and develop the means to change some or all of their structural variables". One major issue that had caught the attention of enlightened police managers through out the world is police-public relations. The transition from the standard model of policing to the community based and introduction of diverse innovative mechanisms to bring police closer to public are manifestations of the above trend. But, in many countries including India, police-community relations remained strained, if not hostile. A proper analysis of major factors which influence the police-public relations and the perception of public on police is imperative before initiating innovations.

Basically all good innovations are based on empirical data collected over time and place and planned on analytical feedback. Thus, the first task before police leaders is to analyze the existing scenario of police-public relations on the basis of such data and ground level experiences; identify the problem areas and address them through well planned innovations and solve them to the advantage of the organization. Several studies and surveys conducted by social scientists, police research scholars and prestigious institutions on the public image of police and inter-related aspects have broadly classified these issues into historical, organizational, personnel and functional connected with the police. As long as the police maintain an eclipsed image due to the confluence of these factors, the task of promoting people's respect for police remains onerous. Thus, the challenge before the police leadership is how to free the organization from these negative influences and change its image.

The historical legacy or the image of police as 'defender of status-quo' or 'tool of oppression' in the hands of ruling elite cannot be buried all of a sudden. Instead the strategy should be to refurbish the popular image of police and improve their acceptability in the society through organizational initiatives, such as amendments in the rules and procedures that govern policing. For example, the National Police Commission (NPC) made a number of sweeping recommendations to reform the police in line with the democratic aspirations of the people. The commission had recommended the adoption of a Draft Police Act incorporating a number of provisions to make police and people-friendly and more service oriented. However, majority of the States which make tall claims on police reforms and modernization are yet to pay some heed to this Draft. Similarly, Police Manuals and Rules which were mostly set in pre-independence era, but still governs the various details of police functions do not bring police anywhere near to the people. It is now established that many meaningful innovations can be introduced on the lines of some of the recommendations of NPC or by making amendments in Police Manuals or Rules without any legal implications. A recent example is Goa Police Act in which a number of innovative provisions have been incorporated to enhance service edge of policing over administrative edge. Similarly, a new Police Act in the direction of democratizing police in line with the aspirations of common people has been enacted in Kerala in 2010 after a lot of debate and discussions among political party leaders, jurists, police leaders, government functionaries and NGO/Civil rights activists. But the mere enactment of an Act or the amendment in the existing legislations governing police will not help reform the police or make them people-friendly, unless the police leaders change their present 'psyche'. The new generation of police leaders should shelve the general trend in police organization treating the archaic rules and procedures as' holy scripts' After all in any dynamic society, changes in rules and regulations are imperative as part of social dynamics leading to development. Side by side, they should encourage a paradigm shift in the role of police from 'traditional law enforcers' to ' facilitators' or 'advisors' in the fields of security, development and welfare for which the personnel should be motivated to actively involve in service and welfare oriented tasks such as assistance to the victims of earthquake, cyclone, flood, famine, rail accidents etc. The proper interaction of the personnel with people in distress and danger and assistance extended to them at the time of crisis and need would help the organization to attain the image of a 'public service agency' much to the liking of large segments in the society.

In professional organizations like police, human resources play a crucial role and the productivity of the organization depends on their performance Thus, induction of right personnel and their proper motivation in line with the organizational goals assume an important task of police leadership. A unique phenomenon of police is that a defaulting policeman becomes symbol of the entire organization and he is being projected by the detractors of the force to malign the image of the police. Thus, the policies regarding recruitment, training, promotion, service conditions and internal discipline and decorum should be rationalized to meet the job requirements of the organization, Gone are the days when every able-bodied youth was found suitable for police work, The new breed of police personnel should have natural attitude and aptitudes, humane qualities, steadiness and mental alertness besides intellectual and academic depth relevant to their work. The concepts like 'catch them young'; train them on modern management and human resources development strategies with a sense of involvement should be implemented.

As management expert, Peter Drucker rightly observed that education in the liberal sense does not deliver 'knowledge' and it is the organization to do it themselves to their manpower, the police leaders should initiate mechanisms to impart true knowledge to the personnel for qualitative improvement in their professionalism and behavior pattern. This is more applicable in the case of Constabulary which constitutes more than 80% of the total force and having maximum visibility and interaction with the public in the society. Therefore, innovative strategies like 'Constable oriented manpower structure' and 'Officer-oriented work culture' by working out proper synergy between officers and constabulary with the aim to develop better qualities of conduct, integrity and professionalism among the latter should be vigorously pursued by the police leadership. Efforts should be made to equip the constabulary to undertake important policing tasks and display a level of conduct good enough to meet the aspirations of the people. For that purpose, the self regulatory mechanisms which have become dysfunctional in the police have to be strengthened after successfully identifying and updating them. Some State police forces in Delhi, Kerala, Punjab, etc have already introduced mechanisms linking transfer/posting of the personnel with their attitude, behavior pattern and professionalism. Adverse traits such as involvement in corruption and rude and indecent behavior towards the public would be incorporated in the Annual Performance Appraisal of the personnel which would form main criterion during posting/transfer. Simultaneously Police leaders should initiate innovative mechanisms that would help to improve the behavior and attitude of personnel towards public. For example, District Police, Patiala (Punjab) in 1999 introduced a novel scheme of all personnel addressing male members of the public as "Shrimanji" or " Sir" and all ladies as "Bhenji" or "Mataji" or "Madam" depending upon their age. This scheme which had created positive impact on the behavioral pattern of police personnel and was appreciated by the public because of the polite and decent behavior of personnel was later introduced in more and more police districts. However one main bone of contention is that such cosmetic schemes in police initiated at the instance of certain career-oriented police leaders with much publicity and propaganda have limitations to create 'permanent positive imprints' in the minds of hardened personnel especially at cutting edge level. We should understand the reality that the indecent and rude behavior of police personnel towards the public is part of the existing police culture and ethos manifesting the authority and powers of the 'khaki uniform' which on many occasions surface in the form of 'third degree methods' and brutalities.

The bottlenecks connected with police professionalism and efficiency especially in the area of detection of sensational crimes quickly influence the public perception on police. The general tendency is that the public instead of appreciating the role and limitations of the police in the entire domain of criminal justice system-in which there are other players like prosecution- arrive at quick conclusions on police and squarely blame them for increase in incidence of crime, delay in investigations and low conviction rate. The public alone should not be blamed for such conclusions and perceptions. It is quite natural that the confidence of public is lost when more than 80% of offences reported to police are declared undetected and only around 10% of the detected cases end in conviction. Moreover, the overall record of the police in their mandatory functions is not up to the mark. Time and again the Courts and Enquiry Commissions have come down heavily upon their 'functional aberrations' during caste-communal riots or the inordinate delay in the investigation of sensational cases. The Apex Court's directions on Bofors, Jain-Hawala, Fodder scam, Best Bakery etc are a few examples.

Innovations in crime management have become an integral part of the functional efficiency of the police. The first and foremost task is de- linking of investigation wing from law and order front and their effective insulation against political interference or any other extraneous forces. The personnel of this wing should be imparted specialized training in interrogation techniques, Forensic Sciences, Finger-printing and other modern scientific aids of investigation so that many unhealthy professional traits such as use of 'third -degree' methods, custodial violence and fabrication of evidence which belittle the image of police can be minimized or dispensed with. Proposals such as formation of District level interrogation centers with a pool of at least half a dozen professional interrogators, association of senior officers in the investigation of sensational crimes and appointment of full-fledged Prosecuting Agency as legal advisors of police department etc should be pursued by police administration to improve speed and quality of investigations and the rate of conviction.

The public perception on police is mainly crystallized through proper and swift response of those who approach the police with grievances and complaints. The police Stations are the cutting edge level of police functioning where common man comes into contact with police. Most of the policing works are done there. In fact, the image of police and their productivity is judged at police station level. Though substantial funds have been earmarked for infrastructural development of police stations and residential accommodation of personnel under Police Modernization Scheme and Special Schemes by the State governments, hundreds of police Stations in rural areas function in rented dilapidated buildings without basic amenities or facilities. While emphasizing the need of improving the condition and facilities of police Stations, the reality is that no amount of modernization or infrastructural development would change the image of police stations unless the personnel manning them would change their attitude and behavior towards the public especially the weaker and underprivileged sections which approach the police stations to mitigate their grievances. Use of abusive language, ill-treatment of persons, harassment of women complainants, non-registration of FIR under one pretext or other, collection of bribe and custodial violence are common in police stations especially in rural areas.

Significantly, a number of innovative mechanisms initiated by police could overcome many such maladies in the functioning of police stations. Specific mention should be made about schemes such as 'Turant chovis' taken up in Aurangabad city of Maharashtra in 2004. This scheme which provides speedy and effective mechanisms at Police Stations with respect to any complaint lodged there, either through a process of conciliation/arbitration akin to Alternate Dispute Resolution (ADR) or through registration of case and commencement of investigations within 24 hours of lodging the complaint, won tremendous applaud from the public, press and the government. An impact assessment of the scheme revealed that out of 959 local and 856 serious complaints received by the police during the period from July 2004 to November 2004, over 99%were heard within 24 hours whereas 88% were disposed off within the stipulated time. The study also disclosed that the innovation helped the police in building confidence among common masses about police and criminal justice system as pending cases at police stations were kept at abysmally low level. In view of the spectacular success of the scheme, Maharashtra government took decision to introduce the innovation in all the districts of the State. Similarly, the Delhi police have also launched a number of innovative schemes to improve the functioning of the police stations with greater emphasis to make the system speedy, transparent and refined, thereby making it more acceptable to the society. Specific reference may be made about 'Sankaraman Kasha' at police station (a meeting room at entry of police stations with enough glass-windows where investigation officers are supposed to meet the complainants), CCTV (to closely monitor the lock-up rooms, sentries and duty officers and the interaction of personnel with the complainants) and E-mail facility for easily lodging complaints The main aim of these schemes which evoked considerable response among the people was to give a new image to police stations by ensuring transparency in functioning.

Just like police stations, District Police Office (DPO)/SSP office is yet another hub of activity in the District Police set up which is frequented by large number of people to get done variety of police related job. A study conducted by Dinkar Gupta, IPS, Punjab in Jalandhar in 1999 revealed that the most common reasons for the public to visit these offices were clearance of arms-licenses, Passport verification, service verification and complaint verification. Patiala police in Punjab launched 'single window system' in order to meet the requirements of the public and to promote police-public friendly relations, quick delivery of service by avoiding wastage of time of the public and reduce the inflow of public to the office. An impact study on the scheme has revealed that it gave fruitful results to the public and evoked high appreciation in the society.

The internal innovations in police which mainly focus on the improvement in infrastructural facilities and functioning of the police constitute only one side of the policing efforts to build up the public image of the police. Equally important are the external innovations aimed at bringing police closer to the public. The community or problem-oriented poling which involves the people in crime prevention, peace-keeping and social defense mechanisms fall under the domain of such innovations. Though not systematically conceived variants of community support for improving police-public relations and law enforcement have been subjected to experimentation in India both by means of formal legislations and through the initiative of innovative police managers in different States. The Karnataka Defence Parties Act, 1964 which had introduced the institution of Dalapathy (Group leader) as interface between the police and rural community was the last formal legislation in this regard. In almost all States, various innovative experiments were undertaken by enterprising police leaders for harmonizing police-community relations. However, most of these efforts could not create any sustainable impact on police functioning or public perception towards police mainly due to absence of institutionalization and systematic support-both organizational and legislative. In fact, many of these schemes went into oblivion when their innovators were transferred or they took up more challenging assignments.

Institutionalization is an essential component for the success or sustainability of any innovative scheme. This is basically an organizational task for which the initiative should come from the organizational hierarchy In the case of police; the leadership can effectively play this role. As Maeterlinck rightly observed; "each progressive spirit is opposed by a thousand men appointed to guard the past introduction of any novelty seems to be out of priority in a regimented and vertical organization like police". Thus, one cardinal task of police leadership is that they should take initiative for the transformation of the organization from a vertical to horizontal one with more flexibility and transparency so that new- fangled ideas and entrepreneurship can find due recognition and acceptance in the organization. Simultaneously, the human resources at various levels of the organization should be properly sensitized on the new concepts so that they should imbibe the spirit of implementation of innovative schemes. The supervisory officers should fix the responsibility of the success of these schemes at each level, as leaving any grey areas would lead deficiency in the implementation.

The efforts by police leadership to change the police organization from a vertical to horizontal organization with flexibility would succeed only when they encourage changes in their present style of functioning. They should shed the mantle of defensiveness and erase the era of mystery surrounding their activities and aggressively solicit public support and involvement. For that purpose, they have to demolish the walls of the 'culture of secrecy' in the force and shelve the 'closed mouth' or 'no comment' policy, which has been exploited by the media and public for 'police-bashing'. In the present 'information era' when the print and electronic media enjoy considerable power and potential in the image building exercise of individuals and organizations, healthy and honest relations with the media would help the police to brighten its image in the society.

Similarly, a change of attitude of police towards the public is necessary to promote latter's respect for police. At present, the police contact with the public is distant and occupies mostly in criminal action. For more formal and effective interaction between the police and the people, police Station level Liaison committees with police personnel and local people with integrity and reputation should be constituted. These committees should function as open platform for the police and public to share their views and grievances and hold free and frank discussions on various aspects of policing including legal constraints, resource constraints and the role of the public in assisting the police to tackle social problems. Such grass-roots level committees with the representatives of the police and public, no doubt, will function as 'facilitators' in cementing the relations between the police and public with mutual respect.

15

Research in Police Subjects:
A Grey Area in Indian Policing

The sweeping changes that are knocking at our doors are perhaps one of the serious challenges confronting organizations and individuals in the present millennium. The rhythm of these changes influences almost all spheres of human activity. Organizations adopt a number of strategies to absorb those changes that are conducive for their growth and betterment. The great management expert, Alvin Toffler rightly commented, "the hyper speed of changes today means that given facts become obsolete faster; knowledge built on them becomes less durable". To overcome this 'transcience factor, new technological and organizational tools are currently being designed to accelerate scientific research and development'. Some common tools that are in vogue and adopted by organization in this direction are market surveys, pilot studies, public opinion polls, and empirical research on a myriad of changes and developments in the society. These mechanisms enable the organizations to arrive at a number of findings and insights in respect of specific issues (concerning the organization or their clientele), which are used as parameters for reforms or innovations meant for improving their professionalism, competence and general acceptance in the society.

Reform-oriented researches in police subjects assume immense importance for police which are engaged in continuous battle against crime and criminals and in search of new insights and techniques in handling a mosaic of offences in the emerging socio-economic environment. These tasks become more arduous in the case of police forces operating in pluralist societies in which centrifugal forces representing caste, community, ethnic, regional and religious groups adopt aggressive and militant postures to uphold their own identity and 'sub-culture' virtually negating the concepts of unity and integrity. Their organized activities ranging from conventional form of agitations to secessionism, insurgency and terrorism pose serious challenge to public order and shatter peace, safety and tranquility especially when they attain the dimensions of Low Intensity Conflicts (LIC) patronized by hostile neighbors across the borders. The country is now passing through such a poignant internal Security scenario with a plethora of complex issues which need in-depth research and comprehensive analysis/assessment. Moreover, the era of globalization and liberalization has given an impetus to transnational crimes as manifest by the steady increase in cyber-crimes, money-laundering, 'hawala' transactions, scams and scandals.

Despite organized efforts, modernization and strengthening of police have hardly kept pace with the exponential growth seen in crime and criminals and dangers all around. The deficiencies in strategic management of law and order and the inadequacies of the force were clear on a number of occasions. The main reason was the inability of the system to formulate right techniques or measures to effectively deal with the early symptoms of unrest or law and order issues which later developed into serious internal security problems such as insurgency and terrorism. As Peter Druker rightly observed; "the important and difficult job is not to find out the right answer, but the right question, for the right question requires the right analysis of the problem". What requires for the right analysis of any serious issue or problem is proper identification of the problem; collection and collation of all relevant material and data connected with the issue from different sources and their proper scientific documentation. The above requirements no doubt, are the basic ingredients of any productive research.

Ironically, the police leadership in the country has never encouraged any such scientific approach while dealing with law and order or other threats to internal security. Instead, the police machinery set into motion to cope with these issues in a casual, routine, ad-hoc and unprofessional way. Their endeavor was not to find out 'why' the problem or situation, but how to deal it. Any number of examples can be cited in this regard. The Telangana peasant uprisings of late 1940s, insurgency movements in the North East, Khalistan movement in Punjab, growth of Left Wing Extremism in West Bengal and other States, Dalit- militancy in some States and emergence of powerful mafias and underworld in metropolises like Mumbai are typical examples in this regard. In fact majority of these movements had originated as local level agitations or campaigns in support of popular or parochial demands or issues spearheaded by a band of rustic leaders or intellectuals. The charisma of A.Z. Phizo, the legendary leader of Naga insurgency was confined for many years to Naga hills and hamlets; whereas the name of Laldenga who spearheaded the Mizo insurgency was within Mizo hills and Jarnail Sigh Bhindranwala who terrorized the entire nation was a rustic Sikh who never dreamt a Khalistan! Had the law enforcing and Intelligence agencies had properly diagnosed and deciphered these movements and their leaders in right perspective and adopted timely, unbiased and effective strategies to neutralize them, these movements would not have attained mammoth dimensions. In the present context, such ambiguities and lack of direction exist at police leadership in the case of LWE. A section of senior police hierarchy in LWE affected States are adamant in their conviction that Left Wing Extremism is a mere law and order issue and should be firmly dealt with by using bayonets and bullets without considering the socio-economic or developmental issues contributing to the growth of the movement or the plight and difficulties of the affected civilian population. They are not prepared to draw lessons from the past or to impartially observe and analyze the present trends in this front, but blindly endorse the plans for the future without understanding ground level realities. Thus, the counter-insurgency operations launched by them in States like Chaattisgarh flopped in total catastrophe leading to the death a large number of police/Security personnel. Such dilemma or professional ignorance of police leadership was succinctly commented by Shri MK Narayanan, former National Security Adviser as; "violent conflicts are shaped as much by conflicts among contending interest groups and cultures as by the inability of the governments and its agencies to think and function effectively. The success of the police hereinafter depend on the kind of insights they can develop about the nature and role of post-State organization; how criminal empires and interest groups are altering the counters of civil societies; how terrorist and insurgent groups erode community interests and destroy the sense of individual responsibility; how niche technologies such as post-modern means of information manipulation and dissemination have become powerful tools of conflict. This is crucial if the police are to uphold the integrity of the nation State."

It is high time that the police organization should develop mechanisms for the better appreciation of major challenges that knock at their doors. Macro and micro level researches in respect of various policing issues would provide right insights for the organization to formulate new strategies for effectively performing their main charter of duties namely maintenance of public order and prevention and detection of crime. A recent report by the US Department of Justice's "Office of Community Oriented Policing Services" (COPS) and Police Foundation on problem analysis in policing clearly highlighted the importance of research programs in police as "problem analysis is actual research in that it involves every formalized methods of study with a goal of arriving at practical solutions". Immense variety and high quality researches on criminal justice system takes place in USA. This has been possible because of the hard work of some outstanding professors and dedicated students who are liberally supported by the governments and other agencies by extending grant and facilities. Partnership/collaboration with Universities and renowned academic institutions helped to enhance the quality of researches. For example, the National Institute of Justice, USA in collaboration with a coalition of 13 urban universities instituted "Improving Crime data Project" (ICD) which helped to improve local access-making and anti-crime efforts in urban communities by raising crime incident data vis-a-vis other sources of data. More over in the campuses of these countries, there is clear ambience that is conducive to serious research-one that promotes innovations and encourages constructive debates. What is more distinctive about these researches is that majority of these works are on down to earth matters that are built around problems which government and law enforcing agencies have to wrestle with each day. Some of the topics that received attention of researchers are the speed of police response to distress calls from the public, biases in the system believed to be weighted against minorities especially African-Americans which lead to brutality and disproportionate incarceration of minorities, overcrowding of prisons, adequacy of criminal convictions particularly capital punishment and crime prevention strategies and tactics. Studies in these areas either by police or academics have undoubtedly yielded to findings which have triggered substantive executive action.

Researches on grey areas of policing with a view to bring out new insights into the role, functions and challenges of police in the changing socio-economic environment in the country are imperative to reform the organization on professional lines. Such grey areas exist in respect of the external and internal matters of policing. For example, debate on the role transition of police from 'traditional law enforcer' to'facilitator' or 'advisor' in areas like security, development, environment, social service etc has become more vocal in the present era of liberalization and privatization. Similarly, the concepts like 'privatization' civilianization' and 'outsourcing' of certain functions of police have been gaining ground within the organization and outside. But many inter-related issues need to be settled before the police leadership go for such innovations. Empirical studies are prerequisite to arrive at right perspectives and strategies on these issues or to identify the tasks and functions of the police that can be outsourced or the areas or duties that can be shared with competent private/civilian agencies without jeopardizing statutory powers of police or interests of citizens. In depth studies are required in many other areas such as transformation of the police organization from a vertical to horizontal body with corresponding change in the behavior and attitude of personnel, better utilization of manpower especially the constabulary in core areas of policing, ,means needed to improve the living and working conditions as well as the morale of personnel at cutting edge level and new forms of 'transcendent literacy' and 're-sighting of training horizons' to equip the force to successfully meet the new challenges etc.

Productive research on core areas of policing and strategic management system in police have become more significant in view of the rapid social changes and widely disparate law and order problems in different parts of the country. Percepts are fast changing. Moral and ethical codes are undergoing revolutionary changes. Majority of the new generation do not find anything wrong in minor vices like gambling, boozing, 'sizzling item shows' or 'semi-nude discos'. Many legal and moral questions come to the fore. Whether police should overstrain their resources and strictly enforce laws in all such matters? Or should they under-enforce laws and concentrate more in core areas of policing? Similar questions arise on the exact role of police on the implementation of various social legislations and Local Acts. As police are accountable to people and rule of law with social commitment, they have to adopt a balanced and judicious approach on these vexed issues which are inextricably interwoven with diverse sentiments and perceptions of different segments of the society. Any callous or blunt policy or strategic management decision on these issues without properly assessing the ground level realities and line of thinking of masses would adversely affect the public image of police. For arriving at right perspectives, police organization need thorough analysis and assessment of the issues for which empirical research on policing issues is more significant.

Ironically, in India, neither productive research on police subjects have attracted the kind of talent it should have nor research based studies have enriched our literature on police matters. No doubt, the publishing industry is flooded with police literature and titles which in majority of cases are either replica of works: from the West or the glorified chronicles on the achievements and adventures of individual police leaders. Seldom they reflect the ground realities on policing or are useful for reforms/innovations in police. Then, there was not much exaggeration when a senior police officer who conducted research on 'Organized crime' made pungent comments as; "not a single book worth its name has been written on organized crime in India all these years. There was no research paper or well researched article except some which contains summaries from news paper reports". Same was the case with majority of police subjects except a few pet themes such as Community policing or pro-active police strategies. Even in these subjects the researchers depended heavily on similar studies in the West. Plagiarism in one form or other was the main facet of these research projects.

Absence of productive and quality research in police subjects in the country was due to a variety of factors, both external and internal to police force. Few Universities or academic institutions have an exclusive department for this discipline. More importantly, funding by government and non-government agencies has been modest. Presently with over 22 lakh police personnel and an annual expenditure of about Rs. 25,000 crores, Indian police spent only rupees one crore on research as compared to over Rs. 2800 crores invested by the Defense forces. More over, police organization does not have any pro-active approach on research matters. Large majority of policy-makers and police leaders interpret research in police subjects as 'wasteful academic pursuit' contributing nothing significant to the organization from professional point of view. Many among them adopt negative tactics in sharing data on crime and criminals with researchers on police subjects. Kiran Bedi, IPS had a bitter experience when a senior police officer of Tihar jail refused to grant permission to her for interviewing under-trial drug-addicts in the jail, as part of her research project. The result was that Ms Bedi had to change the topic of research "Drug abuse and Criminals". The police fraternity did not help her to overcome the tangle. If that be the case of a senior IPS officer like Kiran Bedi in the research field, we can well imagine the plight of scholars and junior research fellows approaching the senior echelons of police hierarchy for collecting empirical data for their research on police subjects. Reality is that collection of data on police or crime related topics such as corruption, police demeanors, fake encounters/custodial violence, human rights violations, Padding of evidence during investigations, police-criminal-politician nexus etc, for any researcher be it a police officer or social scientist is an onerous task. Thus, majority of research scholars seldom select such subjects for their research. Those who conduct research on such subjects fail to show full justice to their project in view of the apparently negative approach by the police hierarchy to share relevant data/material to them.

The existing structural and institutional set up in police to promote quality research in police subjects is inadequate. The reports of National and State Police Commissions and various Committees on Police Reforms contain a lot of macro level data or recommendations concerning general issues of policing. Hardly have they provided any insight into the problems that the police are likely to encounter or confront in future. For example, Dharam Vira Commission which included many eminent personalities could not foresee the myriad of challenges that the police are now confronting or are likely to be faced in the near future especially in the areas of transnational and organized crimes. Instead their main endeavor was to recommend a number of ways and means to insulate police against the interference of the government of the day or political parties. Ironically, the recommendations of the Commission had not been implemented even after four decades since the submission of report. Thus, these recommendations are of now little use in improving the professionalism or performance of the force as many of them had become redundant and lost whatever relevance they had in dealing with policing problems in 21st century. This is equally applicable in respect of the recommendations by other Commissions or Committees, which had had the same fate of Dharam Vira Commission. The latest examples are the recommendations of the Police Reforms Committee headed by K. Padmanabhaiah (former Union Home Secretary) and the Committee on reforms in Criminal Justice system headed by Justice (retd) V.S. Malimath of Supreme Court of India. Though these Committees have come out with a number of recommendations meant for reforming the police and criminal justice system, they are still safely kept in the archives. A different picture emerges in respect of probe reports by Judicial Commissions on police excesses or failures during the enforcement of law and order. These reports usually incorporate a lot of micro level inputs and data on the issue in question, but are of little use for practical reforms in police due to their over-riding judicial perspective and insights. More over, such probe reports open a Pandora's Box of controversies. A recent example is U C Banerjee Commission report on the fire in Sabarmati Express/Godhra riots, which is yet to see the light of the day due to legal and political controversies.

The role of national level institutions notably Bureau of Police Research and Development (BPR&D) and National Police Academy in promoting research in police subjects needs closer look. Both are known centers of excellence in police matters with better infrastructure and financial sources.

The BPR&D as a nodal agency at national level co-ordinates systematic research in police subjects, besides organizing the annual feat of All India Police Science Congress. The Police Congress, attended by Police officers, forensic experts, social scientists etc from different parts of the country is another forum which deliberates upon selected themes closely connected with different aspects of policing and brings out a compendium of findings/recommendations for reforms in police organization. Ironically, majority of these recommendations which focus on more executive powers, better emoluments/perks and more autonomy and financial powers to the higher echelons of the force remain as unfulfilled dreams. In the case of NPA, one of the missions of this institution is to become a centre of research in police subjects. The Academy has been striving to fulfill this mission by undertaking research by Faculty members and offering Police Fellowship etc to selected police officers on specific Police subjects. A review of the research projects undertaken by these institutions reveals that more serious efforts should be made by them to promote quality research that would be beneficial to the organization. A number of macro and micro level research projects undertaken by these institutions focusing on the organizational and personnel issues in police organization do not properly reflect the real challenges the police have to confront in the present society. In view of the rapidly changing internal security scenario in the country with a mosaic of serious law and order issues and a plethora of militant/violent movements/groups, unique to a particular region or State(s), these institutions should explore mechanisms and strategies to promote micro level research on specific challenges to police so that the ground level findings emerging out of these studies can be effectively applied for right executive action. For example, Police cannot apply any common parameters or strategy for dealing with Left Wing Extremism (LWE) in various States, as the topography and socio economic factors contributing to the genesis, spread, consolidation and mass support of the movement vary from State to State and thus the police strategy to counter the movement. The general tendency of research scholars proposing or selecting their own topics for thesis merely for attaining academic decorations or career progression should be dispensed with. Similarly various national institutions should guard against the attempts of police leaders to hi-jack Research projects or Fellowships while they are shunted out from their parent organizations or States on corruption/other issues. Such elements seldom do justice to the research project but leisurely manipulate or misuse the resources of the institutions. Another equally discernible tendency is the hectic lobbying by police leaders to get nominated for research projects funded and sponsored by foreign institutions While those really deserving such recognition are deprived of such avenues, those who get nominated through back doors not only fail to do justice to the research program, but also brings discredit to the organization during their foreign jaunt as part of the project. The heart of the matter is that when the elements of transparency and true professionalism are compromised in the field of nomination of personnel for research and the timely completion of tasks, no worthwhile research on police subjects that are useful to the organization could be undertaken. Unfortunately, we are now passing through such a phase in the country. In order to overcome these bottlenecks and to streamline the entire process of planned research in police subjects, the police administration should take certain positive steps. Firstly, a screening committee comprising police leaders, social scientists/intellectuals and administrative/ Security experts should make objective analysis of emerging trends/challenges in the internal security and law and order fields in different areas/States and identify the issues for formal research from policing angle. Decentralization of research programs focusing on micro level issues relevant to policing/ better enforcement of law and order is the need of the hour.

The concept of decentralization of research is yet to be seriously practiced in State police forces. Hardly there exists any Planning or Research cell in any State police organization. The police leaders who strictly adhere to the canons of regimentation and paramilitary orientation of police, feel that such exercises which are basically academic have no relevance in vertical organizations. This attitude should be changed. There is need for full-fledged research and analysis wing in each State police set up to study and analyze the existing law enforcement arrangement vis-a vis the innovative strategies and mechanisms to equip the police to counter the new challenges and policing problems. Police leaders with right perspective, insight, intellectual and analytical bent of mind, professional aptitude and ground level experience on genuine policing issues in the State should be inducted into this cell. They should have fixed tenure and better perks and facilities. The research and analysis wing should adopt innovative mechanisms to give proper orientation to formal research in police subjects. Micro level research in specific policing problems particular to certain areas such as streets, villages, ghettos-urban and rural-or groups like minorities, dalits, migrants, slum-dwellers, women and children should be encouraged. These research projects should cover a wide spectrum of socio-economic and crime related issues such as steady increase in incidence of crime in a particular district or sub-division, generic factors for the emerging crime, modus operandi of new generation criminals, growth of extremist/militant groups in certain segments of population, proliferation of explosives and illegal arms in particular pockets etc in order to bring out ground level realities of the problem in question. In many instances, the police organization do not have the expertise, resources or right personnel to undertake empirical studies on wide range of challenges/issues that need police intervention. Initially, these tasks can be assigned to professional research groups, NGOs or academic institutions in partnership with police. The insights and findings that are brought out through formal research should be translated into executive action for the larger interests of the organization. The innovations and reforms in police should be based on these findings and not on the basis of ad-hoc or need based arrangements or subjective impressions of police leaders that police are accustomed to. Such a paradigm shift in the strategy of police alone would enable the organization to meet the myriad of challenges confronting the police in the present millennium.

16 Crime and Habitat

From earlier days, criminology showed interest on the geography of crimes. For example, the studies by Gerri (France) and Mayhew (England) in 19th century were well known in this field. Shaw and McKay of Chicago school of Research made decisive contributions on the future studies on crime and habitat. The subject had been revived and revivified in1970s mainly due to the famous works of C.R. Jeffery (Crime Prevention through environmental design) and Oscar Newman (Defensible Space). With these works and other extensive studies, a new branch in criminology namely 'environmental criminology' was born. Essentially, this branch is the study of the 'place in time and space when law offender and target come together' (Brantingham & Brantingham). In other words, it mainly discusses the influence of living conditions and places that perpetrate crimes. The inter-relationship between crime and habitat may be examined from this angle.

The transition of the human society from a primitive to highly advanced one with all complexities in the habitat and living style of the people had largely contributed to the proliferation of crime. In primitive societies, the incidence of crime was comparatively less. The well-known Artic explorer, V. Stefenson reported that at various times that as he traveled away from the civilization of Western society into the farther most regions of Eskimos society, crime had decreased to almost minimum. Similarly, Walter A. Luden, in his study of Australian aborigines showed that there is very little or virtually no criminality among them. The tribal societies of the North East and Central India also showed such trends in crime, for many decades. The advancement of the society through dehumanized development and industrialization with its inherent profit oriented vulgarity and ecological insensitivity coupled with steady population explosion and unemployment led to the speedy deterioration of human values and interpersonal relations paving the way for criminal tendencies, Its manifestations were there in almost all major areas of human life and activity. One noticeable trend was the transformation in the nature of human settlements. There was steady shrinkage of villages; many rural areas became semi-urban; whereas existing urban centers became mega metropolises with a mosaic of industries and other establishments. In the modern industrialized society, urbanization has become an integral part. Thus, the total urban population in the world which was 14% of the world population in 1901 has crossed over 50% during the last one century. The situation is not different in India. The number of urban agglomerations which was 1827 with 25.9 million people (10.84% of the total population) in 1901 has increased to 3768 with 217.6 million (25.72% of the total population) in 1991 and285 million(27.8% of the total population) in 2001.

Such rapid urbanization and the continued exodus of people from the rural to urban areas in search of employment, business etc led to the emergence of sprawling slums both in the heart and suburbs of large cities. These slums in many cities like Mumbai and Kolkota became the breeding ground of a variety of crimes. Majority of the slum-dwellers who constituted the floating population have neither any permanent job nor any regular source of income. Many are in acute poverty and miseries. Those who were uprooted from their rural settings have had an entirely different experience. In fact, it is probably easier to accept poverty in rural, rather than an urban environment. In rural setting, one usually has a bit of land with which to associate. There his struggle is mainly against the forces of nature, drought, floods, cyclone, storms, cold-winds and barren land. On the contrary, the poverty in the 'lonely crowd' of large urban centers is perhaps the worst. In urban setting one can easily make comparisons of his or her desperate condition with that of other privileged and affluent immediate neighbors who live in luxurious sky-scrappers; employ servants; drive the most modern and costly vehicles; send their wards to the reputed and prestigious schools, feed their pets sumptuously; take long pleasure trips; eat in star hotels and restaurants and virtually enjoy every moment of their life in all its color, mirth and gaiety. The cinema and the electronic media which are the most popular entertainment sources of the common man constantly portray the kind of easy life in its extreme sensualist manner even by denigrating the basic human values and culture. People who live in crowded slums, even in hovels, tents, boats under bridges, in the pavements or in the open streets, cut off from their villages and kith and kin, feel the pain of hunger, smell the stench of poverty, suffer the aches of diseases and face the large impersonal and impenetrable, but seemingly self satisfied bureaucracies, are the most vulnerable sections, prone to crime and criminal depredations. They have no empathy or compassion, but only apathy, animosity and anger, towards themselves; to the society and fellow beings. A miniscule section accepts their condition as will of God Almighty. But overwhelming majority turns to crime, hooliganism, prostitution, drug-peddling and all forms of anti-social activities to escape from poverty and social deadlock. People who believe that' they have nothing to lose, but sufferings and miseries' can easily be convinced that their status could be changed by any means-peaceful and violent. The genesis of underworld/mafia, urban terrorism or extremism or similar organized violence could be largely attributed to such trends.

Certain authentic studies on the crime scenario in our mega cities demonstrate the above realities. For example, in

Mumbai, our commercial capital of India, about 50% of population lives in slums located within the city or its suburbs. The 'slum-lords' encroach upon the governmental or private land, raise huts that are sold or given on rent at lucrative amounts. A survey conducted by the Controller of Slums Mumbai in late 1980s revealed that 166390 huts on government and Municipal land were converted into 'pacca-chawls' whereas 48960 huts erected on private land were sold out for prices ranging from Rs. 7500 to Rs. 20000. Through such and other illegal activities, the' Mumbai mafia' had created a parallel economy in which smuggling activities contributed over Rs.100 crores per annum; prostitution Rs. 4.5 crores; 'the matka' Rs. 9 crores, illicit liquor Rs. 12 crores and slums Rs. 2.6 crores. Over the last three decades, the entire scenario had undergone sea change and the powerful mafia and the underworld have become all pervasive virtually controlling the trade and commerce, industry, cinema, and even the bureaucracy. They have established transnational linkages and are the kingpins behind a variety of crimes such as killing for ransom, trade union breaking, clearing of slums for big builders, trafficking in women, smuggling of arms and explosives for extremists/terrorists and underworld. The metro city of Mumbai in late 1980s and 1990s witnessed a series of such incidents such as killings of Datta Samant (independent trade unionist), Gulshan Kumar (Music Mughal) and Vallabh Thakur (industrialist) etc. The situation is not much different in other major cities in the country.

The sprawling slums and the underworld are only one face of the urban habitat. The other face is polished, refined and sophisticated but equally potential to breed crime. That is the 'flat culture' whose implications have been well brought out by Antony E Bottoms, Director of Institute of Criminology, Cambridge University and Paul Wilis, Director for Center for Criminological & Social Legal Studies at University of Sheffield through their well documented studies on 'Housing Tenure and Residential community crime careers in Britain'. One of their major findings was that private rental especially in decayed areas around the city centers and local authority housing sectors which attract transient clientele often resulted in high incidence of crime. Their findings, in many respects, have much relevance to Indian scenario as well. In our mega cities and townships, the mushroom growth of flats and apartments has become a commercial activity, rather than residential. Majority of flat/apartment owners who have bases abroad lease out their apartments to unknown persons through intermediaries or Real estate brokers. We have any number of examples of such tenants using these apartments for illegal activities like running' sex-rackets' (to meet the requirements of privileged clientele), hide-outs for terrorists/ extremists or storage of explosives/arms. Another inherent danger is that some of these tenants pollute the entire habitat through their loose morals, addiction to drugs and liquor etc. Many occasions, adolescent children and women fall victims to their vices. The highly mechanical way of life and lack of social interaction which are the main facets of 'flat culture' help these elements to carry out their nefarious activities without the knowledge of the residents. Such illegal activities have started knocking at the doors of our rural habitat because of the spread of urban culture to more and more areas.

The challenges that we confront in our habitat in the form of crimes and other social issues can be overcome by formulating sound strategies at administrative and law enforcement level. Significantly, the nation States and international organizations have felt the need of such strategies to develop ideal and conducive habitat. The 'World Habitat Conference' organized by the United Nations at Vancouver in 1976 was the first major attempt in this direction. The 'Vancouver Declaration on Human settlements' adopted by the conference emphasized the need of the governments formulating spatial strategies and adopting human settlement policies to guide socio-economic development efforts by nations. Such strategies and policies should form an essential component of an overall development strategy that need to be linked and harmonized with policies on industrialization, environment, agriculture and cultural identity in such way that each should support the other for the greater progress, welfare and well-being of the mankind. Among various other things, the above declaration also suggested the need of improving the rural habitat, reduction of disparities in the living standards and opportunities between the urban and rural areas. In order to overcome many of the psychological and social factors that contribute to the crime, the conference also proposed that the design of human settlements should aim at providing environment in which identities of individuals, families and societies are preserved and adequate means for preserving privacy, face to face interaction and public participation in decision making process are to be ensured. Similarly, the places of worship especially in areas of expanding human settlements should be provided and recognized in order to satisfy the spiritual and religious needs of various groups so that such places would influence the psyche of the people and deter them from criminal activities. However, many developing countries including India pay scant regard to such guidelines in the Declaration and go ahead with human settlements especially for the poor and weaker sections with typical bureaucratic style. Large number of hutments and settlements are erected in remote areas without basic amenities and the residents there are plunged into perpetual misery and sufferings which act as catalysts for breeding crime and criminal activities. Irony is that majority of these hutments which cannot bear the brunt of fluctuating weather conditions due to low cost construction soon turn into semi-dilapidated structures which further frustrate the lives of the residents. Strong administrative measures are needed to plug such loopholes in our system.

At the same time the law enforcement agencies can play a crucial role in effectively preventing and controlling crimes in slums and human settlements by formulating sound strategies. From conventional angle, an effective 'Police informer network' in slums and human settlements for the poor and underprivileged will facilitate the law enforcement agencies to have advanced inputs relating to organized crime. Similarly, beat patrols still have enough teeth to check the intrusion of criminals and anti-social elements to such areas. Such patrols by police personnel having moderately long tenure in a particular area were also found to be effective to check theft, house-breaking and similar offences in residential areas and colonies. However, there is general consensus that conventional crime prevention strategies have limitations to effectively contain variety of crimes especially those related to the habitat. The Sixth UN Congress held in Caracas in1980 on the theme 'Crime prevention & Quality of life' had laid down that it was essential to review the crime prevention strategies exclusively based on legal criteria and advocated that crime prevention and criminal justice may be considered in the context of economic development, political system, social and cultural values and social change especially the impact of the new International Economic Order. The Ninth UN Congress on the Prevention of Crime and Criminal Justice held in Cairo in 1995 also reiterated the need of new strategies to prevent crime and identified the concentration of disadvantaged in certain urban areas without adequate means of subsistence and social support as the major factor contributing to the instability and organized crime. The police forces in various countries are also convinced on the need of evolving innovative strategies and mechanisms to deal with the organized crimes in urban areas. The police organizations in the West, which faced serious dilemma on the habitat oriented crimes in the cities have launched such strategies which are popularly known as 'community policing'. These concepts work on the main hypothesis that police should become partners with the people in the community so that they can address the local priorities related to crime, social and public disorder and neighborhood decay. At practical plane, these new concepts led to the formation of 'Para-police' on the lines of 'Para-medical' or 'Para-legal' with the civilians who perform important but routine or peripheral police tasks usually connected with service to citizens. These forces operated in all the major cities in US and extended timely help to the public especially in distress situations. The Police also functioned as facilitators for the formation of other informal groups such as 'Neighborhood Watch' 'Resident Association', House-owners Association, 'Tenants Association" etc which played pivotal role in strengthening police-community relations on the common plank of prevention and control of crimes. It is significant that police in our country has taken proactive role to float such bodies especially in major cities and other urban centers under the banner of community policing schemes. The Residents Associations which are formed in various cities and urban areas with proper guidance and assistance from the police could operate as front line informal set up in many housing colonies and human settlements to prevent and contain criminal activities. The formation of more such informal groups and their better rapport with police will definitely improve our law and order scenario especially in residential areas and housing colonies.

17

Vision for Police 2020

The Oxford English Dictionary defines 'Vision' as "romantic imagination or apocalyptic supernatural apparitions or Statesman like foresight or sagacity in planning". The very term vision is inextricably intertwined with future. Future, in many respects remains uncertain. In fact, making right predictions into the realms of future through proper vision or right perspective is an arduous task. This is applicable in the case of individuals as well as organizations But, as rightly observed by Daniel Bell, the future is not an overleaping leap into the distance, it begins in the present. Planning for the future does not become a gaze into a crystal ball, but an activity grounded in the past. Thus, the vision for Indian Police 2020 should be based on the events of the past, present trends and different assumptions and premises influencing police in a democratic polity.

Looking into the past, the police force in India which was formed by the British on the lines of Irish Constabulary carried the image of an oppressive instrument meant to safeguard the colonial interests of the British regime in India. After independence, attempts were made to reform the police in line with the democratic aspirations of the masses. But the Police Act of 1861 and the archaic and inhuman practices in the force acted as main stumbling block in transforming the police into a 'people's police' with an egalitarian image. The ruthless measures adopted by the police to quell a plethora of violent and militant movements in different parts of the country augmented its negative image and alienation from the general public. There is no end to such internal security issues which are likely to assume new dimensions by 2020. The first and foremost challenge that the police will be faced in the next decade is the task of safeguarding the integrity and sovereignty of the country against the organized efforts of hostile forces to disintegrate the nation by using the tools of aggression such as subversion, sabotage and proxy wars. Present trends of terrorism, militancy and radical revolutionary movements are clear indicators. Such forces have spread their tentacles from North to South and West to East with transnational links going beyond the contours of continents. They have no dearth of sophisticated weapons, explosives/explosive devices and ingenious remote control mechanisms. Time is not far off when they lay their hands on nuclear or chemical weapons. These challenges have influenced the strategy as well as the style of functioning of police in the country. The crucial question is how far the police set up in the country are capable to deal with these challenges? A closer look at the Strength, Weakness, Opportunities and Threats (SWOT) of the police organization would help us to arrive at a realistic answer to the above question.

SWOT Chart relating to Police in 2011

(Points are self illustrative)

Strength	**Weakness**
(a) Disciplined force	(a) outdated legislations
(b) Structured	(b)Paramilitary orientation
(c) Govt. backed	(c) Rigid/immune to change
(d) Rule-based	(d) Poor image
(e) Vast discretionary powers	(e) Alienation from public
(f) Power & Authority	(f) Politicized system
	(g) Lack of professionalism
	(h) Dehumanized
	(i) Lack of career planning

Opportunities	Threats
(a) Public service	(a) Political interference
(b) Safe environs	(b) Corruption/Nepotism
(c) New challenges to meet	(c) Public hiatus
(d) Traditional resource	(d) Poor preparedness
(e) Tech/ Science backed	(e) Adhoc measures/policies
(f) Innovations possible	(f) improper use of resources

The above SWOT analysis reveals that as compared with Strength, Weaknesses are more robust and crucial, where as Threats are more in comparison to the Opportunities. Thus, more concerted efforts are needed to outdo weakness and Threat and enrich Strength and Opportunities. A thorough introspection is needed as how these weakness and Threats could be overcome and professionalism of the force improved so as to meet the new challenges in the law enforcement field.

While we discuss the vision for police-2020, two major questions come to our mind. What matters more? Whether it is people's vision on police? Or whether it is law maker's vision alone? What is important is a vision that is ideal or acceptable to both the people and law makers. Such a vision on policing alone has proper relevance in a democratic polity, as people-friendly police ensuring the rule of law alone can protect the interests of law abiding citizens as well as democratic institutions. The police who functioned in the country in most difficult situations during the last six decades could make worthwhile contributions in safeguarding the unity, integrity and sovereignty of the nation. Despite such contributions, they could not win over the hearts of overwhelming sections of Indians as all along; Police-public relations remained strained, if not hostile. Thus, the main focus of Vision 2020 for Indian police should be in the direction of developing harmonious relations with the public. This could be attained through a subtle change in the present work culture of police. As rightly observed by Justice (Retired) V.S.

Malimath of Supreme Court; "vision is something like an ideal that needs to be pursued in one's work".

The ideal work culture that should constitute the core of vision 2020 for police was succinctly put forth by former President APJ Abdul Kalam in one of his addresses to the nation as; "The police system should function in a way that good citizens will have faith of nothing to be afraid of. They should not succumb to any external pressure in carrying out their functions. They should protect the honest officials in performing their duties. Citizens should feel comfortable and confident to seek help of police. The aim should be to see that citizens are safe, there is no kidnapping, women are treated with dignity and child labor is eliminated. In order to perform the above roles effectively, the police system has to be empowered with thorough training and congenial working environment."

The ideal situation as envisaged by the former President is akin to Ram Rajya where women walk at night without fear of being robbed of their jewels or molested; children play freely in parks without their parents getting worried over their being doped with drugs; youth travel to and fro from schools/ colleges unafraid of being robbed of their possessions and family members settle their disputes with thoughtful words and not fist or weapons. That is the most ideal situation which may never exist, but the vision of police should be to create a situation nearer to that goal. While pondering over the ways and means to develop such an ideal situation, the first priority of police would be to workout strategic plans to build up their Strength; overcome Weakness; exploit new Opportunities and guard against future Threats. This requires well set strategies and objectives; proper manpower policy; right human resources development mechanisms such as proper training/ in-service courses to develop skills and attitude among personnel and above all a vibrant and dynamic leadership.

The crucial task is to improve public perceptions on police. This can be mainly achieved through the proper and swift responses to those who approach the police with their grievances and complaints. Thus, the police Stations are the cutting edge level of police functioning where common man comes into contact with the police. Most of the policing works are done there. In fact, the image of the police and their productivity is judged at police station level. Though substantial funds were earmarked for the development of infrastructure particularly police stations and residential accommodation of personnel under Police Modernization Programs and Special schemes by the States, hundreds of police stations in rural areas function in rented dilapidated buildings without basic amenities or facilities. While emphasizing the need of improving the condition and facilities of police Stations, the reality is that no amount of modernization or infrastructural development would change the image of police or police stations unless the personnel manning them would change their attitude and behavior towards the public especially the weaker and underprivileged sections who approach the police to mitigate their complaints/ grievances. Use of abusive language, ill-treatment of persons, harassment of women complainants, non-registration of FIR under one pretext or other, collection of bribe and custodial violence are common in police stations especially those functioning in rural and backward areas. The 'Nithari episode' (child-sex and gruesome killing of around dozen of children of poor labor) had exposed as how callous and indifferent were a section of police personnel in complying the basic police practices and procedures in respect of registration of FIR, investigation of complaints and dealing with the common people who knock at the doors of police stations to get justice.

Over the years, police have deviated from the straight path due to a confluence of factors. They have said good-bye to the maxim; "salus populi suprema lax esto" (safety of the people is the highest law. Now time has come that police should strictly adhere to this maxim and build up a work culture and strategy in pursuance of this goal. The vision for Police 2020 should be based on this maxim. Some specific areas that police leadership should look into in pursuance of this task are as follows:

(a) Redefine the concept of police duties. The police in 2020 should not remain as mere crime control agency, but should function like a social service organization for the larger interests of the people.

(b) Induction of women personnel in large numbers in order to effectively deal with the crime against women. At least 20% of police force should consist of women personnel with proper training and motivation so that they can effectively deal with the increasing crime against women.

(c) Acquire knowledge and skills on a continuing basis in keeping with the on-going and future demands of crime control and internal security.

(d) Open/free communication and alliance with citizens in the domain of public safety. This will require total recasting of the mind set of police personnel. Till now the order of the day is overweening secrecy and suspicion of all outsiders.

(e) Ensure research and development in the organization and retain quality of personnel.

(f) Through training and leadership, improve professionalism of personnel to undertake more challenging tasks in line with the expectations of the general public.

(g) Operate as a force with both combat and non-combat capabilities. The range of tasks to be performed by the police is enormous. It literally covers the whole gamut from the cradle to the grave. At one point of time, a policeman may be saving an infant from the clutches of street hoodlums and at another he or she may be helping the old, sick or handicapped in the street. In this required what is expected of a police personnel in 2020 is level-headed, humane and brave generalist officer.

(h) Maintain effectiveness through preventive ethos and minimum use of force.

(i) Maintain alert for rapid entry, professional approach and quick withdrawal during public disturbances so that unnecessary public controversies can be averted.

(j) Maintain impartiality in functioning and secular outlook with due respect to human rights.

(k) Maintain highest degree of discipline, decorum and dedication through appropriate and effective organizational management.

(l) Develop relevant data bank on crime and internal security issues.

(m) Undertake annual financial audit in order to redefine and reintroduce police role and effect mid-course correction as part of organizational development.

(n) Free the police from the undue influence of political parties or other extraneous forces for which reforms and changes in the existing legislations and procedures governing the force should be vigorously pursued with public support and participation.

The underlying spirit of Vision for Police 2020 would be a people's friendly force, professionally competent to effectively face the challenges of the present millennium.

Index